Derashot LeDorot
A Commentary for the Ages
Numbers

OU**PRESS**

MAGGID

Norman Lamm

DERASHOT LEDOROT

NUMBERS

EDITED BY

Stuart W. Halpern

FOREWORD BY

Maurice Lamm

The Michael Scharf Publication Trust
RIETS/YU Press

OU Press
Maggid Books

Derashot LeDorot
A Commentary for the Ages
Numbers

First Edition, 2014

Maggid Books
An imprint of Koren Publishers Jerusalem Ltd.
POB 8531, New Milford, CT 06776-8531, USA
& POB 4044, Jerusalem 91040, Israel
www.korenpub.com

The Michael Scharf Publication Trust
of Yeshiva University Press

OU *Press*
An imprint of the Orthodox Union
11 Broadway
New York, NY 10004
www.oupress.org

The publication of this book was made possible through
the generous support of *Torah Education in Israel*.

ISBN 978 159 264 387 5, *hardcover*

A CIP catalogue record for this title is
available from the British Library

Printed and bound in the United States

Dedicated to the Memory of

Sara Lamm Dratch

שרה רבקה בת הרב נחום ומינדל לאם

Beloved daughter, mother, wife, sister, and aunt

*May her memory be forever a source
of blessing, song and, most of all, laughter.*

෮

Contents

Foreword

Maurice Lamm

Hhow is it possible for one brother to write about another brother? There are just too many memories, too many personal thoughts, and too many subjective opinions – not to speak of the superstition that two brothers sharing the same platform may invoke an *ayin hara* (evil eye); hence the practice of brothers not receiving consecutive *aliyot*. I am not disturbed by any of these concerns. First, as you shall see, I am objectively subjective in my comments about my brother. Second, years ago, my brother, Norman, and I spoke on the same dais at an annual convention of the Orthodox Union. I presented my remarks first, he followed. He introduced his comments by taking note of the practice of two brothers not sharing sequential honors. He pointed out that this restriction does not apply to *hagba* and *gelila*, the lifting and wrapping of the Torah scroll following its communal reading; brothers may share these honors. "And so," he said as he followed me on the program, "my brother has raised the issues, I will wrap things up."

This story is informative in many ways. One, it gives me license to appear, without apprehension, in the foreword of his book. And two, it gives me the opportunity, through sharing this story, to reveal just a bit of his quick wit, linguistic flare, and love of puns, all endearing to those of us who know him.

As youngsters we were practically opposites: I was an independent spirit, athletic, and self-assured...he was not. He was serious, studious, and obedient, traits that were to stand him in good stead as he matured into an accomplished scholar, leading *talmid ḥakham*, prominent leader, inspiring teacher and orator, accomplished writer, and profound thinker. In our early years we shared the typical amount of sibling rivalry. At one point our father became so irritated with us that he cried out, "Cain and Abel, that's what I have for two sons!" Each of us was certain that he himself was Abel, and that the other was Cain.

As we became adults, despite each of us living on opposite coasts, we grew extraordinarily close. We innately understood the future words of Maya Angelou, "I don't believe an accident of birth makes people sisters or brothers. It makes them siblings, gives them mutuality of parentage. Sisterhood and brotherhood is a condition people have to work at." And work at it we did. Our life's trajectories were similar – we both were influenced by learning, religious commitment, and *weltanschauung* by the Rav, Rabbi Joseph Soloveitchik, and by our grandfather Rabbi Yehoshua Baumol; we both entered the rabbinate; we both wrote and published; we even look very much alike. We supported each other, encouraged each other, helped each other, and, most importantly, loved one another. I am genuinely proud of my big brother and his achievements as a brother to me, Tzibby, and Miriam; a husband to Mindy; a father to Chaye and David, Josh and Rivkie, Shalom and Tina; and Sara, *a"h*, and Mark; a grandfather and great grandfather (too many to list, *ken yirbu*), rabbi, teacher, author, and leader whose work has irrefutably shaped the nature of contemporary Judaism, modern Orthodoxy, Torah study, and the worlds of Jewish and general higher education.

Rather than Cain and Abel, we are Moses and Aaron, genuinely joyful in each other's accomplishments. When God informed Moses that Aaron will meet him in the desert and go with him on his mission to Pharaoh, "Aaron will see you and rejoice in his heart" (Exodus 4:14). Rabbi Shimon Ben Yoḥai taught (Song of Songs Rabba 1): "The Almighty said that the same heart that rejoiced at the status of his brother will have precious stones placed upon it, as it is written, 'Aaron will thus carry the names of Israel's sons on the decision breastplate over his heart'" (Exodus 28:29).

Moses similarly rejoiced when he anointed Aaron in his stead as the high priest. We, like Moses and Aaron, are *aḥim le-de'a*, brothers in purpose and destiny, sharing fraternal fate and filial fortune.

Writing this foreword also gives me the opportunity to fulfill a *mitzva*. The Talmud (*Ketubot* 103a) notes that the *vav* in the verse *ve'et imekha* commanding us to honor our parents (Exodus 20: 12) is there "*lerabot aḥikha hagadol*," to direct us to honor our older brother as well (as my own never hesitates to remind me). The obligation is derived from the presence in the verse of a *vav haḥibur*, the conjunctive *vav* (connoting "and"). The presence of this *vav haḥibur* explains why for me this is a *mitzva kala,* a commandment easily fulfilled. Literally, the phrase "*vav haḥibur*" means "the hook that connects" and it is that precious hook of fraternal connection, expressed in brotherhood and friendship, that is one of the most treasured and cherished facets of my life.

I am so very privileged to honor my *vav haḥibur* who is also my *ḥaver* (friend) on the occasion of the publishing of his *ḥiburim*, the written essays of his insightful and inspiring sermons, in this magnificent *maḥberet* (collection). You, like I, will be hooked!

Rabbi Maurice Lamm is an internationally renowned author, president of the National Institute for Jewish Hospice, and professor at Yeshiva University's Rabbi Isaac Elchanan Theological Seminary. He was the rabbi of Beth Jacob Congregation in Beverly Hills from 1972 until his retirement in 1985. Rabbi Lamm is the author of many books including The Jewish Way in Death and Mourning *and* The Jewish Way in Love and Marriage.

Editor's Preface

Stuart W. Halpern

It is an honor to present to the reader this selection of Rabbi Norman Lamm's sermons on the book of Numbers, from among the numerous *derashot* given by Rabbi Lamm between the years 1952 and 1976 in both Congregation Kodimoh in Springfield, Massachusetts, and the Jewish Center in New York, New York.

The book of Numbers recounts the travels and travails of the Israelites in the wilderness, and contains numerous tales of rebellions, crises, and tests of leadership. As such, in his addresses to his congregants about the book, Rabbi Lamm provided his audience with insights into the nature of power, the ingredients of nationhood, the proper balance of humility and confidence and, above all, the importance of eternal fealty to, and belief in, Moses and the Torah.

These sermons are presented as they were first articulated, with only minor editorial tweaks. The "current events" referenced in many of the *derashot* are an integral part of the power and relevance of the pieces, and thus those parts that describe them in detail have been retained so that the reader can best appreciate the historical and communal situation that Rabbi Lamm was responding to at the time. On occasion, the reader will note certain sensitivities of language that have developed since these words first were spoken.

Much gratitude is owed to the many individuals who assisted in the production of this volume. As these sermons were gleaned from the selection on the Lamm Heritage website at Yeshiva University, many thanks go to the Dean of Libraries of Yeshiva University, Mrs. Pearl Berger, whose idea it was to create such a wonderful online collection of *derashot*. Many thanks to Ms. Hilda Tejada for her work in preparing this volume for publication, as well as to Kayla Avraham and Jonathan Schwab for their assistance. Rabbi Maurice Lamm's truly personal and eloquent foreword is tremendously appreciated. And as always, this volume would not be possible without the enthusiastic encouragement from my wife, Ahuva Warburg Halpern, and the entire Lamm, Dratch, Halpern, and Warburg families.

The publication of this book was made possible by the ou Press as well as the support of the Michael Scharf Publication Trust of riets/Yeshiva University Press, which, for many decades, has played a vital role in the production of Torah scholarship under the auspices of Yeshiva University. Lastly, my sincerest appreciation goes to Rabbi Reuven Ziegler, Tomi Mager and the entire Maggid team for their hard work on producing the beautiful volume you hold in your hand.

From the moment they were first spoken, the words in this volume cried out *"kitvuni le'dorot,"* "write me for generations" (*Megilla* 7a). Indeed, may they echo for generations to come.

Bemidbar

Banner in the Desert [1]

In our *sidra* of this morning, the first of the fourth book of Moses, we read of the peregrinations of Israel in the desert. The people were to be divided according to their tribes and march through the wilderness in a set pattern and order. Each tribe, in addition, was to have its own banner, or flag. This banner, or *degel*, was to differentiate it from all the other tribes of Israel.

What is the origin of this interesting commandment? Our sacred tradition gives us an amazing answer. That is, that God did not command the Israelites concerning the banners on His own initiative. Rather, He merely acceded to the request of the Jews who insisted upon banners in the desert. "The Israelites desired that they have banners just like the ministering angels" (Numbers Rabba 2:3).

What a remarkable statement! Are we to imagine that the Israelites conceived of the angels as tin soldiers – and envied them? Do angels really parade as if they were in an elementary school play?

---

1. May 20, 1961.

In order to understand the profound symbol of the banners in the desert and their relation to angels, we must understand that there are two words for a banner or flag in Hebrew and each has a different connotation. Those words are *degel* and *nes*. *Nes* is an external symbol, a sign to others; it is meant for outsiders. Thus, Isaiah (11:12) speaks of the Messiah's function towards the rest of the world at the end of days: "He shall raise a *nes* for the nations from the distance." The *nes* is meant for other nations; it is for the distant, for the outsider. *Degel*, on the other hand, is a symbol of the fulfillment of one's own purpose, his own destiny, the meaning of his own life.

Nes implies a communication with others; you identify yourself thereby to others. *Degel* implies communion with yourself; you identify yourself to yourself – it is a symbol of self-identity.

Nes will cause people to rally. *Degel* will rally people to a cause. *Nes* is appropriate to the *harim*, the mountains, with which it is often associated in the Bible. For when you are on top of the mountain you reach down to others. The *degel* is generally associated with *midbar*, the desert. When you are in a wasteland, there you must first find yourself and discover who you are and what you stand for.

In Jewish tradition, an angel is created for one single purpose, for one solitary *sheliḥut*. The angel, the *malakh*, knows what it is he was created for, and he proceeds to do it. Therefore, the *degel* is indeed symbolic of the angel. The *degel* symbolizes a single-minded purpose – and an angel lives for just that. Hence, "The Israelites desired that they have banners just like the ministering angels," means that the Israelites wanted, like the angels, to know the great purpose for which each of them was brought into the world. Every Jew wanted to know what he stood for, what function he was to serve in the grand drama of Creation.

Purpose does not mean only a career, a profession, a matter of occupational ambitions. One does not have a noble purpose in life by selling real estate, or securities or textiles, or diamonds. These are only the means to an end. And the end, the goal, the purpose – that is the *degel*.

Like the ministering angel, each of us must consider life as a mission, a *sheliḥut*. Each of us must consider himself an ambassador of God who must report back to the Almighty at the end of his earthly pilgrimage, who will then judge us as to whether or not we have carried out our task faithfully.

Of course, it is difficult for everyone to know what single great purpose he is to serve in life. Some people, perhaps the greatest number, are helplessly lost, with no idea of what they are doing in the world. They are like driftwood on the wild waves of a stormy ocean. These are people who lack identity, who seemingly have no pulse, no *degel*. It is about such people that the Russian theologian Nikolai Berdyaev said that they have not only lost the way, but they have also lost the address. They do not know where they are going, and in fact they do not know if one is supposed to go any place at all in life. They live in a vast *midbar* without the benefit of *degalim*.

Many areas of modern life are such bannerless deserts. Television is one such notable example. It was most refreshing to hear Mr. Newton Minnow, who was recently appointed as the Chairman of the Federal Communications Commission, lecture the broadcasters about their responsibilities. It was a speech which will long be remembered by thoughtful people. He reproached them for having no purpose other than that of exploiting the airwaves for financial gain. The words he used to describe the present situation are most appropriate: "a vast wasteland." In Hebrew, that is a *midbar*! What Mr. Minnow was trying to do – vainly, I fear – was to give them *degalim*, banners, a sense of purpose, a set of high goals, in this wasteland. It will be a real pity if the vested interests of industry and politics manage to destroy his plan and return the control of the TV airwaves to those who regard it as nothing more than another source of income.

Most of us, however, and most decent people, are not in that category of those who are completely lost. We know in general where we belong, what our general goals are, what camp we belong to. However, we do not know our individual purposes in life. We know that as human beings it is our duty to reflect the divine image in which we were created, by being decent, compassionate, and kind. We know that as Jews, more specifically, we are obligated to the prophetic challenge: "*atem edai, ne'um Hashem*," "You are My witnesses, says the Lord" (Isaiah 43:10). Our task as Jews is to be witnesses to the presence of God in human history. And, as the sainted hasidic author of the *Sefat Emet* put it, how are we witnesses? By living according to "the words of the Lord," that is, Torah. But if you ask such a person: What specifically is your task, your purpose in life, your specific function in the divine economy of creation? He does not answer because he does not know.

Some individuals, a minority, are truly blessed. They have matured spiritually, and have discovered what it is exactly for which they were created; they know their purpose in life. How fortunate they are!

These last two types – those who know the general trend of their being and those who know the specific purpose for which they were brought into the world – are represented in our *sidra* by the words, "Every man according to his camp, and every man according to his banner" (1:52). These represent the two types we have mentioned (see *Sefat Emet* ad loc.).

"Every man according to his camp" represents those who know the general camp with which they are identified. They have identified themselves with a group. "Every man according to his banner" are those who know specifically their *degel*, their purpose in life. They have identified themselves also within the group itself. "Every man according to his camp" may be in the right location, but that individual tends to fritter away his energies and resources on the wrong task, on trivialities. Such a person is in the right *maḥaneh*, the right group, and the right environment, but has never managed to find his or her own self.

The story is told of the sainted Ḥafetz Ḥaim who, in a time of great and grave community crisis, noticed one of the wealthiest men in the town staying long after the hour of services in order to recite the Psalms. The gentle and pious Ḥafetz Ḥaim approached him with the following rebuke. The Ḥafetz Ḥaim told him that he had no right to spend his time reciting the Psalms when God had blessed him with the wherewithal to alleviate the grave crisis which had struck the community. "Your business," the Ḥafetz Ḥaim said, "is to organize campaigns for charity and disburse it yourself, not to spend all your time reciting the *Tehillim*." And he told him the following parable: "In the army of Czar Nicholas there are many divisions. If a soldier who has been trained for the cavalry and is serving there at present were to decide one fine day that he is going to join the artillery, he may be serving the same Czar and fighting for the same cause, and meaning well all along. But what probably will happen is that his superiors will court-martial him and put him against the wall to face the firing squad. His purpose was determined by the Czar to be cavalry, not artillery. You cannot define your purpose by yourself." "Every man according to his camp" is not sufficient. We must each strive for "every man according to his banner."

This latter class, those who know what their place and purpose is in life, they have indeed achieved the angelic distinction of *degel*. In the Song of Songs (2:4) we read: "*Diglo alai ahava*," "His banner above me is love." The word *ahava*, love, is numerically equal to *eḥad* – "one" (see *Sefat Emet*). The only way to discover the *degel* of *eḥad*, the single-minded application to a great cause, your single greatest purpose in life, that for which you were created, is to experiment with every noble purpose, every sacred task, every lofty cause, until you discover that which you can do best and that with which you can fall in love. You must have a deep loyalty and a profound affection for what you recognize as your purpose in life. The banner of *eḥad* must participate in *ahava*.

Is there any need to enumerate the hundreds of great purposes which beckon to each and every one of us? There is Israel, education – both your own scholarship and assisting others – there is rescue work, there is fighting cancer and heart disease, there is *Ḥevra Kadisha* (assisting in burial of the dead), there is Shabbat, there is the Free Loan Society, there is the ability to make others happy through word or song – there is indeed no lack of *degalim*!

About eight hundred years ago, Rabbi Judah, the author of *Sefer Ḥasidim*, told us that the truly pious man will never neglect any one of the 613 *mitzvot*. Indeed, to have a great cause means never to renege or to be negligent in any of the obligations to which all Jews are committed. However, the truly pious man will choose one of these and, so to speak, "specialize" in it. He will choose one *mitzva* above all others which will become his symbol, his purpose, his *degel*. Perhaps that is why we refer to a young man who has attained maturity as a *bar mitzva* – by right, we should call him a *bar mitzvot* (plural), since on this thirteenth birthday he becomes responsible for the observance of all the commandments. But on this day we tell him that with his assumption of responsibility for all the commandments, he is at the same time urged to find one area of virtue, or goodness, of religious creativity which will define his own purpose in creation.

It is significant that we read the portion of *degalim* on the Saturday before Shavuot. On Shavuot we each realize that our *maḥaneh*, our camp, is one of Torah. But the *sidra* of *degalim* reminds us that it is not enough merely to be a person of Torah. We must also each know our individual purpose – we are each challenged to find and execute our *sheliḥut*. The *sidra* addresses each of us: What do you stand for? Where and what is your banner in the desert of life?

Happy is the person who can answer clearly and lucidly. Blessed is that individual's life – for his mission, his *sheliḥut*, is triumphant. That person's existence is meaningful and worthy. In the words of King David in Psalms: "We shall sing out over Your victory and raise our banners (*nidgol*) in the name of our God. May God fulfill all your requests" (20:6).

Beyond Mitzvot[1]

Our *haftara* for this morning, from the second chapter of Hosea, begins on a high optimistic note: "And the number of the Children of Israel shall be as the sand of the sea, which cannot be measured or numbered" (2:1). For a people who chronically suffer the status of a minority, this prophecy comes as a cheerful source of encouragement.

The verse seems simple enough. Yet the Rabbis of the Talmud (*Yoma* 22b) detected in this statement an apparent contradiction. The first half of the verse says that the number of the Children of Israel will be very large – as great as the sand of the sea. That, indeed, is a large number; but it is not infinite. The second half of the verse speaks of the population of Israel being so great that it cannot be measured or numbered; this implies an even greater number of Israelites.

This is, of course, only an apparent contradiction, because the prophet wants to explain his metaphor and tells us that by the words "as the sand of the sea," he means that the people of Israel will be well-nigh too many to count. But the question of the Rabbis, counterposing the

---

1. May 21, 1966.

idea of a finite with the idea and an infinite number, was meant merely to introduce the answer they offer:

> When Hosea speaks of the Children of Israel being beyond number, he refers to a time when the Israelites will do the will of God; and when Hosea speaks of us being as many as the particles of sand on the seashore, he refers to a time when we will not perform the will of God.

Now this is a stranger answer. When one reads the beginning of our *haftara*, one finds himself in a mood which is favorable to our people who obviously are considered as deserving of divine reward. How, therefore, can the Rabbis maintain that the great promise that we will be as many as the sand of the sea refers to a time when we do not do the will of God?

I should like to propose an answer, which, to my mind, touches the heart of the Jewish outlook on God and mankind and contains an incisive and perceptive comment on the ethics of our Torah. The answer derives from a comment, in another context, by one of the most seminal of hasidic thinkers, Rabbi Zadok HaKohen of Lublin. The Kohen, as he is called, distinguishes between two terms: *retzono shel makom* and *mitzvato shel makom*, the will of God and the commandment of God. All of the *Halakha*, including the 613 biblical commandments and the many more rabbinic commandments, represents God's *mitzva*, His commandment, His directions, His demands upon us. These are the things that we must do in order to justify our existence before Him. But the mere performance of the divine commandment – His *mitzva* – does not exhaust the relation of God and mankind. There is much that goes beyond *mitzvot*, a surplus of meaning, whole worlds that transcend the idea of *mitzva*. This is the area of *retzono shel Makom*, the will of God. God wants of us more than He commands us; His *ratzon* is far greater than His *mitzva*. The divine *mitzva* is something that every Jew can, with enough exertion, perform completely. But that extra something beyond the commandment, namely the *ratzon*, is what each individual must strive to realize and actualize according to his own ability and talent.

For instance, the idea of *mitzva* means that we are commanded to be decent members of the Jewish community and fulfill our obligations. But the will of God, the *ratzon*, is that we be far more than passive participants in the drama of Jewish life; it means that those of us who have any leadership ability must develop it and use it. The will of God is that we not only get but we also give, that we not only belong but that we bring in others, that we not only react to others but that we act on our own.

One of the most obvious places where we may see the difference between commandment and will is the study of Torah. It is important to keep this in mind especially in contemporary times, when despite all our extravagant talk about intellectuals and sophistication, the study of Torah – the real intellectual content of Judaism – is honored more in the breach than in the practice. The Talmud (*Menaḥot* 99b) had already told us that one can get away with a minimum if he so wishes: Merely by reciting the *Shema*, which is a portion of the Torah itself, one can really fulfill the requirements of studying Torah by day and by night. It is easy enough to abide by the *mitzva* of the Almighty. But the function of man is to go beyond this and to try to live up to God's will, His *ratzon*. And in this case, the Jew must realize the verse of Joshua who, speaking of the Torah, said, "You shall meditate therein by day and by night" (1:8). The commandment of God may not be confined to the recitation of two brief passages. The will of God is that we live in the study of Torah constantly, by day and by night – that every spare moment be devoted to the contemplation of the Torah.

Interestingly, both these interpretations found their way into the explanation of Rashi on the *mishna* in *Avot* (1:15) which says that we must set aside regular time to the study of Torah. One comment in Rashi has it that we must study "*bekhol yom,*" "every day"; the other requires of us to study "*kol hayom,*" "all day." The first is the commandment of God, the second is His will.

With this distinction between *mitzvato shel Makom* and *retzono shel Makom*, we may understand what the Talmud told us about our verse in the *haftara*. Both halves of this verse are set in the context of an Israel which is obedient to the Lord. In both cases, Israel accepts and performs the commandments, the *mitzva* of the Almighty. The difference between these two halves is this: The first half, which speaks of Israel being rewarded by a large population, but not a very large one, refers to the time when Israel will perform only the commandments of God but fail to live up to His will. Whereas the second half of the verse, which promises an extraordinarily large increase in Israel's citizenry, refers to the time when the Children of Israel will perform not only the commandments of God, but, even more, *retzono shel Makom* – His infinite will!

This distinction between *mitzva* and *ratzon* affords us a new insight in Judaism that is relevant to us and our times. For one thing, it means that none of us, no matter how observant we may be and no matter how Orthodox we consider ourselves, dare submit to the temptation of self-righteousness. It means that no matter how great our religious accomplishments may be vis-à-vis others, we must always bear and conduct ourselves with the utmost of humility. We must always remember that loyalty to the *Halakha* is not at all an expression of maximal Judaism, but merely minimal Judaism! To observe every last iota of the *Shulḥan Arukh* is to live up to the *mitzvato shel Makom*. And that, most certainly, is not enough! If we observe *kashrut*, Shabbat, family purity, prayer, and all the other institutions of Judaism – we have only reached the level of God's commandments. The real test of genuine piety and authentic Jewishness is when we can get beyond the *mitzva* and reach out for the sublimity of God's *ratzon*! This will of God is far greater than His commandments not only quantitatively, but also measured by the standard of the kind of attitude we bring to the practice of Judaism. If we approach Judaism in the sense of *mitzva*, then it becomes for us an *ole hamitzvot*, a yoke, a burden, an obstacle to our freedom. But when we live the Jewish life with a feeling that we are blessed thereby, that this is what makes us happy – then we have gone beyond the commandments towards the will. The test therefore is: When we live Jewishly, do we feel deprived or privileged? Do we consider that the regimen of religion hampers us or hallows us?

Indeed, it is with reference to the study of Torah that our Rabbis (Song of Songs Rabba 1:53) tell us a remarkable story that illustrates our point. Ben Azzai was teaching Torah when suddenly the people about him noticed a remarkable sight: A wall of fire enveloped him. They quickly came to Rabbi Akiva and reported the incident to him, where-upon Rabbi Akiva hurried to Ben Azzai and asked him: "Is it true what they say, that a wall of flame enveloped you while you were teaching Torah?" "Yes," answered the younger colleague of the great Tanna. "It is perhaps," asked Rabbi Akiva, "because you were studying the *ma'aseh merkava*, the most mysterious portion of the Torah, that part which deal with the most divine secrets, and therefore it was the holiness of the subject matter which caused you to be enveloped in flame?" "No," answered Ben Azzai, "it was nothing as remote and mysterious as that. I was simply studying Torah, *Nevi'im*, and *Ketubim* – just some Ḥumash, some *haftarot*, and perhaps reciting some Psalms. What, then, was so unusual about my study? It was neither the particular subject matter nor the amount of studying I did; rather, it is just that I was so happy, so overjoyed, so enraptured with the Torah, as if this were the very day it was given from Sinai. These words were as sweet and as precious to me as when they were given."

Indeed so! The study of Torah must not be considered merely an obligation which one must dispose of by doing it however reluctantly. It must be considered at all times as a joyous fulfillment of the will of God, as a reenactment of the drama of Sinai, far and above what is *demanded* of me – rather, in the realm of what is *wanted* of me.

This distinction has special relevance to the great Jewish insti-tution of charity or *tzedaka*. If a man gives, no matter the amount, he performs a *mitzva* – and a very, very great one. But the will of God goes far beyond this. To give a coin to a poor man is to perform a command-ment; to help him so that he does not become poor in the first place, that is the accomplishment of *retzono shel Makom*. To give by itself is a *mitzva*, but to give with love, with grace, with kindness and joy – that is the *ratzon* of the Almighty.

Mitzva and will with regards to philanthropy is beautifully reflected in a passage in the Talmud (*Rosh HaShana* 4a): "If one says I will give this coin to charity in order that my children may live, or in order that I may merit the life of the world-to-come, *harei zeh tzaddik gamur* – the man who gives in this manner is completely righteous." Such is the reading of our text of the Talmud. But it is a problematical one; can such selfish and egotistical giving be the work of a man who is termed a *tzaddik gamur*, a completely righteous individual? The commentaries on the Talmud struggle with that question. But an answer is provided by another reading of the same text offered by Rabbenu Hananel and the Meiri. Their text reads, "*harei zeh tzedaka gemura*," that this kind of philanthropy is considered complete philanthropy. In other words, it is a complete fulfillment of the *mitzva* to give charity; but it does not at all characterize the one who gives in this manner as a *tzaddik gamur*! In terms of our own thought, this means that if one gives, but his giving is motivated by some self-concern, then he has abided by the commandment of God but he is still very far from performing the will, the *ratzon*, of God. The *mitzva* was performed, the act was fully done in accordance with every particular of the law – but such giving is without compassion and without love, and therefore has failed to rise to the level of *retzono shel Makom*. For the will of God is to give without the expectation of any reward, even without a spiritual kick-back!

Now we may understand the words of our Rabbis in *Avot* (2:4): "Do His will as you would perform your own will, so that He will do your will as if it were His own will." Our will – our demands of God – are never minimal. We ask not for the material things which will keep us on a bare level of subsistence, but for the luxuries to which we are accustomed and for which we strive. We ask not that we be spared humiliation, but that we be accorded honor and dignity. We ask not that our children not abandon and revile us, but that they love and cherish us now and even after we have gone. We plead not that our children not intermarry, but that they marry well and Jewishly. We present God, as it were, not with a human *mitzva* but with a human *ratzon*. We are not satisfied with the minimum; we strive for the maximum. Therefore the Tanna tells us that we must respond not only to the divine *mitzva* but also the divine *ratzon*! If our material desires are maximal, so must our spiritual endeavors be maximal. Only when our gesture to God is on the level of His will may we expect that He will consider our will.

The First Schlemihl[1]

The word "schlemihl" is a Yiddish – and Anglo-Yiddish – pejorative term for a special kind of personality whose characteristics are apparently self-evident. Maurice Samuel has written of him, "It is the schlemihl's avocation and profession to miss out on things, to muff opportunities, to be persistently, organically, preposterously, and ingeniously out of place."

What is the origin of this particular term? It is hard to say. There are a number of theories. The most probable, to my mind, is a passing reference in today's *sidra*. In the listing of the heads of the Tribes of Israel we read: "The head of the Tribe of Simeon was Shelumiel the son of Zuri-Shaddai" (10:19).

In what way was Shelumiel a schlemihl? It is quite puzzling, because we really know very little from Scripture about the biblical Shelumiel. And the name itself – "God's peace" – tells us nothing about him.

1. May 25, 1974.

However, when we turn to the talmudic-midrashic tradition, we do find some hints about the personality of Shelumiel that may provide biblical dimensions for the well-known schlemihl.

The Talmud (*Sanhedrin* 28b) records the opinion of Rabbi Yoḥanan that Shelumiel had five different names. One of the people with whom this Shelumiel is identified gives us, I believe, a measure of understanding into why Shelumiel has become a model of ridicule and failure, a laughing-stock for generations. And the story itself is very far from a laughing matter.

Shelumiel is identified with Zimri the son of Salu, who is later (25:14) described as a prince of the tribe of Simeon. The story that is told to us in the Torah, later in this book, is that after the incident with Balaam, the Children of Israel began to be attracted to the daughters of Moab and Midian in the pagan rites of Baal-Peor. These rites were immoral, obscene, and all of this was planned by Balaam who, having failed to curse the Israelites, decided upon this device so that they might bring curse upon themselves. These immoral deeds afflicted the very highest echelons. Zimri himself flaunted his prohibited amorous activity with a Midianite woman in the very eyes of Moses and all Israel, whereupon Phineas, in his zeal, ran him through with a spear and killed him.

How does this act of brazen immorality make of Shelumiel a schlemihl? Heinrich Heine, the great German poet who was an apostate Jew, heard of this Talmudic passage about Shelumiel and Zimri, and misunderstood it. In his poem, "Jehuda Ben Halevy," he writes:

> Phineas, blind with fury,
> In the sinner's place,
> By ill luck,
> Chanced to kill a guiltless person
> Named Schlemihl ben Zuri-Shaddai.
> He, then, this Schlemihl the First,
> Was the ancestor of all the
> Race of Schlemihls.

Not so! Shelumiel or Zimri was not at all guiltless or mistakenly killed by Phineas. Heine assumed that Phineas meant to kill Zimri but, by error, killed Shelumiel. He did not realize that the Talmud identifies both men as one and the same.

The Yiddish carefully distinguishes between two allied stereotypes: the schlemihl and the schlemazel. It is the latter, not the former, who is hapless, luckless, a constant victim of conspiring circumstances. The usual example is given of the man who walks along a ledge and inadvertently kicks over a can of paint which falls on the head of a second man. The first one is the schlemihl, the second the schlemazel – possibly deriving from the German and Hebrew, *Schlim-mazal*, bad luck. Heine is thus describing the schlemazel and calling him a schlemihl.

What Heine did not know was the whole story as told by the Talmud. There (*Sanhedrin* 82a) we read as follows:

> The tribe of Simeon came to Zimri ben Salu [Shelumiel] and they said to him, "They are engaged in determining questions of life and death [i.e., Moses and Aaron are sitting in judgment on those guilty of indulging in immorality with the Midianites and Moabites], and you sit by quietly?" What did Zimri do? He arose and assembled twenty-four thousand Israelites and went to Cozbi the daughter of Zur and said to her, "Listen to me." She responded, "I am the daughter of a king [the King of Median], and my father told me never to obey anyone but the top man." He said to her, "I too am a leader, for I am the prince of a tribe; moreover, I am greater than he [Moses], for I am the second born in my family, whereas he is the third born." Thereupon he grabbed her by her hair and brought her to Moses. Zimri said to Moses, "Son of Amram, is this one permitted to me or forbidden to me? And if you will say she is forbidden to me, who permitted you to marry the daughter of Jethro?"[2]

This is the background of Zimri, who was at that point killed by Phineas.

---

2. The obvious answer, to which Zimri or Shelumiel was oblivious, was that Moses had married Zipporah, the daughter of the Midianite Jethro, before the Torah was given and intermarriage was prohibited.

Think of this story, analyze it well, and you will know why Zimri is called a Shelumiel, and why Shelumiel was indeed a schlemihl!

Note, at first, certain positive elements. Shelumiel was not at all a hapless, unlucky goat. He was not a schlemazel. He certainly had leadership qualities – he was, after all, a *nasi*, a prince of a tribe. He clearly had courage: he was willing to defy Moses himself. And, in a twisted kind of way, he possessed what might be called integrity. But when we think a bit more deeply of what he did, we will know why he has truly a schlemihl.

For one thing, when the Rabbis tell us that he had five different names, they are already giving us a hint about his character structure. He was obviously a man of uncertain and unstructured identity, one who does not know what he wants or who he is – or who he wants to be. He fits in and out of roles in a very tricky manner, and we are never certain who he really is. So, anyone can be a schlemihl. But a schlemihl is no one, because he can be so many people! As a result, he keeps on trying out new roles, until he strikes the wrong one, gets himself into hot water, goes beyond his depths, runs afoul of the law – and is executed.

Second, Shelumiel suffers from an inflated ego, and so he lets himself be flattered. "Shelumiel, you are a prince amongst men!" he is told by his fawning aides. And so, like a true schlemihl, he tells himself that he is the equal of any man. He is goaded into challenging Moses. He is so flattered by the attention he receives, by the appurtenances of his office, that he goes along with their nefarious plans. He forgets his limitations. When Cozbi pulls him down a rung or two, which should have shocked him into reality, he claims superiority to Moses on the most ludicrous grounds – that he is second-born whereas Moses is only third-born!

Third, once he gets himself this new identity as a Very Important Person, he can be easily manipulated by sinister forces that remain behind the scenes. He has grandiose conceptions of himself. Yet he is a tool, a pawn, a marionette who is goaded into abandoning every shred of decency and morality, and all the while fancies himself a great leader, even an honorable one.

Fourth, he resorts to force and lawlessness when persuasion and justice fail. When Cozbi speaks out and up to him, he grabs her by her hair and pulls her along. Nothing will stand in his way. The brute, the animal, the cave-man in him comes out when his human dignity fails him.

Fifth, Shelumiel is willing to engage in the most devious distortions of the law in order to prove his point, even when he knows he is wrong. He thinks he can fool everyone and anyone, even Moses, whom he now considers the "enemy."

So we have here, in this story, the characteristics of the first schlemihl. Maybe he is not completely identical with what we today mean by this pejorative term, but it is close enough. And we discover that the schlemihl is not unintelligent but, what is worse, he is unwise; he is not inept as much as he is sinister.

Consider why this *nasi* (which, of course, means "prince," not "president") is a schlemihl, despite his talents and courage and guts.

He is not sure of his own identity and is therefore willing to play many roles, ultimately confusing himself with his own office, as if the *nasi* is identical with the *nesiyut* like another head of state over three thousand years later, the leader of a very powerful country who identified his person with his position. I am thinking, of course, of Louis XIV, the king of France, who said, "*L'etat c'est moi,*" "I am the state."

Second, Shelumiel was so egotistical that he allowed his underlings to isolate him, to flatter him and elevate him beyond his own limitations, to make him think that he was much more powerful than he really was, completely independent of others. He allowed them to nurture within him the illusion of omnipotence.

Third, as a result, the schlemihl can be manipulated by his own subordinates and pushed into genuinely immoral conduct by small men. All the while, his self-awareness as a great man continues unabated – so much so that he is willing to expose his immorality in public, letting the whole world gaze in amazement at his greed and cupidity and ugliness, and he thinks that no one will fault him for it.

Fourth, when all lawful means and ways of persuasion fail, he resorts to brute force, to arbitrariness, to *force majeur* (superior force). He will let no one and nothing stand in his way, for he comes first. He will "stonewall" his way to survival.

Lastly, the schlemihl is one who then looks upon the law as something which he can twist and turn and push and pull at will, to make it conform to his own lack of probity and decency. He calls upon the very law that he violates in order to defend himself. He recognizes no authority other than himself on the law, not even Moses, who now heads his "enemies list."

Such is the biblical Shelumiel. All other schlemihls share one or another of his traits. It is rare indeed to find a schlemihl who, like the *nasi* of the tribe of Simeon, is in a position of power and evinces all the same characteristics. But it can happen. And when it does, it is a cause for grief for an entire people. For so we read that all the Children of Israel were weeping at the entrance to the Tent of Meeting, the center of power and authority in ancient Israel. The biblical schlemihl was a man of unimpeachable schlemielhood, and he was disposed of in an act of zealousness. What could have been an unmitigated disaster was narrowly averted.

Unfortunately, however, while the great disaster was averted, the calamity that struck anyway was great enough. It has to, when a schlemihl rises to power – or, as happened, when one in power becomes a schlemihl. Twenty four thousand corpses in ancient Israel were testimony to this tragic foolishness.

So there is a great moral in the story of the first schlemihl. And it is not at all a laughing matter.

In thinking of the biblical Shelumiel, I am filled with a sense of pity mingled with contempt. Yet, I have greater pity for the people on whom he was foisted and who suffered so on his account.

In a word, I pity the schlemazel more than the schlemihl.

Naso

A Jewish Definition of Power [1]

Our *haftara* this morning tells of the birth of one of the most colorful personalities in biblical history, Samson. He is the only biblical figure known in Jewish literature as a *gibor*, a hero or strongman. His power was proverbial.

This would not be remarkable if Samson were only a rare specimen of brute force who could slay a lion with his bare hands, throw fear into the hearts of his enemies, smite them with the jawbone of an ass, and cause a great building to collapse by pulling down the pillars. But Samson is also known to us as one of the *shoftim*, the "judges." He experienced *hashra'at haShekhina*, divine inspiration and prophecy. And he was, from before his birth, consecrated as a Nazirite, one who for reasons of saintliness abstains from wine and the cutting of his hair. Does this not indicate something unusual about him? Indeed, are we not here offered a new insight into the whole concept of *gibor* and *gevura*, a new Jewish definition of power?

---

1. June 16, 1962.

Our question is: What is that definition? What, in the context of the Jewish tradition, is *gevura*, strength or heroism? It obviously is not mere brawn. What then?

For an answer to our question, let us turn to the Kabbala, that infinitely rich mystical mine of Jewish ideas and ideals. The Kabbala understood creation not as a single event, but as a two-step process. The first step was *hitpashtut*, an overflowing or emanation of God, a flood of divine creativity released at the moment He determined to create the world. However, this alone is not enough. For when an infinite God creates, the creation too tends to be infinite – there is too much, it proceeds without limit, and hence a real world cannot exist. Therefore there must be a second step to counteract this ever-spreading emanation from God, and that is *tzimtzum*, divine restraint, God's self-limitation. Thus, God calls a halt to His own creative endeavors. He limits, as it were, his own impulse to keep on producing world upon world.

The first step, the divine effusion, His overflowing and emanation, the Kabbalists referred to the attribute of *ḥessed*, loving-kindness, and because true love knows no bounds, it always seeks to increase, grow, and intensify. However, while we call it *ḥessed*, the same idea of expansion can refer to any drive or will or passion.

The second element, that of restraint and self-limitation, is referred to by the Kabbalists as the quality of *gevura*, strength. *Gevura* thus means the ability to limit oneself, for it certainly takes moral strength to know when to stop.

This, then, is essentially the definition of power or heroism: self-restraint, self-contraction. And as with God, so with man: *gevura* means not brawn, not grasping for more and more, but on the contrary – self-limitation, self-control. True strength is not the passion for power, but knowing when, and when not, to use it; not the quest for bigness, but recognizing when big becomes too big; not in growth, but in retrenchment; not in dominating others, but in dominating oneself. *Gevura* consists of knowing when to call a halt to man's outgoing and outreaching drives.

This is, of course, true in every aspect of life. Growth is good, but not too much or too fast. The body's cells which proliferate without end are the cause of cancer. An economy which rises too quickly and without inner controls is liable to collapse in the long run. A child who grows but grows without limits is actually sick. A teacher who tries to impart all his knowledge to his charges without modifying his information to fit the child will be a failure.

Even the desire of knowledge, meritorious as it is, must be controlled by man's moral principles. The *ḥessed* of increased knowledge of the world, as it is expressed in modern science and technology, can no doubt be a good thing. We are all beneficiaries of the constantly ongoing programs for unlocking the secrets of nature. But if we moderns also are threatened with sudden and calamitous extinction it is because we have not merged *gevura* with *ḥessed*; because we have not exercised moral restraint in directing the goals and purposes of our scientific research. If more nations were to learn how to make atomic bombs, as they surely will, and each of them were to conduct atmospheric tests, there is no doubt that the function of *ḥessed* would be achieved – more scientific knowledge would be accumulated. But because of the lack of moral heroism in self-control and denying one's self this increased scientific information, the whole world may destroy itself or, at the very least, irrevocably cripple all future generations. *Ḥessed* without *gevura*, in science as well as in the formation of the world, leads to destruction and not to creation.

Consider another example, a more personal one, of the moral courage called *gevura*. Love is a wonderful thing. But it sometimes can be so overdone that it destroys the object of affection – reminding us of the bitter observation of Oscar Wilde that, "Every man kills the thing he loves." I refer to too much love expressed by parents for children, love given in such excess that it becomes possessive and interferes in the life of a child. This kind of unrestrained *ḥessed* has rightly been called "smother love." All parents know this instinctively. More sophisticated ones are aware of it consciously. Yet it bears repetition and reminder. Too much paternal and maternal affection can lead to making too many decisions for the child so that he never learns to think for himself, choose for himself, or decide for himself. An overdose of *ḥessed* can make a child's personality permanently immature. A parent whose heart overflows with tender affection for a child needs the divine quality of *gevura*, of moral courage to discipline, control, and guide his parental love – or at least the expression of it – for the good of the child. Unless a parent controls his outgoing love for a child, unless he limits it intelligently and at the right times, the child will never learn that life has its harsh aspects, that without discipline one cannot live in a civilized society, that one must be prepared to deal with people who will view him critically and objectively and not always with unthinking admiration and affection.

The problems of Jewish education are also affected by the combination of *hessed* and *gevura*. As a rabbi, I have heard every good and legitimate reason for a loving parent not to subject a child to the regimen of the study of Torah: there is too little time for fresh air, there is too great a competition for getting into better high schools and colleges, there are so many other things that one must learn in order to achieve a "rounded personality." And so parents often love their children so much that they deny them the opportunity to learn the meaning of life, the roots of their people, the history and destiny of their own spirit.

Perhaps it is for this reason that in Yiddish, a wealthy man of decent instincts is often called a *gevir*, a word which is derived from *gevura*, meaning heroism and strength. True wealth, in the Jewish sense, is the exercise of *gevura* as we have defined it: moral restraint, refraining from ostentation, self-indulgence, or domination of others; ethical control in acquiring riches and character control in spending them; a quality of graciousness and generosity. This is true heroism, true *gevura*. This kind of man is never *nouveau riche*; he is a true *gevir*.

In today's *sidra* we read the commandment of God that the priests should bless the Children of Israel with the three-fold blessing. The first one is: "The Lord bless you and keep you." Blessing, or *berakha*, has always been understood in our tradition to mean: *hosafa*, increase, growth, expansion. It is a quality of *hessed*. "Keeping," *shemira*, always refers to moral control and ethical limitation, as in "*hishamer lekha pen…*" (see, for instance, Genesis 24:6). Thus, the priests extend to us the blessing of God: May you have a great deal, more than you have now. But may your *berakha* be graced with *shemira*. May you learn how to keep your naturalness and humility intact, regarding your money and your wealth as a trust; may you learn how to retain your dignity and suppress arrogance and haughtiness so that you will achieve true blessing.

Indeed, the quality of *gevura* is a fundamental prerequisite for the religious life of the Jew. What distinguishes the Jewish religion is not the holidays – for other people have them too; not a synagogue – other people have their churches or mosques; but rather, the *Halakha*, the Jewish regimen which extends into every aspect of a person's existence. A life of Jewish law, of *mitzvot*, is an expression of the moral courage we have called *gevura* – for it means that the Jew must learn to restrain himself and his appetites in every phase of life. His desire to eat indiscriminately must be curbed by the inner strength that comes from observing the rules of *kashrut*. His desire to exploit nature, by means of industry or farming or doing business, must be curbed by the inner discipline that causes him to rest on Shabbat in the manner decreed by Jewish law. His lust and his passion, what the Torah in one place has called *ḥessed* and Freud has called the libido, must be restrained by the *gevura* of the Torah's code of sexual morality. The discipline life of the Jew is his greatest strength. "*Ein giborim ela giborei Torah*," "There are none as heroic as the heroes of Torah" (*Avot DeRabbi Natan* 1:23). Physical strength is transitory; military power is ephemeral; political influence is impermanent. Only the moral strength of Torah is abiding and everlasting.

Now, I believe, we may understand why one of the most cherished of biblical characters is called Samson the *gibor*, the man of strength, the hero. If Samson had only possessed *ko'aḥ*, brute physical power, he would have been no better than any Philistine. But he was charged to keep his great physical strength secondary and subordinate to his *gevura*, his spiritual power and moral courage. His greatness lay in that he was consecrated to exercise greater power over himself than over others.

Unfortunately, Samson was not consistently successful. At a crucial moment in his life when he failed, when he forfeited his moral *gevura* and became a spiritual weakling – allowing himself to be tempted by Delilah – his physical power proved to be useless and insignificant too. The strength of Samson lay not in his muscles, but in his morals; not in his biceps but in his spirit. When the spirit and the morals failed, all else was valueless.

No wonder that Samson was commanded to be a Nazirite, to abstain from wine, as were his parents from the moment that – as recorded in today's *haftara* – they were informed by the angel that they would have a child. For wine releases inhibitions, it weakens one's self-control; it makes a man effusive and gives him a feeling of limitlessness and omnipotence. He becomes all *ḥessed*, no *gevura*. The abstention from wine was therefore both a symbol and charge to Samson to exercise the moral self-limitation which is the *gevura* of a religious man.

Perhaps all this can be summed up in the words of the Rabbis in *Avot* (4:1): *"Eizehu gibor, hakovesh et yitzro,"* "Who is strong? He who suppresses his [evil] inclination." The word for inclination, *yetzer*, derives from the Hebrew *yetzira*, creation. The passions and inclinations of man are directed towards self-aggrandizement, reaching out for more power, more conquest, more insight, more affection, more influence. The first impulse of creativity, with man as with God, is *yetzira* or *yetzer* – the centrifugal movement, the outward expansion of force, character, desire, and interest. But a world cannot exist with this alone. It needs the quality of *gevura*, of limitation. And therefore: Who is the *gibor*, the true hero or strong man? He who can suppress his *yetzer*, his *ḥessed*, his desire to go and grow farther and faster.

We conclude with the words of David (1 Chronicles 29:11): *"Lekha Hashem hagedula vehagevura vehatiferet"* – "To you O God, is the greatness and the strength and the beauty." The Kabbala has taught that when both tendencies, that of expansion, called *ḥessed* or *gedula*, and that of contraction, called *gevura*, are united in the proper proportions, the result is *tiferet* – beauty, harmony, majesty. From God's example we human beings may learn the great secret of combining *ḥessed* and *gevura* to produce *tiferet*. May we and all the world be blessed with the quality of *tiferet* – beauty of life, majesty of ideals, and nobility of destiny.

Three Long Lessons from One Short War[1]

The difference in mood and temperament in all our people between last Saturday and this one can be summed up in one verse of King David's Psalms (118:5) that we recite in our *Hallel*: "*Min hametzar karati yah*," "From the straits I called out to the Lord," "*anani bamerhav Yah*, "and the Lord answered me with enlargement." Last week we called out of our anguish, hemmed in by enemies on all sides, encircled by adversaries seeking to destroy us utterly. By this Shabbat, the Lord has given us His blessing, He has enlarged us; we are now able to breathe more safely and securely, having broken out of the ring of death that has encircled us only a few days ago.

What does this sudden deliverance mean? Of course, it is vain to attempt to see the events that have occurred to us this week in their proper perspective. This chapter in history is hardly over; we are still very much involved in its consequences. Yet, time in our days has become condensed, communications are incredibly rapid, and even wars are fought and decided in three or four days; hence,

---

1. June 10, 1967. The Six-Day War ended on this day.

our understanding must keep pace and our evaluation must be accelerated.

We do this although we appreciate how complicated our problem is – especially considering events which can be described as nothing less than *nisim*, miracles. Indeed, they are not the garden variety of miracles, the *nisim nistarim* (hidden miracles), but quite obviously they are in the category of *nisim geluyim*, evident and open miracles which only a blind man can fail to see and only one who is obtuse can fail to appreciate. The victory of Israel was totally unexpected by the victor, by the enemy, or by the observers. The extent of what has happened staggers the imagination. This is the week that Jews for the first time in twenty years visited the grave of Rachel in Bethlehem, and that for the first time in the memory of any person alive today, a Jew entered the *me'arat hamakhpela*, the burial grounds of the Patriarchs of Israel. Above all else, this is the week that Jews once again danced in the streets of Jerusalem *"ke'ir she'ḥubra la yaḥdav"* (Psalms 122:3), a city united. Jerusalem is one; no longer two Jerusalems! This is the week that Jews once again prayed at the Wailing Wall, shedding tears not of anguish but of joy and reunion.

So it is difficult, but necessary, to take the long look, to attempt to recapitulate some of the important lessons of this short war.

The first one was stated quite clearly and simply by King David: *"Al tivteḥu vindivim,"* "You shall not trust in the princes" (Psalms 146:3). You shall not place your ultimate faith in presidents or prime ministers, in generals or commanders, in treaties or alliances.

It is still too early to tell what extent the President of the United States and the Prime Minister of England stood by us, and how extensive was their support for us, given the possibilities of nuclear confrontation with Russia. For whatever genuine help we did receive, we are eternally grateful. Yet it is clear that, in essence, Israel fought alone – and probably will remain mostly alone in the diplomatic battles that are yet to come. The supposed best friend of Israel stood aloof when the crisis came, remotely neutral in his "grandeur"... others, bound to Israel by treaty, waited for other maritime powers to join it before honoring that treaty; it waited and waited and, when no one came, made no move on its own. Our State Department ignored American commitments – in thought, word, and deed.

NASO: *Three Long Lessons from One Short War*

All this – and, I fear, what lies ahead in the days to come – recalls the old adage: May God protect me from my friends, I will take care of my enemies myself. We must realize that in an ultimate sense we are, as a Gentile prophet noticed with great perception, "*am levadad yishkon*," "a people that dwelleth alone" (Numbers 23:9). Of course, Israel needs and should seek alliances, just as individuals need and should seek out friends. But after all is said and done, we are a lonely people. It is that loneliness which is our greatest weakness and our greatest strength, a source of our deepest anguish and our highest joy.

In the first of the three-fold blessing of the priests as given to us in today's *sidra* (Numbers 6:24-26), we read "*yevarekhekha Hashem*," "The Lord bless you," "*veyishmerekha*," "and keep you." Our tradition (*Sifri Zuta* 6:24) has explained this last word as, "*veyishmerekha min hamazikin*," "May the Lord keep you from those who would injure you." "*Mazikin*" generally is translated as "demons, injurious spirits." The Aramaic translator Targum Jonathan identifies two groups of such *mazikin*. He refers to them as "the sons of dusk" and "the sons of dawn." There are two kinds of demons – those who appear in their true colors, black as night, and those who disguise themselves in the brightness of dawn. Some *mazikin* show their blackness openly; Russia and the Arabs are good examples. Others appear as sweet as dawn. India, for example, has always postured as a paragon of peace and piety. Yet, when it comes to Israel, she is nothing more or less than a *mazik*, a malevolent spirit. Close friends of Israel, such as the French government, have proved that underneath the exterior of being "sons of dawn" they are yet *mazikin*, ready to injure us. And even closer friends who are well-intentioned and would genuinely want to remain "the sons of dawn" found themselves ready to abandon us before our strength showed.

The second of the three lessons has to do with the performance of our religious youth. It was amazing how all people of good will rallied to our side: Non-Jews of all walks of life demonstrated friendship, and almost all Jews – with the exception of a sick and psychotic minority which does not deserve to be dignified by mention – were united in their enthusiasm. But the noblest example of all was provided by those many young people who were ready to give not only their substance but

31

themselves, their own lives, placing themselves at the disposal of Israel wherever they might be needed in that war-torn country.

It is a source of profound pride to us that the first to volunteer – when the situation was still dark and dismal – and in numbers highly disproportionate to our percentage of the population, were students of Yeshiva University and other yeshivot, young people who had day school backgrounds, some Jewish education, some anchorage in a life of Torah, some *rei'ah* (spirit) of Torah. I am told that at the beginning of the crisis crowds of young people gathered at the Jewish Agency building to volunteer their services for Israel, and that a leading secular Zionist ideologist opened the door to the office, observed the young people, and turned to an Orthodox member of the Jewish Agency staff, asking, "I wonder where the boys without the *kippot* are!" Certainly we have noticed the presence of young religious Jews in the pictures that appeared in the press and in the rally in Washington, DC. We have always known of the greatness of Torah; rarely have we had this God-given opportunity to observe the graciousness of Torah! What a *kidush Hashem* (sanctification of God's name)!

The second of the three-fold blessing reads, "*Ya'er Hashem panav elekha,*" "May the Lord cause His countenance to shine upon you," "*viyhuneka,*" "and be gracious unto you." Our tradition saw in the blessing of God's bright countenance a reference to Torah – "*Torah ore,*" "The Torah is considered light" (Proverbs 6:23). That is why this blessing is interpreted by the Rabbis (*Tanhuma* 18:24) as "*ya'amid mimkha banim benei Torah,*" "May the Lord give you children who will be students of Torah." On the second half of that blessing, "*viyhuneka,*" they offer a comment according to which the word should be translated not "and God will be gracious unto you," but rather "*yiten hinkha be'einei haberiyot,*" "God will give you the gift of appearing gracious to others!" This indeed is what has happened: Those of our children who deserve the honorific title of *benei Torah* suddenly appeared in a marvelous and wondrous aura of *hen,* of genuine Jewish graciousness and charm. Would that this unusual but thoroughly proper "image" became usual and natural!

The third point is that what Jews could not accomplish, the Arabs did – they united the Jewish people. The sense of purpose and unity was evident to all. Even in Jerusalem, where opinions are sharp and disagreements strong, religious groups of all types were unified. In New York too, with a few painful exceptions, our people were united. A great spirit of fellowship overtook all Jews of all persuasions. Jews who never admitted to being Jewish, neighbors who, according to the custom of this great and faceless metropolis, never greet each other, suddenly smiled at each other with a new and effusive friendship. The blessing of peace, *shalom*, had overtaken our people.

This, indeed, is the third and greatest blessing: "*yisa Hashem panav elekha,*" "May the Lord turn His face unto you," "*ve'yasem lekha shalom,*" "and grant you the blessing of peace."

Quite appropriately, the *Yalkut* (ad loc.) comments that, "Peace is so great, that even in times of war it is necessary to have peace!" Apparently what the Rabbis meant by this remark is that war should never be absolute, even when it is necessary. There should always be some pacifist residue, some irenic core, some opportunity left for establishing peaceful relationships. Even in the course of war, we must find peace.

However, I should like to express a deeply-felt hope based upon a paraphrase of this statement of the Rabbis. I would prefer to read that "now that we have learned to find peace and unity in times of war, may we, in looking ahead, strive for the blessing of peace even during peacetime!" May we learn to cherish this fellowship and oneness even when we are not threatened from without. We must make a new start not for superficial uniformity, but in always asserting the underlying oneness of the people of Israel even while disagreeing and arguing with each other.

Furthermore, our hope for *shalom* must apply to the entire Middle East, as the blessing of peace between Israel and the Arab countries, distant though that seems. A victory can be meaningful only if it results in enduring peace. The Hebrew word for victory, *nitzahon*, derives from the word *netzah*, which means eternity. Military victory is meaningful only if it is followed by eternal peace, or at least harmony, for a long, long time. Our current *nitzahon* will not have been complete unless we can look forward to a *netzah*-type peace which will follow. Of course, if it does not come, we will survive anyway. The Jewish people have changed part of their character these last twenty years. We will no longer submit to enemies in order to satisfy their whims or interests. In the biblical era, it appears that our people had to fight every forty years for survival; nowadays, apparently, the cycle comes every ten years. We can do it if we have to. But this is not our choice. We are not, despite our fantastic military successes, a martial people. Our ambition is always that of *shalom*, that of peace for ourselves and for the entire world, and peace and war cannot long coexist.

So we ask Almighty God on this day for His threefold priestly blessing. We ask Him to bless us and "*veyishmerekha*," to guard us from all those who would injure us, whether these damaging demons growl black as night or smile bright as dawn.

We ask of Him that He cause His countenance to shine upon us, by giving us a generation which will be guided by the light of Torah and which will continue to serve as a source for the special Jewish charm of *ḥen*; for this is the blessing of "*viyḥuneka*."

And above all else, we ask for "*veyasem lekha shalom*," unity in our own camp, harmony in the Middle East, peace in the world.

We conclude with the same words with which that priestly blessings concludes: "*Vesamu et shemi al benei Yisrael*," "And they shall place My name on the Children of Israel, "*va'ani avarkhem*," "and I shall bless them."

May the Name of God indeed be placed upon Israel so that our people will become not only champions in war, but, as the very name Yisrael indicates (as it incorporates His Name, *El*, in its name), we will become the champions of the Lord; and that shall be our great blessing: "*va'ani avarkhem*."

Aristocracy in Jewish Society [1]

T he quality and the character of a society can usually be measured by the kind of people it chooses to honor. A nation's heroes are normally a good index of its mores. You can know a people by observing whether it esteems bull fighters or poets, cloak-and-dagger operatives or philosophers, politicians or musicians, men of wealth and success or spiritual personalities.

With this in mind, it is instructive to inquire what kind of society Judaism envisions for us and how successful we Jews have been, in practice, in conforming to this normative society and the ideals laid down for it by our faith.

At the end of the last portion, *Bemidbar*, we read the commandment to take the census and assign duties to the family of Kehat, of the tribe of Levi (4:2). This morning's *sidra*, *Naso*, continues with the commandments of the census and assigns the duties to the family of Gershon.

---

1. June 9, 1973. This sermon is largely based on the ideas of the late Prof. Feivel Meltzer.

Now, it has been asked: Why is Kehat given precedence over Gershon, especially since Gershon is the firstborn? The Rabbis of the Midrash (Numbers Rabba 6:1) put it this way:

> Although Gershon was the firstborn, and we find in every place that Scripture grants honor to the firstborn (*kavod labekhor*), due to Kehat being the one assigned to carry the ark, which contained the Torah, he was given precedence over Gershon.

We learn, therefore, that *kevod haTorah* is greater than *kavod labekhor* – that scholarship in Jewish life ranks over primogeniture.

Jewish law clearly lays down the priorities of respect and honor granted to different categories of people, and this order represents the ideal hierarchy of Jewish society. In it, primacy is given to the sage, the wise man, the scholar. Unlike Plato, the Rabbis did not place at the apex of society the Jewish version of the "philosopher-king." They did not identify the man of intellect with the man of political authority and civic sovereignty. Rather, they gave the highest esteem to the *ḥakham*, the Jewish equivalent of a philosopher, and second to him was the *melekh*, the king.

We are taught in the *Tosefta* (*Horayot* 2:8) that the order of priority is: sage, king, high priest, prophet. These four are the heroes of Jewish society.

Consider the prophet. The reverence for him is clearly established in our tradition. Indeed, as part of the blessings over the *haftara*, we bless God who "chooses the Torah and Moses His servant and Israel His nation and His prophets of truth and righteousness." Yet, the prophet remains subordinate to the other three. Why is this so? Because prophecy is a response to negative conditions. Prophecy is not, as with soothsayers or magicians in other cults, a matter of forecasting or predicting the future, but primarily its task is to reproach and reprove and rebuke the people and summon them back to God and to Torah. The prediction of future consequences is but one aspect of the prophet's task of *toḥakha*, of rebuke. Hence, the whole office of the prophet is called into being only when the people reveal profound inadequacies and failures and backslidings. That is why the Rabbis said

(*Nedarim* 22b) that if the Israelites had not sinned, they would have had no need for any books besides the Five Books of Moses and the book of Joshua.

The next in order are king and high priest. Notice that the king comes before the high priest. Why is this so? Because Judaism does not assert a sharp dichotomy between the religious and the secular, as other faiths do. We do not believe that we must render unto Caesar what is Caesar's and unto God what is God's. All is God's realm, and the king has his role to play in it. Political leadership has a "religious" function too, namely, that of establishing social peace and harmony and justice. Indeed, the priest has, as his main task, the ordering of the relationship between man and God, *bein adam laMakom*, whereas the king is charged with establishing proper relationships *bein adam lehaveiro*. It is for this reason that the king takes precedence over the high priest.

But at the very pinnacle of the ideal Jewish hierarchy comes the sage, the *hakham*.

The Rabbis (*Avot* 4:13) told us of three crowns: the crown of Torah, the crown of the priesthood, and the crown of kingship. And in *Avot DeRabbi Natan* (1:41) we learn that one can never buy the crown of priesthood. Similarly, one can never buy the crown of royalty (although the effort has been made and it has been done – but illegitimately). Actually, both the high priesthood and kingship go from father to son. But when it comes to the crown of Torah, one not only cannot buy it, he need not pay a penny for it. It is available to whoever desires it. All one must do to seize the crown of Torah is to spend his whole life in it, to experience sleepless nights, to suffer for it, to give up all the pleasures of the world that stand in the way of acquiring greatness and wisdom of the Torah. No wonder that an illegitimate child who is a scholar precedes a high priest who is an ignoramus (*Mishna Horayot* 3:8)!

Of course, not all *hokhma* is creative and constructive. The Jewish tradition knows of a *hakham lehara*, or evil genius (see, for example, *Yalkut Shimoni*, Genesis, 25). True wisdom remains that which is based upon piety: "The beginning of wisdom is fear of God" (Psalms 111:10).

Not only do I refer to piety in the conventional sense, but also to any intelligence applied to the improvement of man's life in the face of God. Thus Jeremiah told us (9:22-23):

> Let not the wise man (*ḥakham*) glory in his wisdom, neither let the mighty man glory in his might, let not the rich man glory in his riches. But let him that glories glory in this, that he understands and knows Me, that I am the Lord who exercises mercy, justice, and righteousness, in the earth; for in these things I delight, says the Lord.

True wisdom is the imitation of God, and God's personality is one which seeks the establishment of love and justice and righteousness in the world. Hence, any human being who uses his mind and heart and intellect and will in order to realize and implement these great qualities is a wise man. Judaism hence approves of the *ḥokhma* of the scientist who improves life as an act of *ḥessed*; the intelligence of the philanthropist and the wisdom of the jurist and the businessman or any citizen whose goal is mercy, justice, and righteousness. But, above all others is the *ḥakham*, the wise individual who is learned in the ways of Torah, who exposes himself to the direct message of the will of God.

Have we Jews succeeded? The answer is a fluctuating one. Generally, I believe that the answer is more positive than negative. For instance, European Jewry, especially pre-Emancipation Jewry, and the part that remained in the *shtetl* of Eastern Europe, as well as central Europe in some cases, was one which came close to realizing this social hierarchy of Judaism. The greatest dream of parents was not that their children become doctors or lawyers or engineers or very wealthy people, but that they become *talmidei ḥakhamim*. Jewish children were put to sleep in their cradles with the lullaby "*Toyreh is the best seḥoyreh*," "Torah is the best reward."

Israel today, with all its problems and its military needs, still reverences learning. Of the four presidents of Israel, the first incumbent, Chaim Weitzman, *alav hashalom*, and the present president, Prof. Katzir, are both men of science. The other two, Dr. Ben Zvi, *alav hashalom*, and that great Jew, Zalman Shazar, achieved renown in Jewish scholarship.

In the United States, we were not so fortunate. It used to be that any national Jewish organization – even Orthodoxy, or perhaps especially Orthodoxy – felt that no convention meeting could be complete without a guest speaker who was preferably wealthy, non-Jewish, and either a politician or a humorist. Organizations vie with each other in getting "name" people in the hope that by honoring them some of the honor would reflect back on themselves. But the people they chose to honor were certainly not those who could fit the prescription of the ideal Jewish structure.

Fortunately, the pendulum is swinging away from that kind of self-abnegation and unworthy attitude. A younger generation is more sophisticated, more accepting of its Jewishness, more understanding, and less sycophantic. They understand that true Judaism calls for the *ḥakham* to have the highest rank in the Jewish world.

At Sinai we were told that we were going to be and must be a "kingdom of priests and a holy nation" (Exodus 19:6), a people who emphasized priesthood and prophecy. Yet our special pride above all else was told to us by Moses before he died:

> For this is your wisdom (*ḥakhmatkhem*) and your understanding in the sight of the peoples, that, when they hear all these statutes, shall say: "Surely this great nation is a wise (*ḥakham*) and understanding people. (Deuteronomy 4:6)

Beha'alotekha

A Definition of Anivut [1]

Our *sidra* this morning introduces us, rather casually and incidentally, to one of the most important and highly celebrated virtues in the arsenal of religion – that of *anivut*. We read in today's portion, "And the man Moses was the most humble (*anav me'od*), above all the men that were upon the face of the earth" (Numbers 12:3). Whatever may be the particular translation of the Hebrew word *anav*, the idea that is usually imparted is that *anivut* is humility, a feeling by the individual that he lacks inner worth, an appreciation that he amounts to very little. Indeed, the author of *Mesilat Yesharim*, one of the most renowned works on Jewish ethics in all our literature, identifies the quality of *anivut* with *shiflut* – the feeling of inner lowliness and inferiority. According to this definition, then, the Torah wants to teach each of us to see ourselves in a broader perspective, to recognize that all achievements are very trivial, attainments mere boastfulness, prestige a silly exaggeration. If Moses was an *anav*, if he was humble and able to deprecate himself, how much more so we lesser mortals should be humble.

---

1. June 8, 1963.

However, can this be the real definition of this widely heralded quality of *anivut*?

We know of Moses as the *adon hanevi'im*, the chief of all the prophets of all times, the man who spoke with God "face to face" (Exodus 33:11). Do the words, "And the man Moses was the most humble" mean that Moses himself did not realize this? Does the *anivut* of Moses imply that he had a blind spot, that he failed to recognize what any school child knows? Does a Caruso[2] have to consider himself nothing more than a choir boy, and an Einstein merely an advanced bookkeeper, in order to qualify for *anivut*? In order to be an *anav*, must one be either untruthful or genuinely inferior?

To a very great extent, modern psychology is concerned with the problem of inferiority. Deep down, people usually have a most unflattering appraisal of themselves. Many are the problems which bring them to psychologists and psychiatrists; yet all so often the underlying issue is the lack of self-worth. Are we, therefore, to accept the Jewish ethical prescription of *anivut* as an invitation to acquire an inferiority complex?

In addition, the definition of *anivut* as self-deprecation and humility does not fit into the context of today's *sidra*. The identification by the Torah of Moses as an *anav* is given to us as part of the story in which we learn of Aaron and Miriam, the brother and sister of Moses, speaking ill of Moses behind his back. They criticize him harshly because of some domestic conduct in his personal life. They are wrong, and they are punished by the Almighty. But what has all this to do with the humility of Moses? The substance of their criticism, namely, the domestic relations of Moses, is as unrelated to Moses' humility as it is to his artistic talents or his leadership ability.

Furthermore, the Talmud relates an exchange that is all but meaningless if we assume that *anivut* means humility. The Talmud (*Sota* 49a) tells us that when Rabbi Judah the Prince died the quality of *anivut* disappeared with him. When this was stated, the famous Rabbi Joseph disagreed. He said, "How can you say that when Rabbi Judah

---

2. Enrico Caruso (1873-1921) was an Italian tenor.

died *anivut* vanished? Do you not know that I am still here?" In other words – I am an *anav*!

Now, if *anivut* really means humility, does this make sense? Can one boast of his humility and still remain humble? Is it not of the essence of humility that one should consider that he possesses this virtue in himself?

It is for these reasons, and several more, that the famous head of the Yeshiva of Volozhin, popularly known as the Netziv, offers us another definition of *anivut* (in his *HaAmek Davar*) which, I believe, is the correct one. I would say that the definition the Netziv offers means, in English, not humility, but meekness. It refers not to self-deprecation but self-restraint. It involves not an untruthful lack of appreciation of one's self and one's attainments, but rather a lack of arrogance and a lack of insistence upon *kavod*, honor. To be an *anav* means to recognize your true worth, but not to impose the consequences upon your friends and neighbors. It means to appreciate your own talents, neither over-emphasizing nor under-selling them, but at the same time refraining from making others aware of your splendid virtues at all times. *Anivut* means not to demand that people bow and scrape before you because of your talents, abilities, and achievements. *Anivut* means to recognize your gifts as just that – gifts granted to you by a merciful God, and which possibly you did not deserve. *Anivut* means not to assume that because you have more competence or greater endowments than others that you thereby become more precious an individual and human being. *Anivut* means a soft answer to a harsh challenge, silence in the face of abuse, graciousness when receiving honor, dignity in response to humiliation, restraint in the presence of provocation, forbearance and a quiet calm when confronted with calumny and carping criticism.

With this new definition by the Netziv, the statement of Rabbi Joseph becomes comprehensible. When he was told that with the death of Rabbi Judah the Prince there was no more meekness left in the world, he replied with remarkable candor and truthfulness: You must be mistaken, because I, too, am meek. There is no boastfulness here – simply a fact of life. Some people are meek, some are not. If a man says, "I am humble," then obviously he is not humble; but if a man says, "I am meek," he may very well be just that. In fact, the Talmud tells us that Rabbi Joseph was at least the equal in scholarship of his colleague, Rabba, but that when the question arose who would head the great Academy in Babylon, Rabbi Joseph deferred to Rabba. And furthermore, all the years that Rabba was chief of the Academy, Rabbi Joseph conducted himself in utter simplicity, to the point where he did all his household duties himself and did not invite any artisan or laborer, physician or barber, to come to his house. He refused to allow himself the least convenience which might make it appear as if he were usurping the dignity of the office and the station occupied by his colleague Rabba. This is, indeed, the quality of meekness – of *anivut*.

And this meekness was the outstanding characteristic of Moses as revealed in the context of the story related in today's *sidra*. Here were Aaron and Miriam, both by all means lesser individuals than Moses, who derived so much of their own greatness from their brother, and yet they were ungrateful and captious and meddled in Moses' personal life. A normal human being, even a very ethical one, would have responded sharply and quickly. He would have confronted them with their libelous statement, or snapped some sharp rejoinder to them, or at the very least cast upon them a glance of annoyance and irritation. But, "The man Moses was the most meek, more so than any man on the face of the earth." Although aware of his spiritual achievements, of his role as leader of his people, even of his historical significance for all generations, Moses entertained no feelings of hurt or sensitivity, of injured *kavod*. There was in his character no admixture of pride, of arrogance, of harshness, of hyper-sensitivity. He had an utter lack of gall and contentiousness. He was, indeed, an *anav*, more so than any other individual on the face of the earth. And he was able to write those very words without self-consciousness! Hence he did not react at all to the remarks of his brother and sister. Therefore, God said that if Moses is such an *anav* that he does not defend himself against this offense, I will act for him!

The quality of *anivut*, as it has been defined by the Netziv, is thus one of the loveliest characteristics to which we can aspire. One need not nourish feelings of inferiority in order to be an *anav*. Indeed, the greater one is and knows one's self to be, the greater his capacity for *anivut*, for meekness. It is the person who pouts arrogantly and reacts sharply and pointedly when his ego is touched who usually reveals thereby feelings of inferiority and worthlessness, of deep *shiflut*. The individual who feels secure and who recognizes his achievements as real can afford to be meek, to be an *anav*.

For it is this combination of qualities – inner greatness and outer meekness – that we learn from none other than God Himself. The Talmud (*Megilla* 31a) put it this way: "Wherever your find mentioned the *gedula*, the greatness, of God, there also you will find mentioned His *anivut*." Thus, for instance, where we are told that God is mighty and awesome, immortal and transcendent, there too we learn that God is close to the widow and the orphan, the stranger and the sick, all those in distress, those overlooked, ignored and alienated from the society of the complacent. God's *anivut* certainly does not mean His humility or self-deprecation! It does mean His softness, gentleness, kindliness – His meekness.

Here, then, is a teaching of Judaism which we can ill afford to do without. When we deal with husband or wife, with neighbor or friend, with children or students, with subordinates or employees – we must remember that the harsh word reveals our lack of security, and the impatient rejoinder shows up our lack of self-appreciation and self-respect. It is only when we will have achieved real *gedula*, true inner worth and greatness, that we shall learn that remarkable, sterling quality of *anivut*.

Let us leave the synagogue this morning aware of that mutual, reciprocal relationship between greatness and meekness. If we have *gedula* let us proceed to prove it by developing *anivut*. And if we doubt whether we really possess *gedula* then let us begin to acquire it by emulating the greatest of all mortals, Moses, and the immortal Almighty Himself, and practice *anivut* in all our human relations. If this *anivut* does not succeed at once in making us truly great, it at least will offer us the dividends of a better character, a happier life, more relaxed social relations, and the first step on the ladder of Jewish nobility of character.

Spiritual Truancy [1]

Whenever the ark is opened in the synagogue, the congregation rises and recites the words of the famous prayer (Numbers 10:35), "*vayehi bineso'a ha'aron*," that when it came to pass that the ark set forward, Moses would utter a special invocation to the Almighty. The origin of this prayer which, together with the brief passage we recite when closing the ark, is in today's *sidra*.

However, beautiful as this prayer is, it is obviously out of place. When we view it in the context of the *sidra*, we notice that it disrupts the biblical narrative. Our tradition too recognized this fact, and therefore in the Masoretic text this paragraph is set off by special symbols.

But why indeed was this particular passage placed here? The Rabbis, quoted in Rashi, give the following reason: "to interrupt the tale of one disaster and that of another." In order not to make the series of catastrophic events that occurred to our ancestors in the desert too depressing and overwhelming, the Torah interrupts its story by telling us of the prayer recited when the ark was set forward.

---

1. May 31, 1964.

What were these disasters? What is the relation between them? And what is the relevance of this particular passage, "*vayehi bineso'a ha'aron,*" to the woeful tales it interrupts?

Were we to look ourselves for the first disaster, the one before "*vayehi bineso'a ha'aron,*" we would be hard put to locate it. All we read in this preceding passage is that the Children of Israel journeyed from the mountain of the Lord a distance of three days. Is this a calamity?

Yes, answers Ramban. These words indicate that the Children of Israel were a bit too overjoyed in travelling away from the mountain of the Lord! Ramban quotes with approval the *aggada* which describes with consummate artistry the quality of Israel's journeying as having been, "like a school child running away from school." They thought they had absorbed enough commandments at Mt. Sinai, and they were afraid lest the Almighty add commandments to those they had already received from Him!

What an insight we are given here! The Children of Israel were more like little children fleeing their school. They were chafed, they were irritated, they were annoyed. They felt that they had received too much homework, that too much discipline had been imposed upon them, and that their freedom of motion was much too restricted. They regarded Sinai, that great schoolroom of humanity, as an intolerable burden – and burdens were made to be disposed of. So the first great disaster was the attitude of spiritual truancy.

Do we not experience this attitude all too often in our own lives, in our own society? All too frequently we approach our religious obligations in a manner more belabored than beloved. Our observance lacks joy, it lacks love, it lacks inner attachment. We, whom this age of automation has given so much leisure, come to the synagogue to worship, and begrudge the time we spend on prayer. We carefully monitor our sessions in the synagogue with our watch. Heaven forbid lest services continue beyond the prescribed time! And this dictatorship of the watch, this tyranny of the schedule, applies to our study of Torah as well. How wisely the Yiddish distinguishes between these two attitudes: between "*davenen*" and "*updavenen,*" between "*lernen*" and "*uplernen.*" One means to pray with one's whole heart and soul; the other means to mumble the words as if they were an obligation that must be disposed of with the greatest dispatch. One means to study with the complete participation of one's intellect and emotions; the other means to listen to a lecture only because it is "the thing to do." The same distinction applies to philanthropy – people who are accustomed to almost unlimited self-indulgence, will, when confronted with a request for charity, plead poverty! No matter what the religious obligation is, we accept it with reluctance rather than with relish.

Even when we do observe the commandments, it is all too often with a jaundiced eye. And sometimes it occurs to us to ask, whether openly or silently, "Why can't the Rabbis make it easier for us?" As if the Torah were the invention of a malevolent group of individuals known as Rabbis who derive some special, obscure, sadistic delight from curbing and restricting their fellow Jews. "Like a school child running away from school."

This holds true not only for individuals but for communities as well. I often have the occasion to speak to various communities throughout the country in an attempt – sometimes successfully, usually not – to improve their religious level, whether it be that of *meḥitza* or *mikve*, and so forth. What resistance I encounter! Sometimes it is almost resentment, as if the whole community asks, are we not doing enough already? Are we not splendid people in that we have allowed God in to our institutions as much as we have?

What synagogue or community cannot stand some improvement – yet, how few are willing to appreciate this!

All this points to a lack of love, an absence of inner commitment – and therefore a religion which is joyless and unhappy. It is the approach of a child who flees from, rather than to, school. It is the grievous error of spiritual truancy. And this indeed is the first great catastrophe of any people.

The second catastrophe, the disaster which is mentioned after the paragraph of "*vayehi bineso'a ha'aron*," consists of the same attitude – except worse, in a more advanced stage of degradation. It is an attitude which came to the fore when the Children of Israel voiced their bitter complaints to Moses and said, "We remember the fish which we used to eat in Egypt free" (Numbers 11:5). What a strange remark, "free." Were they not slaves who worked from dawn to dusk in their back-breaking labors? And if so, can the miserable piece of fish thrown to them by their task-masters be regarded as free?

The *Zohar*, however, gives us a profound insight into that one word. They did not mean that it was free in the sense that it cost nothing. Rather, the word means that they were not required to recite a blessing over the food! Because, they argued, "While we were in Egypt, before we came to Sinai, the mountain of the Lord, there was not yet placed upon us the yoke of Heaven." Imagine! How bitterly they complained over the simple obligation of having to recite a blessing over a bit of fish. Not only were they not anxious to receive new commandments, but they wanted to get rid of those they already accepted! When you have a negative attitude towards your religious faith, then even the responsibility to recite a few words of blessing becomes an intolerable burden.

Hence, what begins with a protest against homework ends as a rebellion against all discipline. What begins as a rejection of school ends as a revolt against the divine Teacher. If the first disaster is that of being a truant, the second consists of becoming a drop-out from the school of Sinai.

A Judaism lived without joy and love and affection is disastrous. It is the way of wildness and irresponsibility. It is the way of "free," the way of "without a blessing" – no benediction, no grace, no charm.

And that is why *"vayehi bineso'a ha'aron"* interrupts the narrative at this point, separating between the two disasters. Now, the words *"vayehi bineso'a ha'aron,"* mean, "and it came to pass when the ark set forward." But the *Moshav Zekenim* has correctly pointed out: Does not ordinary logic and grammar call for a different formulation of the events of the ark's movement? Ought it not to have been stated, "And it came to pass when *the bearers of* the ark set forward?" After all, it was the people who carried the ark who began to move.

But the answer is: No, that was only a matter of appearance. Actually the ark moved by itself! *"Vayehi bineso'a ha'aron"* – the ark, the Torah, the whole Jewish tradition, moves under its own steam, it does not rely for its ultimate destiny upon the people who think that they are carrying it. As a matter of fact, as the Talmud has taught (*Sota* 35a), it was the ark who carried those who thought they were carrying it!

Indeed, this is what we must know if we are to rid ourselves of that pernicious attitude which transforms us into little children running away from school. We think we carry the ark – in reality it carries us. We think that our discipline of *mitzvot* is a gift to God – actually, it is His gift to us: "*Ratza HaKadosh barukh Hu lezakkot et Yisrael, lefikhakh hirbah lahem Torah umitzvot*" (*Mishna Makkot* 3:16). We think that it is we who support Torah – little does it occur to us that, to a far greater extent, it is Torah which supports us. We sometimes speak of the regimen of *mitzvot* as a "yoke" – but we too often forget that a yoke is that which will direct us to the greener pastures of the spirit and allow us to carry along with us, during our long journey through life, highly precious baggage: a life filled with meaning, with purpose, with transcendent values.

Many, nowadays, worry about the survival of Judaism. It is a worthy concern. But actually, it is not the main problem. Judaism will survive, one way or the other. Our main problem is, will Jews survive?

Of course there is profound interdependence between the one and the other. There can be no Jews without Judaism, and no Judaism without Jews. But there is a serious question of how many Jews will survive without Judaism, of how much Jewishness we can retain if we abandon Torah. To what extent can we perpetuate our people if we Jews will not express our loyalty to Judaism with more spirit, more love, more happiness?

The distinguished Protestant theologian Reinhold Niebuhr is reported to have stated that Christians and Jews emerged from the Second World War in opposite ways. Christians emerged fairly intact. But Christianity is in deep crisis. It is the faith which informed a Western world and which allowed this bloodbath to take place. With Jews, however, it is reversed: Judaism emerged unscratched. "The Torah of the Lord is perfect" (Psalms 19:8). The bestiality of Western man presents no challenge to a faith, Judaism, which it has refused to accept and has even denigrated for twenty centuries. But Jews – they are in crisis! And the crisis consists specifically in their negative, begrudging, reluctant attitude towards their ancestral faith.

Hence, we must reverse our old approach. Instead of acting like school children scampering from the classroom at the gong of the bell marking the end of the period, we must be mature adults who can hear the bell tolling and return to the *beit hamidrash* to learn all over again how to serve the Lord with joy. Instead of harboring that dangerous fear of "lest the Almighty add commandments" – that there is too much to observe – let us be more apprehensive about the fact that we are not doing enough, nor have sufficient enough feeling.

Then indeed, "*vayehi bineso'a ha'aron*," will we be carried forth – and forward and onward – by the ark of the Torah. Then will we discover in the timeless truth of Torah in the ark that which will bear us through the storms of life and guide us through the wasteland and wilderness of society. Then the Lord will answer Moses' ancient prayer, "*kumah Hashem*, arise O Lord, and defend Your people against all their enemies." Then indeed Jews will survive, the Torah will flourish, and Israel will prosper.

Then too Israel and all humanity will be the recipients of the divine blessing of *menuḥa* – peace and serenity and tranquility. "*Uve'nuḥoh yomar*, and when the ark came to rest, Moses prayed: Return, O Lord, to the myriads of the thousands of Israel."

A Flair for the Undramatic [1]

I

n a *sidra* replete with the stories of Israel's backsliding, of protest and pettiness, of gossip in high places and unrest in low places, there appears at least one bright spot. It is the story of the first Passover celebrated by the Israelites after their exodus from Egypt.

After this happy and joyous celebration, we read that a number of people approached Moses with a complaint. They said to Moses (Numbers 9:6), we are impure (ritually defiled) because we had contact with a dead body before the holiday, and one who is in a state of impurity may not partake in the Passover sacrifice; why should we be deprived from offering the sacrifice of the Lord amongst all other Children of Israel? Do we not deserve any part in the celebration of the Passover?

Moses did not know what to answer, and he turned to God for guidance. The answer from the Lord was the law of "the second Passover." In response to the complaint, Moses was commanded to declare for all generations that in the event that a person is prevented from participating in the Passover in its usual time because he is distant

---

1. June 19, 1965.

from Jerusalem, or in a state of defilement, he may offer a sacrifice and celebrate the Passover one month later.

The Jewish tradition had only praise for these anonymous individuals who presented their petition to Moses. We are told that whereas almost all other portions of the Torah are ascribed to Moses, this particular section concerning "the second Passover" is credited to these petitioners: *"Megalgelin zekhut al yidei zakai"* – if one is inherently worthy, then worthy events occur on his account (Sifrei *Beha'alotekha* 1:22). The Pesikta also teaches us that these people were "decent, righteous, and punctilious" in performing the commandments properly!

Now the Rabbis are usually sparing in their compliments. Is not, therefore, their praise here somewhat extravagant? Are not these panegyrics somewhat inordinate? Furthermore, the petitioners declared that they were defiled, or impure because of contact with a cadaver. There is no explanation of what caused this incident of defilement. Is there, perhaps, some special significance attached to their defilement that occasioned the Rabbis' encomium?

The Talmud (*Sukka* 25b) provides us with a clue to this fascinating interlude in the life of our ancestors in the desert. They tell us that these anonymous individuals had become defiled because of contact with an abandoned corpse. Now the Jewish law and concept of *meit mitzva* possesses the utmost ethical and spiritual significance. The law states that the greatest act of human benevolence, the *ḥessed shel emet*, is the respectful attention one gives to a corpse which no one claims. When an individual dies without friends or relatives to care for him, then the first Israelite to chance upon the corpse is obligated to bury it with reverence and dignity. It is an act of proper generosity for which one can expect no compensation from the beneficiary. Who knows but this person who apparently had no friends, no family, no acquaintances to care for him, who was probably on the fringes of society, a marginal person, perhaps an outlaw and a derelict? Yet Judaism regards every human being as created in the image of God; this individual, therefore, no matter what his status or achievements, is deserving of the full benefit of our kindness, concern, and attention.

Hence, the heroism and the praiseworthiness of those who petitioned for a second Passover lay in this: Look at the alternative with which they were faced – either to celebrate the Passover or to care for the *meit mitzva*. That particular Passover was the first anniversary of their freedom. It would be a highly festive occasion in which all the fold of Israel, according to their many families, would joyously celebrate the most historical *seder* ever – the first one since Egypt. It would be an occasion filled with drama and excitement, with crowds and with joy. All this, however, would have to be relinquished if they attended to the abandoned corpse upon which they chanced. Caring for the *meit mitzva* meant that they would have to spend their time uninterestingly, even morbidly. Out of dedication to duty they would have to give their attention to something that is dull, depressing, even deadly.

Now, everyone likes a party. Yet these people chose the path that was more difficult – the care for the *meit mitzva*. They were willing to forgo the joys of being with their families on this great Passover *seder*, willing to give up the company of wife and children, of family and neighbors, of joy and celebration, in order to pursue their clear moral obligation. They had a flair for the undramatic! They practiced, centuries earlier, the principle that Solomon later proclaimed, "It is better to go to the house of mourning than to go to the house of merry-making" (Ecclesiastes 7:2).

This readiness to forgo the ceremonial and the pleasurable for the dutiful and the unexciting is even more meritorious according to the one opinion in the Talmud which identifies this *meit mitzva* as the corpse of none other than Joseph! They were the bearers of the coffin of that great Jew who, centuries earlier, had been sold down the river to become second only to Pharaoh, and who, before his death, had made his brethren swear that when the Lord would take them out of Egypt and back to the Holy Land they would bear his remains with them.

One can easily imagine that Joseph was then an unpopular figure. The interpretations of history vary in every age. Joseph was no doubt a faded hero – he was the man who brought the Israelites to Egypt, and they were now marching away from Egypt. Joseph represented the Egyptian phase of Jewish history which they were now trying to reverse and to negate. Probably Joseph had about him the tarnished halo of the *shtadlan*, the aristocratic Jew of great influence in the court of the Gentiles, who would plead on behalf of his benighted brethren – a kind of Jewish Uncle Tom. But this new generation was one of democratic self-determination, one of popular mass activism – so that those who bore his coffin had not only to relinquish the pomp and gaiety of Passover, but they also had to bear the burden of devotion to an unpopular cause – all because of an ancient promise and a feeling of historic obligation. Indeed, they were "decent, righteous, and punctilious" in their observance of the commandments!

The importance of this principle can hardly be overstated. Its significance is increased by the fact that it is not appreciated nowadays. Only recently I had a conversation with a college youth, a member of the current generation of campus activists. He is a person who participates in the many expressions of ferment in colleges throughout the country, in causes that are noble and idealistic – usually. I spoke to him about Judaism. His response was, "But what is there in Judaism that is exciting?" Note the emphasis – the exciting, the dramatic. My answer was that there is plenty in Judaism that is exciting and stimulating and meaningful – but not sensational! Judaism is not a matter of riot and teach-ins and sit-ins and protests and demonstrations and marathons of any kind. It is the excitement of a life lived according to noble principles with a historical awareness, and with a willingness to endure and suffer for a great cause. It represents the excitement of representing God every single day of one's life in a world that turns a deaf ear to the Almighty.

Coincidentally, I had a similar conversation some two or three months ago with an Israeli journalist, a young woman who had been heroically active in the underground during the Israeli War of Independence. She is a woman of great nobility of soul who is genuinely searching for meaning in life, and turning in all sincerity to the sources of our sacred tradition. But I noticed that her approach was indeed that of a revolutionary. She was looking for something breathtaking in Judaism, something gripping, something whereby to express her unrest and dissatisfaction. My answer here, too, was that Judaism is revolutionary. It attempts to throw off the yoke of the established order of indifference and meanness and inhumanity and nihilism both within society and the nation – as well as in mankind itself – the entrenched authority of temptation, of egotism, of arrogance. But this revolution requires people who are inspired, not incendiaries. It requires long endurance, not dramatic one-time battles; a willingness to risk living, not only to risk dying. Judaism requires a world-shaking flair for the undramatic.

The great Gaon of Vilna has expanded the concept of *meit mitzva* to include the concept of *mitzva* itself! The *meit mitzva*, he tells us, also includes those commandments, those *mitzvot*, which have become abandoned, neglected, and unattended. Our Rabbis (*Zohar* 50:134) told us that, "Even the fate of the very Torah in the ark is sometimes a matter of *mazal* (luck)!" So it is with the various observances of Judaism – they are often at the mercy of religious fashion. In some generations, certain *mitzvot* are accorded the greatest honor, while others are rejected, unclaimed, abandoned – true *metei mitzva*. A generation later this situation may be reversed – those previously neglected are now accorded all dignities, whereas those that were prominent are now shunted aside to second place. Jewish greatness and spiritual heroism requires us to direct our attention to those commandments that are in the category of *meit mitzva*, which others reject and neglect.

It is worth mentioning a few Jewish institutions which today would belong in that category of *meit mitzva*. Take, for instance, the command of offering a loan to a person who needs it. In our days the commandment of *tzedaka* is quite popular. It is the focus of awards and testimonials, of dinners and banquets and plaques of all kinds. There is a public relations industry built about the commandment to give charity. By comparison, the *mitzva* to lend money to someone who needs it is a *meit mitzva*. Somehow it lacks the appeal of making the benefactor feel that surge of self-importance and self-congratulation. When it sometimes becomes my task to approach people to offer a loan to a third person, I receive the answer: "Charity is charity – but business is business, and a loan is business." Now that is incorrect! Charity is not "charity," not a matter of love and kindness – for the Jew, charity is his spiritual and moral "business," for it is one's duty to share with others what one has. And a loan does not fall in the category of "business is business"; it is equally the obligation of a loyal Jew to prevent his neighbor from becoming a ward of charity. It is charity with the added element of preventive social and economic medicine, of decency and dignity. Even government recognizes that today, and that is why in the new "war on poverty" the attempt is made to give impoverished people loans in order to build themselves up, rather than remaining second-class citizens.

Even within *tzedaka* itself there is an abandoned *mitzva* – that of "*lo yeira levavekha*," that one should not feel bad that he has to give (Deuteronomy 15:10). When we give we ought to do so joyously, not begrudgingly. Whether we give much or little, it should not be attended by grumbling, complaining that we have to give to so many other causes, and pleading poverty to God. "*Lo yeira levavekha*."

Another such *meit mitzva* in our days is the commandment of the exchanging of gifts, *manot*, on Purim. This is a festive holiday on which all sections of our people participate; but we usually neglect the commandment to exchange gifts. Instead, we defer this particular *mitzva* to another holiday, Hanukkah, for reasons best left unexplained from this pulpit. How important to reestablish the importance of this *mitzva* of Purim in its proper time.

I can think of so many other neglected and abandoned commandments. For instance, there is a law prohibiting us to wear garments with a mixture of wool and linen; or the prohibition of shaving with a razor blade, a deed which entails the transgression of five separate commandments in the Torah. So what if we do not understand the reason for these commandments? Do we always understand why we come to the synagogue, why we fast on Yom Kippur, why we hear the *shofar* on Rosh HaShana? Yes, we ought to study and understand the significance of the various practices of Judaism – but there is no excuse for transgressing them until we have become all-wise.

Another abandoned *mitzva* nowadays is the law which commands us to revere our elders by rising in the presence of an aged lady or gentleman. Our children especially ought to learn that – perhaps they would if we would practice it ourselves more often. We always ought to rise out of respect for an older person, whether that person is learned or ignorant, fine or ignoble.

One can mention many more such examples. For instance, the saying of Grace after Meals has fared rather well. After all banquets and other public dinners of Orthodox institutions – at least then – we recite the "*bentchen*." Yet so few, so pitifully few, remember to wash their hands before breaking bread and to recite the blessing of "*al netilat yadayim*." What a reversal of values for a generation which has all but made a fetish of hygiene and cleanliness!

Or take prayer itself. According to the *Halakha*, the morning and afternoon prayers are equally important. Yet there are so many who would never miss charity who rarely pray the afternoon prayer. One would think that busy American Jews who are always looking to "save time," would prefer this prayer, but there is no accounting for the whim and caprice whereby one *mitzva* is cherished and another lies unclaimed, a *meit mitzva*.

Last but certainly not least in this list of abandoned *mitzvot* is the great and sacred Jewish principle of *tzni'ut*, modesty. Modesty in speech, in manner, and especially in dress is terribly important especially now as we are about to go off for our vacations to the various resorts where this great Jewish principle is observed more in the breach than in the practice. I might add, with full sincerity, that the Jewish principle of *tzni'ut* ought certainly be observed in the synagogue, and most especially in Orthodox synagogues where, to our great chagrin, there is a tendency to overlook this *meit mitzva* and sometimes to dress in a fashion that, for the House of God, is both poor taste and poor Judaism.

Unfortunately, one could extend this list much further. There are, regrettably, many more commandments which are the equivalent of abandoned corpses and which, according to Jewish law and ethics, urgently require our immediate attention over all other practices and observances.

Blessed are those who are willing to forgo the ceremonial and the convenient, the popular and the conventional and the fashionable, in order to redeem the neglected, the remote, the unexciting, and the sometimes incomprehensible *mitzvot*!

As we look into our own hearts we shall discover more than one such *meit mitzva* within our own selves. It behooves us to turn to these precepts, each of which is a divine commandment and an integral part of Judaism, even if not practiced widely, or even if ignored by us heretofore.

Then we shall be acting in the sacred traditions of those anonymous heroes of biblical days who petitioned Moses at the occasion of the first Passover, those dedicated men and women who were "decent, righteous, and punctilious" in their observance of the commandments.

May Almighty God grant that we receive as well our second chance, our personal "second Passover," to enjoy those permissible pleasures which we missed out of our single-minded and sublime dedication to duty.

Upstream[1]

I have spoken several times in the last few weeks on what I consider to be the philosophy of modern Orthodoxy: a total commitment to the *Halakha* while living in this world and participating in it fully – culturally, economically, and politically. We spoke critically, even if warmly and lovingly, of a new tendency noticeable in Orthodoxy in recent years to recoil, to recede from the larger community and ignore all those whose interests do not coincide with ours. Our thesis was that this withdrawal from the world, this refusal to confront contemporary life, is not a viable philosophy for Orthodox Judaism in our times. I believe that this is a theme that needs constant reiteration, continuous consideration, and deep reflection.

Today, however, I wish to emphasize the other side of the coin: the caution that we must exercise never to lose ourselves in the world, not to be overly impressed with the great culture in which we live.

This point is made with consummate skill in a comment by the kabbalistic *Midrash HaNe'elam* on a famous passage in today's *sidra*

---

1. June 4, 1966.

which we will all recognize from our prayer book: "*Vayehi beneso'a ha'aron,*" "And it was when the ark set out" (Numbers 10:35), that Moses offered up a brief prayer, asking God to rise (or reveal Himself), and that His enemies shall scatter before Him. Those who paid careful attention to the Torah reading this morning will have noticed that this brief passage of two verses is surrounded, on either side, by a special mark – the inverted Hebrew letter *nun*. These two *nunin hafukhin*, inverted *nuns*, are part of our Masoretic tradition. What do these strange symbols which appear nowhere else in the Torah mean? The author of *Midrash HaNe'elam* spares no words in describing their enormous significance. They are, we are told, "the very glory of God, and the foundation of the world." It is because of this that Jacob blessed his children with them – for one of Jacob's chief blessings for his grandchildren was "*veyidgu larov,*" "Let them be plentiful" (Genesis 48:16). The word *yidgu* is derived from the Hebrew *dag*, for "fish." Another word in Hebrew and Aramaic for fish is *nun*. Thus the Targum reads, for the blessing we just mentioned, "Let them be as plentiful as the fish of the sea."

Furthermore, this *Midrash HaNe'elam* continues, the Almighty excluded idol worshippers from the fraternity of these two *nuns*, and that is why the pagans always bear enmity towards Israel. And, finally, "The Almighty will redeem Israel and bring the Messiah by virtue of these two *nuns*," i.e. by virtue of these two inverted Hebrew letters.

Thus, in sacred extravagance, holy hyperbole, and marvelous mystery, the Rabbis offer us not a mere play on words to delight our literary sense, but exciting spiritual insights that go to the heart of our problem.

For what they mean is that the letter *nun* means "fish," and therefore the inverted letters, the *nunin hafukhin*, symbolize fish that are willing to swim upstream, against the tide, against the currents and tendencies of their surroundings. It is this remarkable quality which characterizes the true Jew and distinguishes him or her from the pagan. The authentic Jew must be able to dissent; to keep apart; to be unpopular, if necessary; to oppose the time; to swim upstream. An individual who cannot swim upstream cannot affirm his own independent judgment against the mob. That person neither respects nor loves himself, and one who does not love himself cannot love others. And our Torah commanded us (Leviticus 19:18): "Love thy neighbor as thyself," not "Hate thy neighbor as thyself."

The upstream tradition of Judaism means that we must dare to be different. It means that when religious observance is frowned upon we must frown right back and follow the dictates of our conscience and the teachings of the *Halakha*. It means that when religion is popular but for the wrong reasons – such as social and esthetic reasons – we must not hesitate to say so openly and urge people to practice their religion for the proper motives. When others, for instance, consider it good style to indulge in uninhibited and unrestrained lavishness, whether in the pagan extravagance of the funeral, or the vulgar exhibitionism of the gala *bar mitzva*, we must not fear to affirm our upstream mentality – to assert the delicacy of Judaism's democratic traditions, its insistence upon simplicity, and the emphasis upon the spiritual and the religious. Whenever we find society in violation of the sacred ideals of Judaism, we must become the *nunin hafukhin*, those who are willing to go upstream and not downstream. We must do so even if we are excoriated, even if the pagans bear us enmity because of it.

The upstream tradition of Judaism also means to dare to be alone. The very heavy emphasis of the midrash on the theological significance of the *nunin* – that they represent the very glory of God and the foundation of the world – shows that true religious distinction comes not when it is easy to be religious, but when one's loyalty is tested in the crucible of heroism. That is why profound religious thinkers and philosophers from Professor Whitehead[2] to Rabbi Joseph B. Soloveitchik speak so often and so broodingly of loneliness as a major component of religious thought and experience. To be different, to go against the tide, often leaves people with a feeling of aloneness; but that is what makes mankind worthy and life worthwhile.

To be different and unpopular and risk loneliness is often extremely difficult and painful – hence, the quite normal desire for assimilation by the minority to the majority, the desire to emulate the

---

2. Alfred North Whitehead (1861-1947) was a renowned English mathematician and philosopher.

non-Jew and adopt whatever is not particularly Jewish. This tendency is reflected in an anecdote which is part of the bittersweet folklore of our people, which often possesses more wisdom then many a philosophy book. It is told of a *maskil*, an enlightened non-believer, that he received the honor of reciting the blessing over the Torah. He performed this act with great devotion, concentrating with obvious piety and sincerity upon the words "*asher baḥar banu*," in which we thank God who has chosen us from all other people to give us the Torah. When he was asked by the congregants why he, a non-believer, demonstrated so much piety in reciting this blessing, he answered that he very genuinely meant what he said. "Now that God has given the Torah and the commandment to Jews, I feel I need not observe them; had He given them to the Gentiles, I would have been impelled by my desire to emulate everything non-Jewish to accept upon myself the terrific burden of studying Torah and observing the *mitzvot!*"

This, indeed, is the downstream tendency so typical of many Jews who may not admit to it openly: flowing gently with the tides of the times into cisterns of assimilation and the backwaters of oblivion.

But the way of Torah is different – it is the way of differentness. There was a Gentile prophet who said of us that we are an "*am le'vadad yishkon*," "a nation that dwells apart and by itself" (23:9). What Balaam was referring to was Jewish originality, spiritual uniqueness, and validity. The upstream tendency of Judaism means that a Jewish home must be different from other homes; that the Jewish synagogue must – in its structure, its worship, its ritual – be unlike other houses of worship; that Jewish education must be different from the usual education; that Jewish *tzedaka* must not be the normal kind of charity; that a Jewish university must be more than just a good ordinary university; and that Israel must be more than just another political entity. This is what the midrash meant when it said that God would bring the Messiah by virtue of the inverted *nunin* – that the Jewish vision of redemption is that we, finally, will be true to ourselves, that every nation will be itself and every individual himself or herself. The differentness of the State of Israel does not mean that it can have no diplomatic relations, no foreign aid, no exchange students. It does mean that, involved with the world, it nonetheless must not surrender its own soul and abandon its own uniqueness.

This, then, is the meaning for us of the inverted letters. We must never swallow Western civilization whole. We must always stand aside. We must never forget that it was Western civilization that produced that obscene execration called Auschwitz – and it was the philosopher Santayana who warned us that he who forgets history is doomed to relive it. The nation that gave us Auschwitz was the most advanced in the world – scientifically, technologically, and culturally too. Only recently I read that one of the leaders of the Gestapo, Heydrich, of accursed memory, used to gather his friends to his home twice a week for a festive listening of Bach, Mozart, and other priceless musical compositions. When he became Governor-General of Czechoslovakia, he set for himself two priorities above all others: to liquidate every Jewish man, woman, and child in his territory; and to rebuild the Prague Opera House as a center for music lovers of all Europe. Now this does not mean that music and culture, science and engineering are *treif* (not kosher). It does mean that we must keep somewhat aloof, that we must adopt a critical stance and not embrace general culture blindly. It means we must exercise dissent and criticism, intelligence and judgment. It means that we must confront all of modern culture, but not necessarily capitulate to it; we must face all the facts of contemporary life but select for ourselves only what is worthy while rejecting all that is morally abominable, never succumbing to that which affronts our conscience as Jews and as humans. It means that "*vayehi bineso'a ha'aron*," the march of Judaism and Israel through history, must often be characterized by *nunin hafukhin*, by going upstream, by opposing the tides of the times.

This afternoon we shall read in *Avot* the famous *mishna* (2:1), "Which is a right way that a man should choose for himself? Whatever is fitting and proper for the one who does it, and fitting to him *min he'adam* (from the man)." The last idiom is usually taken to mean that his actions are regarded as appropriate and proper by society. But more careful study of the idiom reveals an entirely opposite meaning! What the Rabbis meant was that the right way for a man in life is not only one that is fitting for him generally, but that is also fitting for him "*min he'adam*," from the man – it must accord with his own inner self, it must issue from the deepest recesses of his own spirit and conscience. The right way is one that is not dictated by the taste and temperament of others, but by my own inner conscience – by my convictions, not those of my contemporaries; by my standards, not those of my society; by my faith, not those of my friends.

This is the way we must choose for ourselves. It is the way of "*vayehi bineso'a ha'aron,*" the way of the ark of the law in its travels through the wilderness of time. Whether it is with the tides or against them, upstream or downstream, our way should always be *haderekh ha-yeshara*, the right way.

Violence – Jewish Insights into an Un-Jewish Theme [1]

In recent years, months, and weeks the violence that lies latent at the heart of the American character has begun to surface. The recent spate of assassinations has brought into the open and into real life the celebration of violence in American myth and folklore. In hypnotic fascination, as if we were watching what has been previously but a bad dream suddenly turned into real life, we have seen the myth of the cops-and-robbers game and the cowboys-and-Indians battles transformed into the reality of political and social violence.

Of course, it is true, as many commentators have told us, that we must see the problem in perspective. Violence is not a particularly American quality. The killing in our days in Biafra and in Indonesia, the mutual slaughter of the supposedly peaceful Indian Hindus and Pakistani Moslems, and the wholesale massacres in Nazi Germany, were just a few instances of the universal phenomenon of violence. Furthermore,

---

1. June 15, 1968.

it is not just now that Americans have learned the art. Attempts had already been made on the lives of Presidents Theodore Roosevelt, Franklin Delano Roosevelt, and Harry S. Truman. But the successful assassinations of President John F. Kennedy and Dr. Martin Luther King do bring the whole problem into sharper focus. And we must admit that it is no tribute to us that just now we have become concerned with the problem. It seems that we have, all of us, indulged in the national sport of sweeping unfavorable aspects of American life under the national rug, and that is why violence failed to attract our attention when the Ku Klux Klan was on its disgusting rampage of pillage and murder.

Yet, whether it is universal or specifically American, new or old, the recent assassinations of important people in American life represent a tragic and serious blot on our civilization and society. It is a reminder to us that we should never desist from pondering and attempting to eliminate or diminish violence.

Today I wish to speak about the problem not as a psychologist or a sociologist, but as a rabbi, presenting a few Jewish insights into violence, an un-Jewish theme.

For violence certainly is an un-Jewish phenomenon. Interestingly, there is no single Hebrew word that adequately translates the word "violence." The nearest to it is the Hebrew *hamas*, which has both a narrower and broader signification than "violence." That the whole idea is un-Jewish is attested to by our *haftara* of this morning, which concludes on the triumphant spiritual note, "For not by power nor by might but by My spirit, says the Lord of Hosts" (Zechariah 4:6).

This idea is carried over into traditional Jewish typology. The Jew is represented by Jacob, whom the Bible describes as a *"yoshev ohalim"* (Genesis 25:27), literally, a "tent-dweller," but which in Jewish tradition symbolizes the eternal student. At the same time, Esau is a man of *tzayid*, the hunter, the man of blood lust, the one whom his father recognized as a man of violence when he told him, "And by the sword shall you live" (Genesis 27:40). Just as Esau, the father of the Western nations, is a man of pillage and battle, so is Ishmael the father of the Arabs, a man of virtual insensitivity. The Torah describes him as *"pereh adam"* (Genesis 16:12), a wild man, whose hand is in everyone else, and against whom everyone else's hand is set.

This same Jacob, father of the Jewish people, while blessing his other children before his death, expressly resented two of his sons who had indulged in violence. Concerning Simeon and Levi, the old patriarch said, "Simeon and Levi are a pair," "*kelei ḥamas mekheiroteihem*" (Genesis 49:5), normally translated as: "The instruments of violence are their habitation (or, their kinship)." The last word of the Hebrew is puzzling and by no means certain. The Rabbis, however, interpret the word in a manner which sheds light on the entire theme of *ḥamas*. According to this interpretation, Jacob said, concerning the *kelei ḥamas* (weapons) that Simeon and Levi used to destroy Shechem: "*Gezulim hem biyedkhem,*" they were stolen by the brothers, they did not belong to them. For who are weapons of death more appropriate? For Esau, who sold his birthright (Genesis Rabba 98:5). The word *mekheiroteihem* comes from the root *m-kh-r* which means "to sell," and thus refers to Esau. When a Jew takes up weapons, he is indulging in an un-Jewish theme; he is appropriating what is more in accord with the character of an Esau.

Despite this, it would not be correct to say that Judaism subscribes to pacifism. It does not go to the other extreme. That is why Jewish law gives the courts the right to impose *mitat bet din*, capital punishment. That is why the *Halakha* (*Berakhot* 58a) teaches that *haba lehargakh, hashkeim vehargo*, one may kill in self-defense. And Judaism knows of a "just war," one which may be fought either for self-defense or because of divine command. In biblical history there are seven political assassins whom we cherish, such as Yael, who did away with Sisera, the enemy of Israel. Judaism recognizes that in an imperfect society we must sometimes employ violence against the criminal and the enemy in order to prevent him from killing the innocent.

The question of when to accept and when to condemn violence is therefore a sensitive and delicate one. It was the same Jacob who, according to the tradition, was confronted by this very dilemma. Of Jacob we read, as he was preparing for the confrontation with Esau (which he expected to be a bloody one), "And Jacob was sorely afraid and it distressed him" (Genesis 32:8). Why the repetition, both "afraid" and "distressed?" The Rabbis (as quoted by Rashi ad loc.) say: Jacob was afraid lest he be killed and distressed lest he have to kill Esau. Neither of these alternatives appealed to him very much. Not to employ violence meant possibly to submit to death; to use violence went against his whole nature and all his ideals. On the one hand, pacifism leads to the entrenchment of a permanent tyranny. On the other hand, to approve of violence means to embrace murder and corruption as accepted facts of the social order.

Hence, Judaism can approve of violence only in the most restricted form. That is why, although it legislated *mitat bet din*, it kept capital punishment down to a minimum. Thus, Rabbi Akiva and Rabbi Tarphon declared that had they been members of the Sanhedrin, they never would have put a man to death. Although the *Halakha* does not agree with them, it nevertheless tells us that a court which passed the death verdict once in seven years (according to others, once in seventy years) was known as a tyrannical or bloody court. Thus too, although Judaism recognized the "just war," it permitted it only in the case of self-defense; otherwise the king had to receive the consent of the entire Sanhedrin. Also, the prophetic ideal, the whole Jewish vision of the perfect society, was one in which universal peace would prevail. This was more than a projection into the future; it affected contemporary practice as well. Interestingly, the *Halakha* (*Shabbat* 63a) declares that under usual conditions it is forbidden to carry on Shabbat. Nevertheless, this prohibition does not cover *takhshitin*, ornaments or jewelry. But this dispensation excludes one type of ornamentation which is forbidden on Shabbat – that which comes in the shape of a sword or a spear – for Shabbat is primarily a day of peace, and war violates the entire spirit of the Sabbath. Shabbat is a time that we anticipate the prophetic ideal of the Messianic Age, and we must outlaw all symbols of violence on such a day.

Furthermore, Judaism is suspicious of the vigilante. Violence, it is true, must sometimes be used to curb or punish violence – but only with the utmost care. The Midrash (Genesis Rabba 22:12) tells us that after Cain murdered Abel, the first instance of human violence, the birds and the beasts gathered about Cain in a kind of kangaroo court. They cried for vengeance. But then the Almighty noticed that in this zoological Sanhedrin there also appeared the serpent – and then God denied them their wish and declared that whoever killed Cain would himself be punished. Why so? Rabbi Abraham Ḥen, in his *sefer BeMal-khut HaYahadut*, explains that contemplating the serpent, God realized that he was not concerned with the blood of Abel that was spilt, but with the blood of Cain that was not. The serpent was disguising his blood lust as a passionate call for justice.

So Judaism requires a sense of balance, and where violence is unavoidable it must be legally restricted and restrained, and it must be employed only by responsible, decent, and moral people. That is why I would prefer to translate that verse from our *haftara*, "*lo beḥayil velo bekoaḥ ki im be'ruḥi amar Hashem Tzeva'ot*" (Zechariah 4:6) as meaning that strength and power by themselves are improper, and that only when they are utilized in the spirit of the Lord of Hosts can they prove acceptable to the Jew.[2] It is because violence always carries with it the danger of spreading that the members of the Sanhedrin, who alone were empowered to pass the death penalty, had to be people of impeccable moral stature – and even then the death sentence could be issued only when the Sanhedrin convened in the Temple itself, so as to impress them with the gravity of their decision. Jewish law in our time too reveals the same bias. The *shoḥet* (ritual slaughterer), who is empowered by the law to spill blood, though it be but animal blood, must be a God-fearing man. Indeed, the Jewish code of law places higher requirements of piety upon the *shoḥet* than it does upon a rabbi.

Applying this principle to American life, it appears that the first thing we must do is to get guns and all other lethal weapons out of the hands of minors and maniacs. How weird, how grotesque, that in 1968 this great country, which pretends to be the leader of the civilized world, still does not have an adequate gun control law, and that apparently the will of the great majority of our people threatens to be frustrated by the lobbies in Congress. If Congress should fail this week to pass a decent

---

2. Compare the interpretation by the Gaon of Vilna of the verse in Proverbs, "*sheker haḥen vehevel hayofi, isha yirat Hashem hi tithalal*" (31:30). This does not mean that charm is always deceitful and beauty is always false, but rather that these qualities are reprehensible only in a woman who is not pious; but "*isha yirat Hashem hi titha-lal*," if a woman fears the Lord, then she should be praised as well for her charm and her beauty.

gun control law, democracy will have proved a failure, our law makers nothing more than common criminals, or, at best, a collection of rural primitives, and our whole country utterly insane. The excuse that such weapons are necessary for hunters or sportsmen is totally inadequate. As Jews we ought to outlaw any hunting in the first place, whether or not it leads to violence against man. The failure to curb illicit dealing in weapons of death will mean that the culture of this country, which has always prided itself on drawing upon the so-called Judeo-Christian tradition, but which also carries with it a pagan strain, will finally have resolved the tension between its two cultural ancestors, Jacob and Esau, in favor of the latter. We will have opted for that verse which describes Esau, "And by the sword shall you live" (Genesis 27:40) except that the "live" part will be questionable.

Violence, for Jews, means more than the destruction of the life of the victim alone. According to the *mishna* in *Sanhedrin* (4:5), the word for "blood" in Hebrew can be singular (*dam*) or plural (*damim*). When God charged Cain with the murder of Abel, He said to him, "The voice of the bloods (*demei*) of your brother cry out to Me from the earth" (Genesis 4:10). Why the plural? The *mishna* answers that with his act of violence, Cain had spilled both the blood of his brother and the blood of untold generations which might have sprung from Abel's loins.

In the same vein, we can understand the statement of the Sages (*Tosefta Yevamot* 8:7) that, "Whoever spills bloods, diminishes the Image" – i.e., he detracts from God in whose image man was created. Here too we notice the plural, *damim*. Why so? As Rabbi Moshe Ḥaggiz, in *Eleh HaMitzvot*, explains, it is because violence implies spilling the blood of the victim, and, as it were, spilling the blood of the One in whose image man was created.

If we, therefore, in the United States, continue to countenance the subtle incitement to violence in our communications media, in TV and radio and cinema, we will be responsible not only for the victims, but we shall also destroy the soul of our country and diminish its image. For too long now we have been upsetting the equilibrium between the extreme poles of censorship and licentiousness by opting for a policy that "anything goes." The tension between the two ideas has been resolved in favor of the latter. We have permitted murder and mayhem on TV, in our literature, and in our movies. Our literary critics have proved irresponsible; they have identified sadism with realism, and realism with art, making an aesthetic out of violence. We have taken the chaotic cruelty of the jungle and transformed it into ordered brutality, properly programmed and systematically scheduled for given channels – and then we reward the authors with Oscars and Pulitzers. I do not favor a puritanical restrictive censorship over communications media, but I do believe that our liberalism has become a bit too doctrinaire and unresponsive to the realities of society and the perils it faces.

Finally, the problem of violence is not only of concern to the potential assassin or his intended victim, it is a matter for each and every one of us, even the most serene and non-violent.

Permit me to explain. The generation of the flood was destroyed because of various sins, and one of them was *ḥamas*, which is generally translated as "violence." In context, however, the Sages preferred to define *ḥamas* more narrowly as *gezel*, robbery. Thus, when the Lord pronounces doom upon that generation by saying, "The end of all flesh has come before Me, for the earth has become full of *ḥamas*" (Genesis 6:13), Rashi explains that this means that the verdict of universal destruction was issued specifically because of the sin of *gezel*, robbery.

Yet, our Rabbis did not accept this as a perfect identity. They saw a fine distinction between *ḥamas* and *gezel* (Genesis Rabba 31:5). The latter term refers to robbing a man of property that is *shaveh peruta*, worth at least a penny, whereas the term *ḥamas* refers to violently taking from a man that which is worth less than a penny.

What the Sages are saying, I submit, is that from a moral perspective violence is not purely a matter of murder or grand larceny; it begins with and consists of petty crime, the guarded insult, the murder of a man by little bits. In the eyes of God and Torah, *ḥamas*, violence, is not only a matter of the dramatic assassination that makes the headlines, but it is as well the thousand little assaults that we perpetrate every day against our neighbor's sensitivity, a friend's ego, a mate's peace of mind, a parent's dignity, a child's self-respect, a colleague's self-worth, a competitor's equal opportunity. Practically and legally, there is a difference between *shaveh peruta* and that which is worth less than a penny; but morally and spiritually there is not. Every time we smirk at a human being, we spill a drop of his blood; every time we utter a cutting and unkind remark, we kill the victim a little bit; whenever we humiliate another person, we do violence to his or her self-image.

A human *beit din* can punish only for *gezel*, for violence of a larger proportion, that which is *shaveh peruta*. But the Almighty can despair of man and bring utter judgment upon the world even for *ḥamas*, even for less than a penny, even for those who kill another human being not all at once but in little tiny bits.

In the words of Isaiah (11:9), "They shall not hurt or destroy in all My holy mountain" – and when shall this vision of non-violence be realized? "For the earth shall be full of the knowledge of the Lord as the waters cover the sea" – when people will learn and live Torah, when powered by the spirit of the Lord of Hosts, we will strive for the knowledge of God rather than for might or power, when we will learn to respect the inviolate dignity of God's creatures.

To quote the same prophet Isaiah (60:18), "Violence shall no longer be heard in your land, nor desolation or destruction within your border; for in the place of your defensive walls will be the salvation of the Lord, and in the place of your protective gates shall be the praise of Almighty God."

Shelaḥ

Having Self-Respect[1]

There is an old proverb, in the finest and juiciest vernacular, which expresses a great and unfortunate truth – "As the Gentile goes, so goes the Jew." This pointed and biting comment on the Jew in exile is amply attested to by our history. The Canaanites worshipped idols – and later the Israelites did. In the middle ages, the Christians developed ascetic sects – and then some Jews propounded a form of asceticism which smacked of Christianity. The Poles and Cossacks wore a certain type of clothing, and then the Jews adopted and sanctified it and continued to wear it – even long after it had passed out of style. Whether culturally or sociologically or religiously, the Jew has often fallen prey to this form of mimicry which calls for adopting and adapting the least attractive forms and features of other peoples.

Our Sages, in the beautiful homilies they usually employ, underscore this point. In this week's biblical portion we read of the twelve *meraglim* (spies) who were sent to the Promised Land by Moses. Their mission was clear and to the point. They were to spy out the land and

---

1. June 21, 1952.

report their findings to Moses and the people. Two of these special investigators, Kaleb and Joshua, were profoundly impressed by the beauty of the land, its great possibilities and the tremendous potentials of the Israelites in developing and thriving in that country. The other ten spies, however, did not take such a sanguine approach. They were cowed by some giants they had encountered. They brought back reports which sound like a biblical version of *Jack and the Beanstalk*. Disconcerted, discouraged, and disheartened, they submitted a gloomy and pessimistic report. Now pessimism is a highly contagious disease, and soon they infected most of their fellow Jews. The results were tragic and the wrath of God was incurred. But what caused this state of affairs? The *meraglim* must have undergone some special experience which contributed to this campaign of fear and hysteria which they engendered. The Rabbis (as cited by the Ba'al HaTurim on Numbers 13:33) supply the "missing link" in the biblical narrative. One giant, they relate, ate a pomegranate and then threw away the shell. And then the *meraglim* climbed into that shell to seek shelter in it.

What our Sages want to indicate with this story is that the *meraglim* were people who had no self-respect. They were "*golus* Jews" or "*shtadlanim*" even before the Jews settled in Israel. Some Jews, they mean to tell us, will accept even a hollow shell, as long as it was once used by a non-Jew. They are willing to accept it even after it has been emptied of its life-giving pulp and after it has been discarded. Indeed, "as the Gentile goes, so goes the Jew." Twelve staunch princes of their people seeking shelter in a second-hand pomegranate shell! What a shame and disgrace; what a notorious self-debasement! And the Bible itself does not fail to predict the results of an attitude of this sort. By their own testimony, the *meraglim* indict themselves when they say, "And we were in our own eyes as grasshoppers, and so we were in their eyes" (Numbers 13:33). Certainly! For if a man thinks of himself as no more than an insignificant insect, it is the inviolable law of nature that his fellows think of him as being no more than a mere grasshopper. If a man is willing to cringe in the pomegranate shells thrown to him, then thrown to him they will indeed be.

That lesson of self-respect, of not accepting the shells of strange ideologies, of not dancing to someone else's tune, is something which must be impressed upon us with all firmness. A glaring example of that lack of self-respect we Jews display on occasion happened some short while ago when a Jewish mayor of a Jewish city in the Jewish state visited this city. The bus driver of that mayor's city demanded of him, legitimately, that they be granted their one day off on Shabbat. The mayor of Haifa agreed that they deserve a one-day-a-week respite – but not on Shabbat! Any day, but not Shabbat! Here is a man who has done his utmost to keep the streets of his city clean and the avenues of his soul muddy. And leaving aside the fact that the voices raised in protest were few and far between, the committee selected to lay out the welcoming mat to this mayor, saw fit to do him honor with a non-kosher reception. Again the protests were feeble when a storm should have been raised and when every pulpit in the country should have thundered against this unmitigated *chutzpah* and brazen effrontery and presumptuousness.

Why was there no open and clear repudiation of this sort of arrogant audacity? Because, I firmly believe, we had buried our heads in the empty shell of nationalism thrown to us by others. Nationalism can be Jewish too. But only when it is vested with the holiness and sanctity and spirit which is typical of our people. Nationalism without these elements – secular nationalism – is only a hollow shell of an idea which was already out of vogue and being discarded by others when we picked it up. The real lovers of Zion were those who did protest this travesty. The others were, and are, not. How can we expect the respect of others for our people and our religion, if we do not manifest any respect for them?

One can cite example after example of Jews, especially American Jews, indulging in sycophantic mimicry and imitation of everything which tastes of non-Jewish sophistication. This month of June is particularly appropriate for mention of some of the more flagrant examples of Jews adopting Christological ceremonies and features and integrating them in the marriage ceremony. The notorious "double-ring" ceremony, for one, is a Gentile ritual which seems to have some fascination for some Jews. Or take some modern authors – and here I have in mind one of the finest books on Judaism expounded in modern terms ever to appear – who mar otherwise excellent remarks by constant and consistent reference to a "Judeo-Christian" tradition. Here too one detects an attempt, however unconscious, to cringe and beg acceptance from the non-Jew by hiding in the discarded shells of their pomegranates.

One wonders what happened to our Jewish pride and self-respect. We appeal not for vanity, but for self-respect; not for the negation of others, but for the affirmation of ourselves – for the free expression of our desire to pick our own fruit and not grovel in the waste baskets of others for mere shells long discarded. When that day comes, Israel will be ours indeed in the fuller, more meaningful sense. Then we will have gained more than a land – we will have won back ourselves.

On Showing Your True Colors[1]

This morning's portion concludes with the famous passage concerning the commandment to wear fringes, *tzitzit*, on our garments. The Torah demands that one of the four threads, which are to be doubled over into eight, should be colored *tekhelet*, a heavenly blue. The law requires that this dye be prepared from the blood of a special mollusk or snail called the *ḥilazon*. Today we no longer know exactly the identity of this *ḥilazon*; even in the days of the *Mishna* it was scarce. Therefore, the overwhelming majority of Jews today do not wear any *tekhelet* in their *tzitzit*, although some few groups maintain that they can definitely identify this mollusk and therefore do wear one thread of *tekhelet* in their fringes.

Now, far beyond the emblematic or symbolic value of the *tzitzit*, this commandment is full of deep religious meaning and mystical significance. But in addition to this, permit me to commend your attention to a sensitive ethical-moral point regarding the *tekhelet* proposed by the Talmud (*Bava Metzia* 61b). The Sages quote God as saying, "I

---

1. June 4, 1967.

will punish one who affixes a thread of blue dyed with *kala ilan* and announces that it really is *tekhelet.*" Now, the *tekhelet,* coming from the rare mollusk *ḥilazon,* is expensive and scarce; *kala ilan* is a common and cheap vegetable dye, called indigo. One who dyes his fringes with *kala ilan* and proclaims it to be *tekhelet* is therefore palming off the artificial as genuine. The statement in the Talmud is, therefore, a protest against hypocrisy and deception.

How often we witness – or, indeed, are ourselves the victims of – such sham piety and duplicity. We all too often have personal experiences with people who pretend to be righteous and decent, but are really quite ignoble and selfish. And we wonder: Why should such people get away with it? The Talmud, therefore, promises us that God, in His good time, will exact justice on such people. He, as the embodiment of *emet,* truth, will not abide for long such dissimulation by unprincipled people.

Two instances of recent events come to mind, in both of which we Jews collectively were the victims of this prevarication of people posing in *kalan ilan* as if it were *tekhelet,* in indigo substituted for true blue.

The first of these is the official proposal of the Vatican this week that Jerusalem be internationalized. The Vatican is, of course, deeply troubled by the safety of the shrines in the Holy Land. Indeed, how touching, how moving! So profound is its concern that it desires all of Jerusalem to be put under international control. For twenty years no Jews were permitted to visit the Wailing Wall, whereas members of other faiths were permitted access to their shrines. During all this time, the Pope was silent. He acted like a true reincarnation of one of his predecessors who will go down in history as the Pope of Silence. The man who considers himself the symbol and leader of all religions of the world did not utter a single word of protest as long as an Arab flag was flying over Jerusalem, but the minute the Israeli flag was hoisted over the Holy City, he has become exercised. He apparently was untroubled by the slaughter of human beings; he is moved by concern for holy places – provided it is the Israelis who are in control.

No, this is not the *tekhelet* of righteous concern; this is *kala ilan* – his true colors are showing! Let all those amongst us who were the proponents of theological dialogue with the Vatican, all those who considered those who were reluctant to engage in these dialogues as discourteous and uncivilized in not accepting an invitation to talk – let them ponder what has happened this week. Talk, unfortunately, is cheap. Actions speak far louder. The Vatican is the one who proposed "fraternal dialogue" as part of its new doctrinal structure. Look what has come of it – it is the ersatz-blue of *kala ilan*, not the authenticity of *tekhelet*.

The second item that comes to attention is the important speech of the French ambassador to the United Nations a day or two ago. Now, I do not refer to the major contents of his speech. As a compassionate people, we must be profoundly sympathetic with an ambassador who must attempt to make logical, moderate, and ethical a position taken by his chief of state which is not only illogical but almost absurd, totally immoderate despite its protestations of "objectivity," and not only not ethical but treacherous because it represents a unilateral abrogation of a solemn treaty with the State of Israel. What I say, therefore, I intend as a footnote to an important address.

In the course of his speech, the ambassador averred, in attempting to demonstrate France's objectivity and neutrality, that France has never been guilty of racialism against the Jews. What a jejune and empty remark that is! Forgetting the famous Dreyfus case, his statement is particularly infelicitous considering that this very day, June 24, 1322, exactly 645 years ago – after the Jews were accused of poisoning the wells, after massacres and slaughter of Jews in many cities in France, and after the French government levied an enormous fine on all Franco-Jewish communities – on this very day in 1322 another head of France by the name of Charles, King Charles IV, expelled all the Jews from France! For thirty-seven years thereafter, no Jews were to be found in this country.

No, not every country, especially in Europe, can boast of no anti-Semitism tainting its questionable past. It would be much better for France never to use its own lily-white record as proof of its "objectivity" towards Israel. The ambassador's *tzitzit* are showing; and though he would like them to appear blue, they are *kala ilan*, not *tekhelet*.

However, there is no need to berate a human failing that is all too common. I know you will agree with me in condemning hypocrisy, and that I am therefore preaching to the converted. Permit me, rather, to commend to your attention what was said on this talmudic passage by the late and sainted thinker and scholar Rabbi Abraham Hen in his *sefer BeMalkhut HaYahadut*, namely that the reverse is true as well! God is also displeased with one who possesses the genuine *tekhelet* and yet proclaims that it is merely the artificial *kala ilan*. God not only will punish the hypocrite who passes off the artificial as genuine, but He also dislikes the coward who disguises the authentic as the inauthentic. In other words, there is a strong, neurotic tendency for some people to have the courage only of other people's opinions – but not their own! They are afflicted with a moral weakness – they are ashamed of their elementary decency, they are apprehensive lest they have too good a reputation; they are fearful lest their virtue prove anti-social.

Does that sound strange? Yes – but it is a fact nonetheless. There are, apparently, those who wear *tekhelet*, but proclaim that it is only *kala ilan*.

Have you ever seen a man enter a restaurant in the company of colleagues or business associates, be handed the menu, and with nervous eyes darting in all directions clear his throat and apologetically whisper that he is a vegetarian? Of course, the real reason is that he is kosher. Why attribute to *kala ilan* what is really *tekhelet*?

Or, a man is invited to participate in a Friday night engagement, and he declines by explaining that Friday nights he reserves as "family night." Family night? How about Shabbat? Why not call *tekhelet* by its own name instead of announcing it as *kala ilan*?

There are some parents who send their children to day schools and who explain to their neighbors that they do so because they prefer "smaller classes." But why not say outright that the only way to survive meaningfully is through providing a Torah education for your child? Why call it *kala ilan* when in fact it is *tekhelet*?

There are even some people who believe their own propaganda when they proclaim that they support Israel, "because it is the only democracy in the Near East." How foolish! And if Syria were a democracy? And if Nasser were elected by parliamentary procedure, as was Hitler? And if Israel were not American-style democracy in all essentials? Would we then be unconcerned with the fate of Israel? Is our loyalty only political and nothing more? Does not the love of Israel and our solidarity with the people and the state transcend the political considerations? Let us call *tekhelet* by its right name!

It sometimes happens that a Jew comes to me after I have "caught" him in an act of *mitzva*, and he will apologetically assert, "Rabbi, don't get me wrong: I am not really religious!" What *kala ilan*! I just do not believe it. After witnessing the fantastic religious spirit that overcame our people when we liberated the Wailing Wall, I firmly believe that every Jew possesses the spark of Godliness, the *nitzotz* of Jewishness. I know of no non-religious Jews. I know only of Jews who have fulfilled their religious potential to a greater extent, and those who have not yet done so. Jews wear *tekhelet*! I cannot bring myself, in all honesty, to declare it *kala ilan*.

There is one biblical personality who symbolizes this attempt to disguise *tekhelet* as *kala ilan*, and that is Judah. You recall that he played a special role in the unfortunate episode of the maltreatment of their brother Joseph. The brothers had planned to kill Joseph. But Judah, who was a natural leader, saved Joseph's life by telling the brothers (Genesis 37:26), "What profit will it bring us if we kill him?" Let us better sell him into slavery.

Now, the Rabbis were quite harsh on Judah for this statement. They declared (*Sanhedrin* 6b) that "whoever praises Judah is considered a blasphemer," and they applied to such person the verse from the Psalms (10:3), "He who blesses the profit-taker has blasphemed the Lord."

But why, indeed, were they so harsh on Judah? Did he not, after all, save Joseph's life?

The answer, I suggest, is that Judah did not really believe what he said – that they ought to save Joseph only because it will bring them profit. In fact, immediately after his statement of "What profit…?" he says to them: "Let us not injure him, because he is our brother, our own flesh and blood." In other words, Judah was posturing. Out loud, as his ostensible reason for not killing Joseph, he said it will bring us no profit if we kill him; but sotto voce, whispering quietly his real reason, he said that Joseph must not be harmed because one does not destroy his own brother, his own flesh and blood! Judah thus was a man of *tekhelet* – but he posed as nothing more than a penurious person of *kala ilan*! His reasons were noble, but he expressed them in the sinister language of the marketplace. No wonder that the verse ends with the words, "And his brothers heard." But of course they heard – he was, after all, addressing them! What the Torah means is that they heard Judah's real reason. They listened with an inner ear. They were not impressed with the "profit" argument, but understood the real, underlying motivation of Judah – the ethical reason that one does not harm his own brother.

That is why our tradition considers him a blasphemer – for indeed it is a blasphemy and a desecration of the divine image to disown your own innate nobility, to deny your inner genuineness. We must, by all means, show our true colors!

As we make our way to vacation or travel this summer, and no doubt come into contact with many new people, let us take along with ourselves this lesson of *tekhelet* and *kala ilan*. Never, never, Heaven forbid, may we dissemble and declare as *tekhelet* what is but a cheap imitation. Neither is it incumbent upon us to flaunt our *tekhelet* in the eyes of others, to draw unnecessary attention to our Jewishness. But, we must also not submit to the moral cowardice of disguising our *tekhelet* as *kala ilan*.

We have often heard about resisting the *yetzer hara*; let us not strive so mightily to resist the *yetzer tov*.

Let us show our true Jewish colors – and be proud of them.

Does It Pay to Be Good?[1]

Does it pay to be good? This is a question one often hears – and asks – as a sign of frustration. Usually, it is just an expression of momentary disappointment and serves a cathartic function. But sometimes, and with some people, and especially if repeated often enough, it is elevated from a query of complaint to a philosophy of life, and from a passing mood to a firm moral judgment. So let us ask ourselves the question rather seriously: Does it pay to be good?

We must first divide the question into two parts by posing a counter-question: "pay" for whom?

"Does it pay to be good?" may refer to the benefactor, to the one asking the question; or it may refer to the beneficiary, the one who is the recipient of my goodness and generosity.

The first question – does it pay for me to be good – probably should be answered, for most cases, in the negative. If you expect dividends from your ethical investments, you are seriously in error. The good life is not necessarily the happy life. John Kennedy, born into a wealthy

---

1.   June 10, 1972.

family, high society, and catapulted into historic political prominence, decided that "life is unfair."[2] Much earlier, the Rabbis broodingly concluded that the reward for virtue simply is not in evidence in this world (*Kiddushin* 39b). I myself, being professionally engaged a good part of the time in doing favors for people and arranging for some people to be kind to others, learned long, long ago that one thing I must never expect (if I wanted to lead a life free from constant minor disappointments) is gratitude. I now never expect anyone to show gratitude. Therefore, when, as often happens, I meet people who are possessed of that noble virtue, I am delighted beyond words at the great discovery of a genuine human being. But ingratitude neither overwhelms me nor surprises me any longer because, truth to tell, and without the least trace of cynicism, it is the rule rather than the exception. Were a person to be good only because it pays, or because it will be recognized and acknowledged, he would have to stop being good!

But essentially the question does not even deserve an answer – for, no matter what the answer may be, our immediate reaction must be to ask: "So what?" Who says that it has to pay in the first place? An individual who plans to be moral because it pays to be good will end up either an evil person or one who will suffer constant frustration. Judaism taught us, "Do not be like servants who serve the master only in order to receive a salary or a wage" (*Avot* 1:3). Don't be good merely because it pays. Judaism never urged upon us that old maxim, "Honesty is the best policy." A Jew must be honest even when it is not a good policy. Morals and goodness are matters of principle, not prudence. Yes, we believe that ultimately there is spiritual reward – but this must never become the motive for being good in the first place.

The real question that is worth pondering is the second one: Does it pay to be good for the beneficiary of my kindness? At first glance, it is a simple matter of definition – obviously it is good for someone if I do

---

2. On March 21, 1962, at a press conference in which he was criticized for sending more troops to Vietnam, President Kennedy justified his decision by stating, "Some men are killed in a war and some men are wounded, and some men never leave the country, and some men are stationed in the Antarctic and some are stationed in San Francisco. It's very hard in military or in personal life to assure complete equality. Life is unfair."

that person good. Yet it is not quite that simple. We must consider such factors as excess, timing, and short-term indulgence which may lead to long-term damage. And here there can be no uniform answer. Here what is required is wisdom and maturity and deliberation in order to foretell whether our benefaction will ultimately prove helpful or harmful.

The incident of Moses and the spies he sent into Canaan provides an illustration of a case where it did not pay to be good. God told Moses, "Send for yourself people to spy out the land of Canaan" (Numbers 13:2). But according to the way the Rabbis (as cited by Rashi ad loc.) interpreted this incident, the relations between God, Israel, and Moses were quite complex, and the role of Moses was anomalous. Thus Rashi states:

> God said to Moses, "Send a delegation of spies if you wish. But do it on your own responsibility. For Myself, I am not commanding you to do so." For the Israelites themselves demanded such a delegation, and when Moses consulted the Divine Presence, He replied: "But I have already told them that it is a good land! Therefore, if you wish you may let them have their spies, but not without great risk."

In other words, the sending of the spies was a concession, like the permission to appoint a king over themselves, or the granting of permission for the eating of meat to the children of Noah, or the law of the beautiful captive. And, while we may be grateful to God for being an understanding Father, it is not always clear that such indulgence is for our own ultimate good.

Obviously, here Moses was being too good. He submitted to pressure by the Israelites, when perhaps he should not have done so. He was too good – and it didn't pay!

The commentators are undecided about the moral qualities of these spies. Some say they were truly just, some say merely innocent, and some say they were wicked. But I prefer a fourth interpretation, that of *Midrash Tanḥuma*, which declares them "*kesilim*" – a word which means both knaves and fools, primarily the latter. The spies were immature and childish. And Moses over-indulged them, pampered them and babied them, like a father who is too good to his little children.

In Deuteronomy 1:23, Moses, in recollecting the story of the spies, said: "*Vayitav be'einay hadavar,*" which usually is explained as, "And the plan found favor in my eyes." But if Moses admitted that the plan was valid in his opinion, how does Rashi tell us here that Moses did not really favor it, and that he consulted with the Divine Presence which discouraged him? I submit that, perhaps, the expression of "*vayitav be'einay hadavar*" means, in essence: I, Moses, considered the matter and decided to be good to you. And of course – Moses erred. For to be good is not always the same as to do good. It is sometimes better to be hard-headed than soft-hearted.

Indeed, Moses already knew the harm that can come from excessive softness. After the sin of the Gold Calf, when Moses acts as the great advocate and defendant of his people, he tries to shift part of the blame for the making of the calf on God Himself! He maintains that God helped to spoil this people. "Moses said to the Almighty: O God, the gold and the silver which You gave them to excess [when they left Egypt and crossed the Red Sea], so much that they had to exclaim, 'enough!' – that is what caused them to make a golden calf" (*Yoma* 86b); You spoiled them and led them to think that such material valuables are a true criterion of greatness, and so they deified them!

So, all of us must learn in our personal and professional and especially family lives that it does not always pay to be good. Sometimes we intend to be kind and generous, and are only inviting trouble later on for the very one whom, out of love, we seek to benefit.

We tend to sin in this respect especially as parents. It is an old Jewish syndrome of which the Bible records numerous examples: Eli with his sons, Samuel with his sons, David with his sons. In our days, we often try to give our children what we did not have, and so we fail to give them what we did have. Our generation of affluence is over-pressing material good on the younger generation, and thereby denying them a sense of discovery, of self-worth, of the achievement of earning and deserving the goods of the world. We think, "*vayitav be'einay hadavar,*" we are being good to them, when we are really helping them build a Golden Calf. We send teens on a trip around the world but then there is nothing for them to look forward to other than ennui and boredom. We saturate them with luxuries until they are sated and cry, "Enough!"

What else is there left for them to live for, especially since non-material values were never seriously considered? We send our children to the best universities with only the minimal attention to Jewishness, Jewish society, and the opportunity for Jewish observance. And later, even the finest Orthodox families wonder where they went wrong and why they now suffer from the problems of intermarriage.

But this idea of short-term kindness leading to eventual harm has to do not only with individuals but applies to collectivities as well.

One such case is the problem of the priorities that our liberal Jewish community sets for itself. We are generally a kindly people, and therefore concerned with the well-being of all peoples. And that is as it should be. But we have sinned in the area of priorities. We have tried to be good to others and denied our kindness from our kin. We have acted politically, socially, and economically on behalf of all the underprivileged – except for the Jewish poor; on behalf of all political causes – except our own; on behalf of all marginal people – except for those of our own people who have not yet "made it." And so it did not pay for us or for them to be good.

A second such instance concerns the hijackings which now proliferate in the world. The policy of most governments has been to be soft, accommodating, and gentle with hijackers. Most nations told themselves, obviously in sincerity, that they were protecting the passengers on the immediate plane endangered. Yet they failed to see that in this way they were inviting further hijackings and endangering the lives of untold numbers of other, future passengers. Apparently, only the government of Israel took the right attitude: no concessions, no submissions, no negotiations. They realized that it does not pay – even for the passengers of an endangered jet – to submit to the criminals.

In this respect, I wish to single out for special condemnation and censure a recent editorial that was distinguished by viciousness and inanity rolled into one. A week or ten days ago, *The New York Times*, in an editorial after the Lod massacre,[3] had the temerity and audacity to suggest that Israel itself must accept part of the blame, because when it

---

3. On May 30, 1972, members of the Japanese Red Army recruited by a Palestinian terrorist group killed 26 people and injured 80 others in Tel Aviv's Lod airport.

decided to storm the Sabena jet some time earlier,[4] this provoked the terrorists to attempt the Lod massacre.

What unmitigated gall! While the *Times* was pontificating in its editorial columns, its news columns were informing us that the Lod massacre had been planned long before the Sabena jet incident. Now we know, factually, that this was the case. Furthermore, this week the airline pilots of the world set June 19th as a deadline for a new policy against hijackers – once more in consonance with that of the State of Israel – and that they will strike if this policy is not worked out.

Perhaps it is a consolation for us to recall that *The New York Times* was usually wrong on Israel, from the beginnings of the Zionist movement until this very day. Thank the Lord that, with all our reverence for the sage advice given to us from the Olympian heights of the *Times* editorial room, we have been wise enough to disregard it and ignore it. Perhaps it is a measure of the justice and rightness of Israel's cause that it evoked the displeasure of the *Times* editorial writer. When we satisfy the *Times'* standards, perhaps then we ought to question whether we are on the right track.

To summarize, we respond to the question, "Does it pay to be good?" as follows: If the question is asked whether it pays for me to do good, the question is invalid – it is a pseudo-question because it really makes no difference what the answer is. It is irrelevant. I do not do good because it pays, but because as a Jew I am commanded to do good.

But if it means: "Does it pay to be good toward the beneficiary?" the answer is that it depends upon that individual, upon his maturity and sense of proportion, upon that person's absorptive capacity for kindness and goodness. It is a question which demands wisdom and knowledge of the particular case in order to know how to act properly.

For, as we indicated, it is so very difficult to know when we are truly doing good and when we are going to excess, that even God was

---

4. On May 9, 1972, Sabena flight 571 from Brussels to Tel Aviv was hijacked by PLO Black September members outside of Vienna. Israeli Defense Minister Moshe Dayan arranged a rescue operation, which included future Prime Ministers Ehud Barak and Benjamin Netanyahu, that captured or killed all the terrorists, and rescued all the passengers.

faulted by Moses in this respect. Yet, we must always rely upon Him and pray that He be good to us without overindulging us and causing us eventual harm. So we pray, in the blessing of Rosh Ḥodesh, for "*ḥayim sheyimalu mishalot libenu letova*," a "life in which the desires of our hearts will be fulfilled" – but not all of them, not everything we want, not without measure, but only: "*letova*," for what is truly our real good. *Amen sela.*

Koraḥ

Reenacting an Old Drama [1]

The rebellion of Korah and his co-conspirators against Moses and Aaron, of which we read this morning, is the first great, direct test of the leadership of Moses. The quelling of the rebellion of this band of malcontents reestablished and reaffirmed the leadership of Moses of his people in the desert.

And yet, according to *Yalkut Reuveni*, the Sages of the Kabbala taught that this great battle between Moses and Korah had ancient roots. The struggle between these two, they say, was merely the reenactment of the old drama of the strife between Cain and Abel. They identify Moses with Abel and Korah with Cain.

The detailed kabbalistic analogy is beyond our limited comprehension. Nevertheless, it is obvious to all of us that the Sages of the Kabbala have here enunciated a great truth. For indeed, as we analyze the two dramas, we find confirmed the similarities between these two sets of biblical characters.

---

1. June 22, 1963.

Thus, for instance, we can detect at least three elements which unite Moses with Abel and Koraḥ with Cain. The first of these is *kina* – jealousy or envy. The fratricide committed by Cain against Abel had its roots in Cain's envy of Abel – the Lord accepted the offering of Abel, but did not accept the offering of Cain. The same feelings provoked Koraḥ to his abortive insurrection. Both Moses and Koraḥ were brothers in the sense of being members of the same tribe of Levi. Yet Moses was the undisputed leader of the people, while Koraḥ was not. He was consumed by the fires of jealousy – even as later he was consumed by the fires of the Lord when he met his end.

The second observable element that unites these two pairs is *ta'ava* – concupiscence, desire, a ravenous appetite for more and more. In the story of the sons of Adam, the Sages tell us that they divided the world between the two of them. Cain owned a full half of the world – yet he begrudged his brother the other half and desired it for himself. Koraḥ, according to Jewish tradition, was exceedingly wealthy, so much so that "as rich as Koraḥ" has become a byword in Yiddish. Yet Koraḥ was not satisfied with his wealth, and instead he was overwhelmed by a *ta'ava* for political power as well.

A third similarity is the striving for *kavod*, for honor and recognition. More than envy or desire motivated Cain to his tragic act. He was, in addition, the older brother of Abel – and he regarded Abel's distinction as an insult and an offense against his position. He did not receive the *kavod* he thought was his due. So, Koraḥ felt deeply unhappy because of the lack of recognition he felt he deserved. He wanted *kavod*, and did not receive all that he expected. How clearly this comes out in the first accusation that Koraḥ publicly directs against Moses in his denunciation, "Wherefore do you presume to raise yourselves over the congregation of the Lord?" (Numbers 16:3).

The Abels and the Moseses, the people of good will, must always be prepared to cope with the malcontents, the dissatisfied, those who always grasp for more than they deserve. As the Rabbis taught us in *Avot* (4:21), "Envy, desire, and undeserved honor drive a man out of the world." This was literally true in both our cases. Cain was forced out of his world – he was sent into exile, to wander over the face of the earth. No place could he call his own, no house could he identify as his home.

Korah too was driven out of the world – indeed, he literally was swallowed up by the earth and vanished from the world of men.

The quarrel between Moses and Korah was not something localized in ancient history – it is a universal drama, as old as man himself. So long as there will be people who will allow themselves to be dominated by unworthy aspirations, someone is going to be terrorized and victimized. The two cases of Cain and Korah are, in essence, a biblical insight into the personality of the aggressor.

Yet there is one question that remains to be answered. If indeed the story of Korah and Moses is but the reenactment of the old drama of Cain and Abel, why are the results so different? Why is it that Abel was the victim of Cain in that ancient story, while the man identified with Abel, Moses, is the victor over Cain's representative, Korah? Why does the good lose in one case, and triumph in the other?

Before we answer that question, we must find yet one more similarity between these two couples. And that lies in the element of disguise, of cloaking evil in piety. The most characteristic element in both stories is the projection of selfish, egotistical, aggressive intentions in the guise of the noble, the good, the decent. For his own nefarious purposes, the devil will quote scripture, and the aggressor nation will announce itself "leader of the peace-loving camp." Thus, Cain's motivations were, as we have seen, completely selfish in nature. Yet, Cain did not announce his intentions as boldly as all that. Tradition teaches (Genesis Rabba 22:7) that Cain and Abel divided the world in the following manner: Abel was to receive all chattel, or moveable objects, while Cain was to possess all land, all real estate. Therefore, Cain decided to press his claims in the form of justice and righteousness. Wherever Abel went, Cain told him, "You are standing on my land. Please move on. If you continue to trespass I shall protect my rights against you." From a formal, conventional point of view, Cain was apparently within his rights. He had justice on his side. If that was the agreement between the two brothers, Cain had the right to insist upon its complete execution – so his *kina* and *ta'ava* and *kavod* were all wrapped up in the cloak of legalism, piety, righteousness.

Korah, according to the Bible and Rabbis, did the very same thing. He did not call a press conference and announce that he was going to initiate a *coup d'état* in order to satisfy his ambition for greater power and influence. He did turn his eyes heavenward and act as the protector of a true demagogue, he denounced Moses and Aaron saying, "Have you not taken enough power for yourselves? Do you not realize that all these people are holy, that not only the two of you are holy?" He set himself up as the great democrat, defender of the people. Jewish tradition further records that Koraḥ tried to make Moses and Aaron appear as tyrants who needlessly exploited the people for their personal gain and profit. He cast himself in the role of the advocate of the ordinary, common man against the tyranny of Moses.

So both in the case of Cain and Koraḥ, the real motives of envy, desire for power, and the grasping for honor, are disguised in a veneer of righteousness. They are hypocrites.

Perhaps this is the reason we find in both these stories a strange grammatical construction – a verb without an object. In the story of Cain and Abel we read: "And Cain said to his brother Abel, and it was when they were in the field that Cain rose and killed his brother Abel" (Genesis 4:8). What did he "say"? We read that he said something, but we do not read what he said. So too, in today's *sidra* we read: "Koraḥ and the people who were conspiring with him, took…and they rose up and rebelled against Moses" (Numbers 16:1). But what or whom did they "take"? We are not told.

Perhaps what the Torah means to tell us with these unusual constructions is that the reasons they gave, what they said, the "front" they presented, the excuses they offered – were all empty, meaningless, and of no concern to us. What Cain said was totally irrelevant – he never said what he really meant. The fact is that he was fraudulent and hypocritical. What Koraḥ said or whom he took along with him was equally inconsequential – the important thing is that in order to satisfy his own desire for power he deceived and almost destroyed his entire people. It is the action, the deeper motive, unspoken and unarticulated, but disguised in the cloak of piety, that is so terribly and unspeakably evil. It is that which really counts. The rest is unworthy of being recorded in Scripture.

Here, then, we can discover why Moses was the victor, while Abel was the victim of his aggressive brother. In all our readings of the Torah and our midrash we do not find that Abel truly fought back against Cain. We do not find him calling Cain's bluff. Instead, in all likelihood, he tried to counter his brother Cain on his terms. No doubt he rebutted his arguments with legal arguments of his own. And when you try to fight the devil on the devil's terms, you are bound to lose.

But Moses had learned the lesson of Abel. He refused to discuss Koraḥ's complaints in the manner they were presented. Instead he pierced the mask, he went straight to the heart of the matter, and ripped off the disguises of these evil men. He said to them (Numbers 16:8-9), "Listen here, you sons of Levi, is it not enough for you that God has chosen your tribe above all others, that you seek as well to become the priests, the sole leaders?" He stripped them of all their pious pretentions and let all the people see what these rebels really wanted – power, power, and more power. And then he turned to the people and said to them, "Depart from the tents of these evil, wicked people." That is all that they really are. Moses learned from the story of Cain and Abel – and we must learn from the story of Koraḥ and Moses – never to be impressed by pious frauds, for even their piety is fraudulent. Evil should not be debated – it should be exposed.

This is a lesson for us in all aspects of life. In order to survive, physically and morally and spiritually, we must insist upon the truth and look for it with all the power at our command.

In recent years, Jewish writers and "intellectuals" who are very uncomfortable with their Judaism have pronounced publicly on our faith in many ways. Worse yet, certain organizations which should know better have turned to them as the oracles who will decide for us the real nature and future of Judaism. The magazine *Commentary* started this with a symposium, and the results were sad indeed. Now the American Jewish Congress has instituted a "dialogue" between American and Israeli Jews in Jerusalem. From the most recent reports of *The New York Times*, the dialogue this week included American writers, novelists, and columnists. All of them, according to the report, were "rather nebulous about their identification as Jews." One author – whose recent book portrays a rabbi in a role that would make any sensitive reader blush with embarrassment – declared the "essential nature of Jewishness" to be a feeling of alienation, of being in exile, an outsider. Thus, he declared, most Jews in Israel and the United States, being insiders, in their respective societies have "ceased to be Jews."

What a romantic definition! It certainly sounds appealing. But then, by this definition, King David, King Solomon, the Gaon of Vilna and countless others were not Jews! They were not alienated from their own society. This particular writer is a Jew, but they are not. Furthermore a Jewish society is impossible – for a society cannot be alienated from itself!

Another writer, who recently no doubt made a great deal of money with his "best seller," declared that to be a Jew one must be a "dissenter from the affluent society." By such terms, Rabbi Judah the Prince, who according to the reports of our tradition was very wealthy, was not a Jew – although he was the editor of the *Mishna*!

It is useless to show the emptiness of this dilettantism. It is humiliating to hear Jews alienated from Judaism describe Judaism as a state of being alienated from Jews. It is embarrassing that the American Jewish Congress saw fit to invite only one observant Jew – a Professor of Physics from the Hebrew University – to participate in this "dialogue."

We must learn, and should have learned by now, that all this is a façade. It is an elaborate circumlocution for assimilation – a word no longer popular nowadays. It is a roundabout way for saying, "I desire to commit spiritual suicide but haven't the courage to face up to it. I would like to forget that I am a Jew, but the cruel world won't let me. In my heart of hearts I want to be reborn a 'WASP' – a white Anglo-Saxon Protestant – but my infantile wishes are constantly frustrated."

It is a sad but true fact that those who ponder the definition of their Jewishness have usually lost it by that time. The Jew who practices Torah and *mitzvot* does not normally concern himself about the definition of his Jewishness. It is when an individual has assimilated in fact, but is unwilling to acknowledge it in words, that that person wraps up his assimilation in this existentialist rhetoric of "alienation."

Our policy ought to be not to discuss "Who is a Jew?" on such terms. We should, rather, recognize assimilation for what it is, call it by its real name, and avoid unnecessary dialectic.

Those of us who are true to the Jewish tradition and loyal to our Torah need not participate in this new fad and fashion on inventing new definitions of Jewishness. Like Moses, we prefer to go straight to the truth. We will not call Judaism "alienation" or "dissent." We will recognize such terms merely as excuse for assimilation, for the surrender of Torah and *mitzvot*, which alone constitute Judaism.

It is for good reason that the *Aggada* (*Bava Batra* 74a) tells us of Rabba bar Bar Ḥannah putting his ear to the ground in a spot in the desert pointed out to him by an Arab as the burial place of Koraḥ and his cohorts, and hearing them declare from the bowels of the earth, "Moses is true and his Torah is true." Our Torah is truth, and our truth is Torah. We shall not become ensnared by the slogans, "images," and posturing of the Cain's and Koraḥ's and others of their ilk. Through our Torah of truth we shall become perceptive. With its wisdom, its insights, and its eternal blessings we shall learn to live our lives in a manner pleasing to God. We shall forever proclaim, through all time and all the world, "Moses is true and his Torah is true."

Rebel and Revolutionary [1]

The rebellion against the leadership of Moses and Aaron is one which had tragic consequences and which left an indelible impression upon the collective Jewish memory. The Torah lists the names of those involved in the conspiracy in the desert. But who indeed were the members of this conglomeration of the displaced, the dissatisfied, and the disaffected? What motivated them, and what was their relation to each other?

Rabbi Naftali Zvi Yehuda Berlin, the Netziv, found three distinct groups in this mutiny of malcontents, and he describes them to us in his commentary *HaAmek Davar*. The first consists of the two hundred and fifty princes of the congregation. These community leaders were not at all malicious people. They were well-intentioned but misguided. They were great Jews, great even in their piety. That is why the Torah (Numbers 16:2) refers to them as "princes of the congregation, the elect men of the assembly, men of renown." They were Levites who desired to be *kohanim* not because the priesthood offered them positions of

---

1. June 14, 1964.

influence and status, but because it represented an opportunity to come closer to God in the course of serving Him in the Sanctuary.

The second group consisted of two brothers from the tribe of Reuben – Dathan and Abiram. These two were known as trouble-makers even before the Exodus from Egypt. They were not at all people of ideals or convictions. They were merely power-hungry schemers – nothing more, nothing less.

The third element in this mutiny was Korah himself. He was a man of great fame in Israel and yet was, in a way, the worst of all, for he tried to appear to the people a man of sincerity and genuineness, who had legitimate and selfless complaints, like the two hundred and fifty princes – but in fact he had the same base ends as Dathan and Abiram, namely, the usurpation of the authority of Moses and Aaron.

This analysis – of which we have mentioned but the bare outline – is not only an act of exegesis, but also a valid insight into character that is relevant to the human condition in general, whether in the days of Moses or our very own times.

Permit me to expand on this by referring to a recent essay by Dr. Erich Fromm, "The Revolutionary Character," whose ideas we shall accept in part. Fromm distinguishes between two types – the rebel and the revolutionary. The rebel is one who is innocent of any ideological convictions. This individual is resentful of authority and wants to over-throw it so that he can become the authority himself. This person is dissatisfied not with the office, but with the office-holder. His goal is a naked power-grab.

The revolutionary is completely different. This person is not necessarily one who participates in revolutions; the term is used psy-chologically, not politically. The revolutionary is one who thinks inde-pendently. He is unimpressed by those in control and will not accept an idea just because it was pronounced by someone in authority. This individual's mood is a critical one, not that of bland acceptance. The revolutionary will even be able to see through "common sense" when that term is used to describe what is but nonsense repeated often enough by those who are influential enough. The revolutionary is one who can transcend the parochial limits of his own society and milieu, and thus criticize both his own and any other society. The revolutionary character is one that enables a person to say "No," and not automatically assent to authority, to the status quo, to their environment, to "conditions."

Of course, not always is the revolutionary angelic. This person can be right or wrong, good or evil, constructive or destructive, depending upon what he says "no" to, and upon whether his criticism is valid or invalid. Simple "orneriness" is not a virtue. But at least the mood of the revolutionary character is authentic. He thinks and reacts as an individual, not a cipher, not just another sheep in the flock.

With this distinction we can, I believe, better appreciate the Netziv's analysis of the Koraḥ episode. Dathan and Abiram were what we have called rebels. No ideals or principles or ideologies informed their treachery. They lusted for power directly and without inhibition. The two hundred and fifty princes were revolutionaries. They refused to accept without question the denial to them of the priesthood. But they misplaced their energies. Their criticism was well-intentioned but grievously misdirected. And Koraḥ played an opportunistic, political, demagogic game. He cloaked himself in piety and tried to disguise himself as a revolutionary character, like the two hundred and fifty princes. But in essence he was no different from the rebels Dathan and Abiram. He was the McCarthy of the biblical period.

Indeed, the Koraḥ-type is no stranger to our contemporary world. Far too many greedy, corrupt, and power-hungry men, from Iraq to Ghana and from Indonesia to Latin America, have taken over the reins of government without in the least benefiting their own people – and all this under the pretense of nationalism and anti-imperialism. The slogans are the slogans of revolution, but the goals are the goals of rebellion. Our age, so stormy and tempestuous – born in the French and American revolutions, sired by the industrial revolution, agonizing now in the scientific and nationalistic and civil-rights revolutions – offers great temptations to the Koraḥ-type character. As Fromm puts it, "Twentieth century political life is a cemetery containing the moral graves of people who started our as alleged revolutionaries and who turned out to be nothing more than opportunistic rebels."

Now these three classes represent what is wrong with the protest against power and authority: the two hundred and fifty princes who were misguided revolutionaries, the avaricious rebels Dathan and Abiram, and the demagogic and deceiving Koraḥ. But the constructive, creative aspect of the revolutionary character also has a place of honor in the Jewish tradition. In fact, it is a distinguishing feature of Judaism in the world and one of the major functions of Orthodoxy within the Jewish community.

What is the prophetic tradition if not the expression of a revolutionary character? It had its genesis in Abraham – who was an iconoclast. It reached its heights in Moses who defied Pharaoh and both the military might and cultural hegemony of Egypt. Elijah was a revolutionary when he challenged Ahab, Isaiah when he thundered against the drunkards who ruled the northern kingdom of Israel, and Ezekiel when he dissented from the popular worship of Baal and Marduk. For three and a half thousand years Judaism has been out of step with the world – and has thus managed to be its repository of sanity and sanctity.

In like manner, today it is the mission of Orthodoxy to perpetuate this tradition of dissent and the revolutionary character within the Jewish community. Of course, if there are those who believe that this is the best of all possible worlds, that our American-Jewish community leaves nothing to be desired, that synagogue services must be rallies and that rabbis must be propagandists, then there is nothing more to be said. But for those whose love for Jews does not leave them blind, who are painfully aware of some of our faults and defects, there remains the problem of who will fulfill the role of the little boy who dared to proclaim that the emperor was naked. That role, I submit, is incumbent upon Orthodox Jews whose convictions force them to measure mankind and events by the criteria of Torah rather than by their own subjective tastes and shifting contemporary standards. It is we who have the obligation, painful though it be, of being the critics – constructive critics, of course, but critics nonetheless. It is part of the fate, the destiny, and the mission of the Torah Jew to say "no" when others sheepishly nod their heads in agreement, to arouse whilst others drowse in moral stupor, to irritate and goad when others seek only to pacify and tranquilize.

The founder of Chabad Hasidism, Rabbi Shneur Zalman, in his *Likutei Torah*, saw this idea implicit in the famous words of the prophet in the second chapter of Jeremiah (verse 2), "Thus says the Lord, I remember for you the affection of your youth, the love of your espousals, *lekhtekh aḥarai bamidbar be'eretz lo zeru'a,* how you went after Me in the wilderness, in a land that was not sown." Those last three words, "*be'eretz lo zeru'a,*" says Rabbi Shneur Zalman, mean not only "a land not sown," but also a land in which the word and idea and imperative "*lo,*" "no," was sown! The most memorable achievement of our people was our willingness to accept a Torah and a tradition that emphasized the "no," that enshrined the power of dissent, that glorified nonconformism with the popular and the conventional. "*Eretz lo zeru'a*" – the "ground" – principle of Judaism is: "*lo,*" "no." There in the desert, the vast and lonely *midbar,* we learned to be ourselves, to forge our own souls and characters under the tutelage of God alone. There we learned to say *No* to the idols worshipped by the crowds; *No* to the ever-present threat of assimilation; *No* to the passions and lusts that tyrannize a man; *No* to the avarice which inheres in his character. There, in that "*eretz lo zeru'a,*" man learned to say *No* to the hidden fears that creep up on him in secret and threaten to paralyze his will and ruin his peace of mind; *No* to his grief when it turns excessive and overwhelms him; *No* to his worries and concerns when they give rise to despair and the kind of hopelessness that moves black clouds over his heart and his mind and his soul; *No* even to his perverse tendency to say "No" when there is no cause for it!

Today's American Orthodox Jew must not forget his ancient origins in the "*eretz lo zeru'a.*" We must say "no" to the bankrupt Jewish secularism that surrounds us, often in clerical garb; "no" to the unreflective, obtuse, and self-disdaining tendency of certain Jewish organizations publicly to violate our most sacred tenets; "no" to Jews who dare call themselves observant or Orthodox but who perpetrate miserable, unethical business practices; "no" to renowned leaders of powerful Jewish organizations who seem to have lost every shred of self-respect. I refer, in this last instance, to the leaders of the American Jewish Committee who had an audience with the Pope in Rome to discuss Jewish-Catholic affairs just two weeks ago – on Shabbat! How horribly incongruous – leading Jews meeting with leaders of another religion on a day that they ought to be spending in the synagogue and in Sabbath rest! Can anyone blame church leaders for silently questioning whether they ought to take Jews seriously at all? Certainly we dissent. We counter pose a most vigorous "no" to this shameful exhibition of self-denigration and inferiority.

There may be those who will complain that this is a negative, unproductive attitude. But that is a shallow conclusion. For, when it issues from a commitment to Torah, every *no* is really a "yes." "No" to the idol is "yes" to God. No to assimilation is "yes" to the promise of a Jewish future. "No" to Jewish self-denigration is *yes* to Jewish dignity and self-respect. "No" to despair and fear and hopelessness is "yes" to faith and trust in God. Our "*lo zeru'a*" issues from "*ḥesed ne'urayikh*" and "*ahavat kelulotayikh*," from a relationship of love and affection. Our revolutionary character, unlike the rebellious character, seeks to correct, not abolish; to build, not to destroy. It is motivated by love, not enmity.

It is a difficult challenge which our historic tradition places on us – to be revolutionary without being rebellious, to know when to be critical and when to conform, when to dissent and when to assent, when to say "yes" and when to say "no." But God in His goodness has given us a standard by which to judge. It is something Koraḥ and his children learned, albeit too late. For, as the Talmud (*Bava Batra* 74a) tells us in a most meaningful legend, when centuries later Rabba bar Bar Ḥannah put his ear to the ground where Koraḥ and his cohorts had been swallowed alive, he heard a voice that issued from the bowels of the earth. And that voice called out, "Moses is true and his Torah is true."

That is our measure, our criterion. With that truth we shall know when to say "yes" – and when to say "no."

Too Wise, Too Foolish [1]

The rebellion of Koraḥ constituted a trauma of major proportions in biblical history. The whole enterprise of Moses – the spiritual reconstruction of his people, their political liberation, their psychological emancipation from a slave mentality, the development of a "holy nation and kingdom of priests" – was jeopardized by the demagogic Koraḥ and his band of malcontents.

In retrospect, Koraḥ was doomed from the outset. Moses, after all, was not a leader by his own choice, but had this mission imposed on him by Providence. So, in effect, Koraḥ was rebelling against God. Hence, Rashi (commenting on Numbers 16:7) was moved to quote the Sages in exclaiming: "Koraḥ, who was so clever, how did he become involved in such foolishness?"

But the Kotzker Rebbe rephrases that quotation from Rashi which provide us with a new insight. His question is phrased as, "How did Koraḥ, such a clever man, get involved in the foolishness of being clever?"

---

1. June 22, 1974.

He means to say that, at the time, Korah appeared to have everything going for him. The people were afflicted with widespread discontent, with fear, with want, with jealousy of Moses, with feelings that Moses and Aaron and Miriam were nepotistic. Yet the fatal mistake of Korah was not foolishness as such, but quite the opposite: he was too sharp, too brilliant, too capable.

Korah, according to the Kotzker Rebbe, is teaching us that it is foolish to be too clever. Korah's very sharpness was a sign of his dullness, his very astuteness was a symptom of his want of intelligence, his very shrewdness was the stuff of stupidity.

This danger of being too clever is an old phenomenon that was known to the sages of all cultures and all times. Thus, for example, Jeremiah taught us, "Let not the wise man glory in his wisdom" (9:22), Aristotle taught that vice is virtue taken to excess, and Greek culture had a tradition that hubris (pride, arrogance) leads to the revenge of nemesis (punishment, suffering).

Our whole society suffers from this tendency to value intelligence as an end in itself, without moral dimensions. It is true of our science and technology, which have for so long proclaimed an indifference to the moral consequences and social implications of their activities; to business, which piously proclaims only one goal, that of profit; to law and to journalism and to a hundred other professions.

That is why I personally subscribe to the thesis of James Madison, one of our Founding Fathers, that democracy is based not on the naïve and romantic faith in mankind's innate goodness, but quite the contrary, on an expectation that groups of people, like individuals, will be motivated only by their self-interest. Each group tends to extremes in order to achieve its aims. Democracy means that we allow all the groups of society to come into a tension with each other, and in the interplay of forces, each group cancels the overreaching of other groups. This is the theory of checks and balances. Yet, despite all of this, it sometimes happens that one or several groups rip apart the social and political fabric by just being too smart and too successful.

The Yom Kippur War proved it for Israel. The Israelis fought valiantly and heroically. But they realize now, as do all of us, the danger of the stupidity of cleverness, the arrogance that comes from being too smart. We foolishly tried to be clever, and imagined that our superiority was unmovable, ingrained, and permanent. We therefore become negligent and careless.

But if for Israel our over-shrewdness was expressed in negligence, no such mitigation can be provided for what happened in the USA.

Here, a band of sharp-headed but small-minded men over-reached themselves by trying to do in the opposition with impunity. But the Watergate gangsters succeeded only in out-smarting themselves. During the entire course of the exposure of this sordid affair, we are often moved to wonder: How foolish of them to be so clever! At every step, at every fresh revelation in this sordid and dirty business I have been shocked at how supposedly brilliant men do such foolish things. But I am convinced the solution lies in the Kotzker Rebbe's insight: They are being too smart, too shrewd – foolishly so!

The same worry about an excess of success, a superfluity of brilliance, leads one to apprehension and ambiguity about our Secretary of State. One must of course admire his unquestioned genius. But is that a guarantee of peace? Of the welfare of the United States? Of the survival of Israel?

His recently proposed compromise figure of 45,000 Jews to emigrate from Russia every year sounds good, yet it also sounds quite hollow when you read that, in anticipation of President Nixon's arrival in Moscow, Russian-Jewish activists are being chased, persecuted, arrested. Some good omen for the success of Kissinger's policy!

In religious life too we must beware of the foolishness of being too wise, too smart.

Knowledge remains the highest goal of the Jewish spiritual enterprise. But never is it valued without a spiritual-moral commitment, and never with arrogance.

I have always been fond of the statement of Rabbi Naḥman of Breslov that no matter how educated a man is in the ways of Torah, in the ways of God, and in the ways of the world, when he rises for prayer "*yashlikh et kol haḥokhmot aḥar gabo,*" let him throw out all his knowledge, all his sophistication, all his wisdom, over his shoulder – and stand before God childlike, simple, plain. All our philosophy, all our learning, all our ratiocination is as naught before Him. Surely each of us knows some people who think they are sophisticated when they are only indulging in sophistry!

Permit me to cite a famous *mishna* in *Avot* (4:1) which I shall consciously misinterpret in order to illustrate my point.

Ben Zoma said: "Who is a wise man? One who learns from every man." My "misinterpretation" (in the sense that this was obviously not the original intent of the author) is to read that: "Who is a wise man? One who learns from everything" – from all of life, from all of experience, from all individuals – that "man." We are only human beings. We are only men and women. We are limited and moral and finite and inadequate and fallible.

The merely shrewd individual thinks he has monopolized understanding and learning. The wise man is one who knows how much remains inaccessible to human beings and is forever closed to their probing intellects. The fool imagines that his smartness will save him. The wise person distrusts an exaggerated view of wisdom itself.

Koraḥ thought he could outsmart the whole world. So he proved to be a fool. But the truly wise individual knows how easy it is to fall into the pit of stupidity, knows that with every advance in knowledge or insight we walk on a thin line, on the rim of an abyss of foolishness, so that one error, one misstep, and our wisdom has begotten us eternal folly. Therefore, the truly wise individual humbly acknowledges that there is no true knowledge without faith, no wisdom without morality, no advancement of mankind without the greater knowledge that there is the ever-present danger of being overly clever.

Perhaps this is what Isaiah meant in his great messianic vision (11:9), "The world will be filled with the knowledge of the Lord (*de'ah et Hashem*)." Why the "*et*"? That small word sometimes means "with." Hence, the world will be filled with knowledge – all kinds of knowledge: religious and secular, spiritual and scientific, economic and psychological – "*et Hashem*," "with the Lord" – accompanied by, and restrained by, and graced by, the healing trust and faith in God and the humility that comes with it.

Only when faith is combined with knowledge, when the Lord is acknowledged along with the exercise of one's own intelligence, are we ready for the Messiah. Only then are we worthy of redemption.

The Rebel within Each of Us [1]

In the course of his counseling, a rabbi has all kinds of problems that are brought to him, both religious and personal. Sometimes I find, paradoxically, that one is a disguise for the other. A person can come to me with a religious problem, and upon analysis I discover that it is not at all a religious question, but fundamentally a psychological problem. The reverse is also true – someone may come to me with a request for help in a personal situation, and I discover that at the bottom it is really a religious issue. The weight of my experience serves to confirm the famous statement of the Swiss psychiatrist Carl Jung that most of the thousands of cases he has treated were, in the final analysis, religious or spiritual questions.

One of the main things I have learned from all this is that no one is really immune to the virus of antagonism to God, Torah, and Judaism. No one is unaffected by the sense of rejection of his Jewishness. There is a rebel in each of us. Were I to put it in terms of today's *sidra*, I

---

1. June 14, 1975.

would say that every Jew possesses not only a piece of Moses, but also a bit of Koraḥ.

Take the most fundamental aspect of religion: faith itself. How many of us can honestly say that we have never had any doubt? Faith, as I have pointed out in my book, *Faith and Doubt*, is not a static fact, but a dynamic quality. It is something which waxes and wanes, which grows stronger and grows weaker, depending upon circumstances and dispositions. There are times when the Moses within us becomes dominant – we look at the world around us, at the marvelous complexity of nature, the grandeur of the cosmos, and we are shocked that it could ever occur to anyone to question the existence of the infinitely wise Creator. And there are other times that the Koraḥ within us takes over and asks, as per *Menaḥot* 29b, "This is Torah and this is its reward?" With all the injustice that is rampant, can anyone truly believe that events are governed by a good and just God? We feel desolate and alone in a world bereft of meaning and goodness – and God.

Of course, one must respond, and the response is far too complicated for us to expound in the course of a brief talk. But I most strongly recommend the attitude of one of the greatest of all Talmudic scholars, Rabbi Akiva Eger, who explained that he never became ecstatic when he discovered a solution to a problem, nor did he ever become overly depressed because he could not solve a problem.

This normally occurs when people discuss the Holocaust. It represents one of the greatest impediments to faith. Of course, there are times when the question lacks authenticity. When I see a man puffing on a big cigar, looking very well-fed, having secure employment and a great deal of leisure and recreation and a bank-book, and he asks me how I can believe in God when history proved so cruel to Jews, I cannot accept the question as real or as meaningful personally. But the question, nonetheless, is a real question, no matter who asks it. To attempt to answer is to risk either triviality or immorality. We must learn from the contemplation of the Holocaust, as it affects religion, that the courage to ask questions must evoke the courage to live without answers.

It is important to note that thinking and reflecting and pondering and brooding over the problems of faith and doubt is normal. It is acting impetuously on the basis of undigested rumination and half-baked thinking that is reprehensible.

Korah, historically, was not a philosopher, but a rebel. The Torah introduces the whole narrative with the words, "And Korah took" (Numbers 16:1). What did he take? There is no answer. What the Torah is trying to tell us is that these were not thoughts that occurred to Korah in the privacy of his own mind and the intimacy of his own heart. They were resentments that he immediately put into practice when he organized this conspiracy. He expressed his rebelliousness in his nefarious conduct.

It is quite possible for a person to have a doubt, to struggle with it, to feel the encounter deeply and personally and painfully, and to emerge with a loss of faith. When that happens, I regard it as deeply regrettable, but I respect the person who has undergone such a serious encounter. I cannot have respect for one who has abandoned his faith – and in Judaism, faith is more than mere intellectual assent to a set of dogmas, but a whole way of life that can prove quite onerous – because of what are fundamentally reasons of convenience, because one does not want his growing career to be affected adversely, because that individual is unwilling to sacrifice for what he knows in his heart are great and holy principles. Of course, these are dishonorable motives, and therefore what one does is rationalize and attribute the loss of faith to intellectual questioning.

Each of us, quite naturally, has moments of doubt and hesitation and weakness. But we must treat intellectual doubts on the intellectual realm, in the realm of thought, and when we speak them out, we must discuss them with those who can help us in finding a solution. It is good to recall what the great author of the *Beit HaLevi* once said: "Not all that one thinks must he say, not all that one says must he write, not all that one writes must be printed and published."

Another element of Korah within us concerns authority. There can be no Torah, no Judaism, without authority. The idea that everyone can write his own *Shulhan Arukh*, that religion is a private thing and therefore no one can tell me how to act – one of the dogmas of the so-called "traditional Jewish liberalism" – is a wrong-headed combination of the misreading of the American constitutional guarantee of freedom of religion as a spiritual rather than a political statement, and the influence of Protestantism. Above all, it is a throwback to the attitude of Korah, who, in his demagoguery, said to Moses: "The entire congregation is holy." When you say that everyone is holy, that is tantamount to satisfying that no one is holy. Korah was trying to make a point under the guise of a popular egalitarianism – that everyone has a right to formulate his or her own religion.

Certainly, there is a difference between authority and authoritarianism. But Korah identified one with the other and rejected both. And that rebellion against religious authority exists in each of us – even as we sought to reject parental authority when we were adolescents.

Baiting and berating *gedolim* is as popular in one segment of the Orthodox community as apotheosizing them is in the other. In the right wing of Orthodoxy, a new concept has taken hold which makes of religious authorities supermen and attributes to them a doctrine heretofore considered exclusively Catholic – infallibility. I have always been uncomfortable with the institution founded by Agudath Israel, the *Mo'etzet Gedolei haTorah*, "The Council of Giants of the Torah." What man, with any measure of normal humility, will allow himself to be inducted in a group which announces itself as "giants" or "greats?" Yet, our camp is equally guilty of such adoration and such cult of personality when we blame the *gedolim* for all sins, from being anti-Zionist to being unenthusiastic about emigrating from Europe to the United States of America – as if greatness in Torah automatically implies the gift of prophecy.

Unquestionably, religious authority in Judaism is not unquestionable. But it is equally true that there is authority. *Emunat hakhamim*, faith in the wise, means that those wise individuals are authoritative. It commands us to have reverence for religious authorities even if we do not feel we can accept their opinions. It means to follow them even though we often do not agree with them. At all times it means that we must have respect, simple *derekh eretz*.

I grant that it is not always easy to do that. In *Avot* 6:5 we are told of the various ways in which Torah can be acquired – one of them is *emunat hakhamim*, faith in the Sages, and right next to it comes *yisurim*, pain. Acquiring Torah is indeed painful at times, but it is a pain which must be risked and embraced.

Another and more subtle element of rebelliousness is that which is against the continued study of Torah. Every intelligent person aspires to know more, to acquire greater education. But, insofar as we are human, we resent the process of achieving that greater level of knowledge. It is wonderful to know, but it is hard to learn.

At a recent conference on Jewish education at the American Jewish Committee, one of the most distinguished personalities in general education today – who is a concerned Jew – leveled certain criticisms against Jewish education, primarily of the afternoon Hebrew school variety. His major point was that it is not enough fun, there is not enough joy, so that as a result "the kids are turned off."

There is a large element of justice in this criticism. But I regard it as shallow and unfortunate. If the "kids" are "turned off" by the difficulty of learning, it is because their parents have raised them on the idea that everything is fun, and that which is not fun is not worth trying. Yet, all of learning is to some extent arduous. The major aspect of the study of Torah is not so much knowing it, but rather is working and sweating and toiling in Torah. King Solomon taught us that, "If you want to gain more knowledge, you must risk more pain" (Ecclesiastes 1:18). All creativity, from math to music, from Torah to philosophy, involves pain and frustration and suffering. As the Rabbis put it (*Avot* 6:4), the way of Torah is to live a life of deprivation and want and suffering and frustration. The creative act is, indeed, not always "fun."

Spiritual and intellectual creativity are similar, in this respect, to biological creativity – the process of birth, whether of an idea or a baby, can hurt, it can be messy, it can be disconcerting. But after the process has been brought to a successful conclusion, the product is a source of great joy and exultation.

One can mention a host of other Koraḥ-like qualities that we can find in ourselves if we search hard enough and honestly enough – self-righteousness, arrogance, cleverness, demagoguery, and so forth.

But enough! The point is made: We must not feel exceptional if we discover these ugly attributes in ourselves; we must not allow them to prevail, they must never become dominant. Being aware of their existence should lead us to control them.

According to the Talmud (*Bava Batra* 74a), Korah and his group still call out, to this very day, from the bowels of the earth into which they were swallowed: "Moses is true and his Torah is true and we are deceivers."

Korah lives, in the depth of each personality. The task of Jewish growth and spiritual development is not to destroy him or even to silence him, but to educate that Korah within, so that he pronounces his ultimate confession: Moses is right, the Torah is true, and I am wrong.

Ḥukat

Weakness – The Fatal Flaw [1]

Our *sidra* this morning tells of one of the most painful episodes in biblical history, one which was seared into the consciousness of the people of Israel. It is the incident of *mei meriva*, "the waters of contention" (Numbers 20:13). The Israelites, after the death of Miriam, complained about the lack of water. From a mere water shortage, they escalated their complaints to a general attack on Moses, expressing a preference for having remained in Egypt as comfortable slaves over being in the desert as starving and thirsty freemen.

Thereupon, the Lord told Moses and Aaron, "You shall address the rock [or, speak concerning the rock] before them, and it will give forth its waters" (v. 8). Moses and Aaron then turned to the Children of Israel and said, "Listen here, you rebels, shall we bring forth water for you from this rock?" Then Moses raised his hand with the staff in his hand he smote the rock twice and the water came out.

The punishment ordained for Moses and Aaron was severe: "Because you did not have sufficient faith to sanctify My Name before

---

1. June 24, 1972.

the Children of Israel, therefore you will not enter the Promised Land but will die on this side of the Jordan" (v. 12).

What was their sin? The biblical text is unclear, and many interpretations have proposed by commentators both ancient and modern. Rashi offers the most popular explanation: Moses was commanded to talk to the rock, and he hit it instead. However, Nahmanides is unhappy with this interpretation because everything Moses did during his ministry was performed by the striking of the staff. Besides, as we indicated above, Moses and Aaron were not commanded to speak *to* the rock, but *about* it. Maimonides maintains that the sin of Moses and Aaron was their anger. They lost their temper when they said, "Listen here, you rebels." Nahmanides, however, criticizes this interpretation as well because, first, Moses was right in expressing his anger, and second, there are other occasions when Moses appeared to lose his temper and he was not reproached. Nahmanides therefore follows the interpretation of Rabbenu Ḥananel and maintains that the sin of Moses and Aaron was to use the first person, "Shall we bring forth water," rather than, "Shall He (the Lord) bring forth water."

My own interpretation, which I respectfully submit to you, is an expansion and modification of that offered by Abarbanel and certain modern exegetes: The misdeed of Moses and Aaron was that of weakness. The first reaction of Moses and Aaron when they heard the rebellious plaints of the Children of Israel was not the immediate response of challenge, but of fear and retreat.

Moses and Aaron retreated from before the congregation to the entrance of the Tent of Meeting and there they fell on their faces. When they should have stood up, they fell back.

More precisely, I believe we can pinpoint the sin of Moses in the second strike of the staff. Permit me to explain.

Moses and Aaron started to assert themselves when they confronted the Children of Israel and said, "Listen here, you rebels." However, they kept themselves back. They restrained their response. Now psychologists, especially psychoanalysts, have taught us that inhibited aggression is usually directed against the self or against inanimate objects. If I am angry at someone and secretly wish to harm him I will stamp my foot or slap my thigh.

Now, the first time that Moses struck the rock was understandable. Everything he did, from splitting the Red Sea to bringing forth water, was performed with a strike by the staff. However, the second time he hit the rock, it was an act which expressed misplaced hostility, originally felt toward the Israelites, now redirected towards the rock.

Why was that wrong? What should he have done? Simply this: He should have expressed his anger directly to the Israelites, rather than the inanimate rock. Crudely put, he should have wielded the staff not on an innocent rock, but on the heads of this ungrateful and recalcitrant people who, after thirty-eight years in the desert, still proved that they were immature slaves, still whining, "Why did you take us out of Egypt?" One could expect this from a generation that was born in slavery and still primitive and immature – not from a generation born in freedom in the wild desert.

Moses and Aaron should not have fled, not have feared, not have conceded, not have compromised, not have taken it out hysterically on a rock. They should have encountered the Israelites with force and indignation.

In other words, Moses and Aaron were taught – and through them, we are taught – that weakness in a leader can be a fatal flaw.

Jewish leaders have always been commanded to be tender and loving. Moses and David are, in our tradition, the archetypes of gracious leadership. Both were taken from the sheepfold to become the shepherds of Israel. Just as a shepherd must learn to look after every stray lamb, to pick it up tenderly and hold it close to his breast, so must the leader of our people be a shepherd to human charges. But not always! There are times that strength and power and courage and resistance are called for in a leader. So, the first King of Israel, Saul, was deposed because he was too merciful, too compassionate, too soft, towards Amalek, where he should have been firm and strong. The Talmud (*Ketubot* 103b) tells us about the death of Rabbi Judah the Prince, who was both the most eminent scholar of his generation and the *nasi*, the political leader of all of Israel. On his deathbed, his children came in to bid him farewell. Rabban Gamliel, his son, entered, and his father transmitted to him the orders of leadership, telling him how to conduct himself as his successor. And he said to him, "My son, conduct your presidency with strength." Lead from on high, with dignity and power and pride.

Leadership is not meant for diffident weaklings. A leader must often act against the masses. A leader need not necessarily be a "consensus president." He must be at the head of his people and sometimes demand of them, reproach them, rebuke them. That *vox populi vox dei*, that the voice of the people is the voice of God – is not a Jewish idea!

This interpretation I have offered is both text and pretext for my comments on certain Jewishly significant news that has come to our attention this past week or so.

The abdication of Jewish religious leadership years ago and today as well has produced an ugly harvest which we only now are reaping.

In the beginning of the opening up of the Jewish communities to the Western world, Jews began to acculturate. Now, from our point of view, that was perfectly understandable. To cull the best of Western culture – that is commendable. But what happened was that certain people began to approach the Western world with inferiority feelings, and with the desire to break down the discipline of *Halakha*. Thus, the same Jewish leaders cut out almost all Hebrew from the prayer book, did away with mention of Zion and Jerusalem (because, after all, Germany was our motherland and Berlin our Jerusalem), legislated that the Sabbath always begin at 6 PM and end at 6 PM winter and summer; and then changed Saturday services to Sunday.

What was the rationale for this radical surgery performed on the Jewish tradition? Simply, that this is what people demanded – as reflected in the popular saying, "Give youth what it wants!" What they forgot was that, first, youth does not always know what it wants (that is the special privilege of youth); second, youth changes its wants every few years; and third, the word of God is permanent and the plaints of whining youth are temporary. *Halakha* must always remain superior to fashion.

Is this yielding to the fads of youth leadership or pettifogging Milquetoastism? If these people were really leaders, they would have raised their staff over the heads of their congregations and brought it down in a sharp line and said, "No!" Even the most liberal denominations of Judaism have certain limits. Even the breaking of *Halakha* cannot go beyond a certain point.

Let us not lose our sense of proportion. Sometimes, Orthodox Jews chafe at the *maḥmirim* (stringent ones) in our Orthodox camp, those who always take the more strict or stringent view and seem to delight in issuing prohibitions. I object to that too. But there is an infinitely more serious charge against the other extreme, those of the non-Orthodox groups who seem to have one answer for all problems: "Everything is permitted." But in such an attitude of permissiveness, religion cannot grow. If everything is permitted, there is no religion, there is no morality, there is no civilization.

If, for example, a young Jew or Jewess wants to marry out, he or she can do so. This is a free country. But to provide a rabbinic presence is to grant him or her the illusion of religious sanction, and that is dishonest. For a "rabbi" to be present and preside at such an occasion is a matter of fraudulent posturing, as if the berobed eminence of a sacerdotal rabbinic personality is the imprimatur of the Jewish tradition granted to one of the greatest transgressors of our faith and our tradition. The occasion calls for sitting *shiva*, not for co-officiating with a priest or minister, with a caterer, band, dancing, and drinking. And compassion or the desire to keep a Jew in the fold this way – that is not an answer, but is a self-defeating and fraudulent rationalization. Solomon had already taught us (Ecclesiastes 7:16), "*al tehi tzadik harbei*," don't be too much of a *tzadik*, too moralistic, too self-righteous.

The bitter failure of liberal Jewry to maintain a commitment to the Jewish religion is no consolation to us Orthodox Jews. It increases our sense of pessimism and depression about the survivability of the American Jewish community. But it must be a lesson to us in many ways – religiously, communally, and in matters of family and personal life. For the Torah teaches us something of historic importance in recording the punishment meted out to Moses because of that second strike. Weakness is a fatal flaw in Jewish leadership. Sometimes you think you are being good when you are really doing evil. You think you are helping, and you are destroying. You submit to momentary compassion, and in the process you lose the Promised Land.

A Jewish leader must be gentle but must also be strong. He must be considerate but must know how to use power. Power, of course, can corrupt. But the attainment of a good life requires the benevolent use of power. Without it, we are in contempt of *emuna* (faith) and we have failed to perform *kedushat Hashem* (the sanctification of God's Name).

When we do use power benevolently, then it becomes a source of blessing: "Blessed are You, O Lord, *ozer Yisrael bigvrura* (who girds Israel with strength)."

And blessed is Israel when it responds with its own strength.

Balak

From Curse to Blessing[1]

The opening verse in the daily order of public prayer is the familiar "*Ma tovu ohalekha Ya'akov, mishkenotekha Yisrael,*" "How good are your tents, O Jacob, your dwelling places, O Israel" (Numbers 24:5). It must be quite an important verse to be so strategically and significantly placed, as it is the very first thing we say as we enter the synagogue. And indeed it is just that. For as the opening chord in the overture to the Morning Services, "*ma tovu*" sets the key for the entire day of prayer, the symphony of the Jew's mind and heart and soul rising harmoniously with those of all of Israel towards our Father in Heaven.

Just what does this verse mean? Our Sages (Pesikta Numbers 129) interpreted "tent" and "dwelling place" to refer to synagogues and religious schools. "How good are your synagogues and your halls of study" is the meaning of this blessing. May they increase in influence and grow in beauty and splendor. And this blessing, which is found in today's *sidra*, comes from a most surprising source. It was first uttered, our Bible tells us, not by a Jew but by a non-Jew – and an enemy of Israel, at that. It was

---

1. July 10, 1954.

133

Balaam *harasha*, the wicked one, who, upon seeing Israel's tribes arrayed in the desert about the Tabernacle, exclaimed "*ma tovu.*" And there is yet something more surprising in the entire episode, something that makes the choice of this verse for our opening prayer even less understandable. Tradition consistently reports, in all its comments on this episode, that Balaam fully intended to curse Israel. He had been hired to do so by the Moabite king Balak. Seeing Israel proudly and devoutly arrayed about the Tabernacle, Balaam arose and wanted to curse Israel, saying, "May you *not* have any synagogues and schools, may they diminish in influence and in scope." But instead of a curse there issued forth from his mouth, by divine command, the blessing of "*ma tovu.*"

But if so, then it is difficult to understand this choice of "*ma tovu.*" Was it not intended as a curse? Was it not uttered by an enemy of our people, by the ancient forerunner of the modern intellectual anti-Semite? Indeed, one of the outstanding halakhic scholars of all generations, the Maharshal (Rabbi Solomon Luria, sixteenth century), wrote in his Responsa (#64): "I begin with the second verse and skip "*ma tovu,*" which was first recited by Balaam, and he intended it as a curse." This is the weighty opinion of a giant of the *Halakha*!

And yet our people at large did not accept the verdict of the Maharshal. We have accepted the "*ma tovu,*" we have given it the place of honor, and as we well know, it has become the "darling" of cantors and liturgical composers. And if all Israel has accepted it and accorded it such honors, then there must be something very special about it that somehow reflects an aspect of the basic personality of the Jew and a deep, indigenous part of the Jewish religious character.

That unique aspect of our collective character, that singularly Jewish trait which manifests itself in the choice of "*ma tovu*" under the conditions we mentioned, is the very ability to wring a blessing out of a curse. We say "*ma tovu*" not despite the fact that it was intended to harm us, but because of that very fact. It is Jewish to find the benediction in the malediction, the good in the evil, the opportunity in the catastrophe. It is Jewish to make the best of the worst, to squeeze holiness out of profanity. From the evil and diabolical intentions of Balaam, "May you not have any synagogues and schools," we molded a blessing of "*ma tovu,*" which we recite just as we enter those very halls of worship and study.

Hasidism, in the symbolic language of its philosophy, elevated this idea to one of its guiding principles. We must, Hasidism teaches, find the *nitzotz* in the *kelipa*, the "spark" in the "shell" – that is, we must always salvage the spark of holiness which resides in the very heart of evil. There is some good in everything bad. The greatness of humanity consists of our ability to rescue that good and build upon it. In fact, that is just how the entire movement of Hasidism had its beginning. European Jewry, suffering untold persecutions, was desperately seeking some glimmer of hope. There was a tremendous longing in every Jewish heart for the Messiah. There was a restlessness and a thirst for elevation. Two false messiahs,[2] one a psychoneurotic and the other a quack and charlatan, proclaimed themselves messiahs and led their people astray. All European Jewry was terribly excited about these people. Soon one led them into Mohammedanism and the other into Catholicism. The common, simple Jews of Eastern Europe – those who suffered most and who bore the most pain – were completely depressed by this tragedy of seeing their only hopes fizz and die. Now there was nothing to turn to. And here the Baal Shem Tov stepped in, took these yearnings and longings and pent-up religious drives and directed them not to falseness and apostasy and tragedy, but channeled them into a new form, into sincere and genuine religious expression which, all historians now admit, literally rescued all of Jewry from certain annihilation. He wrung a blessing from a curse. He found the good in the evil. He saw opportunity in catastrophe. He knew the meaning of "*ma tovu.*"

Jewish history is rich in such examples of making the best of the worst, of transforming the curse into a blessing. The Temple and its sacrificial service was destroyed, so our forefathers reacted to the catastrophe and found new avenues for religious expression in prayer, the "sacrifice of the heart." Jerusalem and its schools were ruined, so they decided that Torah is unprejudiced in its geography, and they built Yavneh, where they accomplished even more than in Jerusalem. British Foreign Minister Ernest Bevin refused to permit 100,000 Jewish refugees to immigrate into Palestine, so, having no choice, we proclaimed and built a State of

---

2. Sabbatai Zevi and Jacob Frank.

Israel for over a million Jews. Remember the mourning and sadness and gloom when Bevin refused us? And remember our joy and thrill in May of 1948 when the State was declared? Blessing from a curse. We have never completely surrendered to curse. We have always poked around in its wreckage, found the spark we were looking for, and converted the whole curse into one great blessing. That is what is implied in reciting *"ma tovu"* as the opening chord of our prayers. God, continue that power within us. Let us make the best of the worst – blessing from curse.

Perhaps one of the most outstanding examples of a human being who was able to transform curse to blessing is the renowned Jewish philosopher Franz Rosenzweig, who died in 1929. Rosenzweig was a German Jew, an assimilationist, who was profound, scholarly, and sincere in his intellectual pursuits. He is the one who, concluding that he was going to convert to Christianity, decided to follow the historical process, and so attempted to acquaint himself with Judaism as a stepping stone to his new faith. Interestingly, he experienced a great religious feeling during the *Ne'ila* service on Yom Kippur in some small Orthodox synagogue in Germany, and thereafter became one of the leading Jewish philosophers of our time, a man who attracted many great students and colleagues and, in his criticism of Reform, led people back to our origins. Rosezweig was an extremely active man. He was a thrilling and popular lecturer. He was a talented speaker, writer, and administrator, as well as thinker. But, at the prime of his life, in 1922, tragedy struck. In the wake of a cerebral hemorrhage came partial, and then complete, paralysis. The widely traveled searcher could not move. The able lecturer could not speak. The writer could not move his hands, could hardly even dictate notes. Surely, this should have killed him. Surely, this should have marked the end of a fruitful and promising career. But no – Rosenzweig had rediscovered Judaism, and with it its inarticulate but very real insights. And so he learned to wring fortune from this misfortune. He dictated numerous letters, scholarly articles, and books to his wife by virtue of a special machine. His wife would turn a dial, with the alphabet, and he would nod ever so slightly at the letter he wanted. Thus, mind you, were letters, articles, diaries, and books written!

Nor was this only a flurry of panic activity, something to "make him forget." No, it was a state of mind, it was the Jewish genius ever seeking the "spark" in the "shell," the blessing in the curse. Shortly after the onset of illness, he wrote the following: "If I must be ill, I want to enjoy it. In a sense, these two months have been quite pleasant. For one thing, after a long spell, I got back to reading books." This from a man who couldn't move a limb, and who couldn't pronounce one consonant intelligibly! And listen now to what the same man wrote seven years later, just before his death: "I read, carry on business…and, all in all, enjoy life…besides, I have something looming in the background for the sake of which I am almost attempted to call this period the richest of my life…it is simply true: dying is even more beautiful than living." What a conversion of curse to blessing!

It is so, and should be so, with every individual. Misfortunes, may they never occur, have their redeeming qualities. Death brings an appreciation of life. Tragedy can bring husband and wife, father and child, brother and sister, closer together and bring out dormant loves and loyalties. Failure can spur one on to greater successes than one ever dreamt of. In the inner shells of curse there lies the spark of blessing.

The aim and goal of prayer, as our Jewish sages have pointed out through the ages, is not to change God, but to change ourselves. We come before God as humble petitioners, terribly aware of our short-comings, our inferiorities and our sins. Whoever prays truly knows that somewhere, sometimes, he or she has been caught in the web of curse. We feel tainted with evil. And so we pray. We pray and we want God to help us change ourselves. What sort of change is it that we want? The change from evil to good, from curse to blessing. We want to transform ourselves. That is the spirit of the prayerful personality.

And that is the reason for beginning the day of prayer and petition with "*ma tovu.*" We enter the House of God which stands and survives despite and because of its ancient and modern enemies. The synagogue itself is the symbol of that transformation. We begin now to pray, with the object of such transformation in ourselves. Hence, "*ma tovu.*"

How good. Indeed, not only good, but how fortunate is a people who can forever hope and smile, knowing that even if, Heaven forbid, curse could be its lot, it will wring out of it every drop of blessing. This, indeed, is the greatest blessing. "*Ma tovu.*" "How good."

Vacation as Vocation and Avocation [1]

Most people regard vacation as a time for relaxation, fun, and "good times," but hardly as a time for profound thinking. Yet the fact remains that, as an important aspect of leisure, vacation presents a most pressing problem. A growing literature, both in scholarly periodicals and heavily annotated tomes, testifies to the increasing concern with vacation and leisure. The new scientific, industrial, and economic conditions of our day have made more time available for more people than was ever dreamt of by our parents and grandparents. And even more is expected in the coming years. Predicted for the near future, for instance, is a four-day, twenty-hour week. In addition, early retirement alongside an increasing longevity means the addition of many non-work years to the ordinary life-time. What shall we do with all this time?

Vacation is therefore an important sociological, psychological, and even religious-spiritual problem. Of course the subject is too broad and comprehensive to attempt to exhaust it within the confines of one talk.

---

1. June 27, 1964.

Nevertheless, permit me to explore with you some general Jewish guidelines to the theory and practice of vacation.

There are basically three attitudes to vacation. The first is held by a respectable minority. This group consists of those who are frightened by leisure and who are annoyed by anything but long hours of intensive work in which they feel comfortable and secure. They have no patience for relaxation, which they regard as mere idleness. They are happy only when they are occupied in their profession or business or skill.

Now is this an attractive point of view? Of course, anyone prefers a work-horse to a playboy. The late Lord Beaverbrook, in his book *Don't Trust to Luck*, very correctly said that, "A man will come to less harm by over-work than by over-play."

Yet a Jewish approach is incompatible with this attitude, according to which work tends to become obsessive rather than creative, an end rather than a means, a form of neurotic escape from having to decide what to do with one's life. If one spends all of one's time in work it can make him a mere human beast of burden and squelch any aspects of personality which are hidden and yearn for expression. Indeed, if, according to our point of view, to rest on Shabbat is divine, then to relax in the middle of the week is human!

The second attitude towards vacation is entertained by many more people than the first. It regards vacation as a vocation, as a goal, indeed as the highest ideal and true purpose of man. It is an approach which issues from a dissatisfaction with labor, from a man's unhappiness with his work. Such people would like to have life-long leisure – vacation as a full time vocation or occupation.

The ancient Greeks, for instance, shared this view. They had more days of celebration than work-days in their calendar. The Romans, by the fourth century, counted 175 holidays in every year.

A thousand years ago, Saadia Gaon (*Emunot veDe'ot*, section 10) cited a group – presumably Jewish – who held the theory that "rest" (what we would call leisure or vacation) is the ideal human condition. There is a deceptive simplicity to their argument: Since all good people strive for rest, and since the higher one climbs on the social and economic ladder, the more time one has for rest, and since rest is a condition in which there is no fatigue or anxiety, and since the Almighty gave us Shabbat and *Yom Tom* during which we rest, hence it follows that this state of rest is the true desideratum, and vacation ought to be permanent. Saadia, of course, dismisses this as senseless. It is logical, he says, that rest should be valuable only after a period of exertion. Furthermore, it is unhygienic, and at best this kind of philosophy is a rationalization of laziness. Saadia might have added that more fatigue or anxiety results from an excess of rest than from an excess of work. It is an essentially negative attitude towards labor, which now becomes a chore and not a joy. Even more important, the *Halakha* could never accept such a point of view. Jewish law regards a professional gambler as *pasul le'eidut*, automatically disqualified as a witness in court. The reason is not so much the suspicion that a professional gambler is a man who has no scruples about taking someone else's money or property, as much as that such people do not engage in productive activities, in the kind of creative work which advances civilization. That is why vacation cannot be an ideal, and ought not to be considered the goal of one's life.

The third attitude, and the most advisable, is that which views vacation as an avocation, as a necessary diversion; as a hobby, as it were. This point of view retains a positive attitude towards work. It loves it and revels in it. Yet a person must not remain a slave to work. Indeed, Shabbat and *Yom Tov* are the models of this kind of leisure-vacation by virtue of the Torah's *issur melakha*, the prohibition of labor. Yet this prohibition does not imply a derision of labor – on the contrary, just as it is a *mitzva* not to work on Shabbat, so is it a *mitzva* that, "You shall labor for six days" (Exodus 20:8). But a free individual is one who requires free time, away from work. Therefore the ideal is the kind of combination of Shabbat and work-day that our Bible and tradition has ordained for us – a rhythm of work and play, of time-on and time-off.

Indeed, a normal, healthy person wants and deserves both work and play. During work he looks forward to leisure; during his rest, he looks forward to resuming work. The English poet Robert Browning, in his poem "The Glove," put it this way:

> When a man's busy, why leisure
> Strikes him as a wonderful pleasure.

'Faith, and at leisure once is he?
Straightway he wants to be busy.

Let us go a step further. Not only does he "also" need leisure, but it may be more important, in the ultimate scale of values, than his work! When the ancient Jewish philosopher of Greek Alexandria Philo came to explaining Shabbat, he maintained that it was a divine commandment to rest on the seventh day so as to recuperate and refresh ourselves in order to draw strength for the next six days of labor. This, however, is not really an authentic Jewish idea. According to it, Shabbat was made for the purpose of the weekdays. A much more genuinely Jewish idea was expressed by Abarbanel. He pointed to the first description of Shabbat in the Torah in Genesis, where we read, "The heavens and earth and all they contain were completed (*vayekhulu*) by the seventh day" (Genesis 2:1). The word "*vayekhulu*," however, actually means more than, "they were completed." It is related by its root to the Hebrew word *takhlit*, purpose. In other words, the purpose of the creation of heaven and earth during the six days of work was the Sabbath rest! Indeed, as Abarbanel points out, our prayer books support this contention. In the *Amida* on Friday nights we say, "You have sanctified the seventh day for Your name, [it is] the purpose (*takhlit*) of the creation of heaven and earth."

Perhaps the best proof to confirm this whole approach is from the Bible itself. For, whereas Shabbat is the last day of the week according to the divine scheme of Creation, it was the first day in the life of the first man. Since Adam was created on Friday before dark, the Shabbat was his first full day on this earth! So the leisure represented and symbolized by Shabbat is the higher purpose for which a man works all his life. That is why the Shabbat in our tradition has, in addition to the negative element of refraining from labor, such vastly important positive elements as *kedusha*, holiness – for the sanctity of Shabbat is the first instance of holiness mentioned in the Torah and the most important source of holiness in all of Judaism; *kibud* of Shabbat, the enjoyment or *oneg* of Shabbat; and the charming and profound teaching of our tradition that on Shabbat every Jew receives a *neshama yetera*, an additional soul. It is the quality of our leisure activity that lends it or denies it dignity.

Here we come, then, to the major problem: What do we do with all this new time that is available to us? How do we spend this leisure? One need not describe in all its gory details, especially not from the pulpit on Shabbat, what goes on in our resorts, those places sacred to American leisure. Of course, the sports and the relaxation are legitimate and highly commendable for our physical and psychological well-being. But what happens beyond that? Can this kind of activity be said to be the *takhlit*, the purpose, of man's life? Or is it the very negation and antithesis of purposefulness in life? One writer on the leisure problem has correctly stated that modern technology has mastered the art of saving time, but has failed to tell us how to spend our time. That is a matter of values – and values are beyond technology.

The religious – and human – insight into leisure begins with the observation that modern man has too many holidays but too few holy days. Our great question is: How do we recapture for our weekday leisure and vacation some of the meaningfulness of the Shabbat with its holiness, its honor, its joy, its "additional soul"?

Part of the answer can be derived from the fact that Hebrew has no special term for leisure. Indeed, the Hebraic mind cannot comprehend the whole idea. The whole problem of leisure is irrelevant to the Jewish way of thinking. What does "spare time" mean? How can there be a problem of what to do with time, when there is Torah to study? The study of Torah is the most rewarding activity of man. If man was given ten lifetimes to live, and he worked at the study of Torah incessantly, he would never exhaust it.

For us the answer is the same: The most important activity of mankind awaits its attention – the study of Torah, each person on his or her own level. I cannot believe that we of this generation, who have universal free education and an ever-growing number of university graduates, people who read more and who take more courses than ever before – that we should not be able to study the Torah with some kind of intensity. Those who can ought to study Gemara, those who are able ought to study the Torah commentaries, those who prefer ought to read through the Soncino *Nakh*, and whoever finds that difficult ought at least to study the portion of the week with the Hertz commentary.

There are some people who think that whatever study of Torah we engage in is reserved for the shul during the "season" of Rosh HaShana through the end of June. But I beg to differ: *Talmud Torah* has no "season." It must be engaged in at all times: "*Vehagita bo yomam valayla,*" "You should meditate in it by day and by night" (Joshua 1:8). In today's *sidra* the heathen prophet Balaam turns towards our ancestors and says to them, in words which we repeat every morning before entering the synagogue, "How good are your tents O Jacob, your dwelling places, O Israel" (Numbers 24:5). Our Rabbis (*Sanhedrin* 105b) saw in this a reference not merely to physical dwelling places, but to our spiritual homes. The words for "tent" and "dwelling places" refer to synagogues and schools. It was those, our places of prayer and Torah-study, that so impressed our heathen adversary. But then Balaam added two significant words: "*kinhalim nitayu,*" "they are stretched forth as streams." And here our tradition points out that the word for "stream," *nahal*, refers to a very special kind of stream – the kind that never dries up, neither during the hot season nor during the rainy season, neither during summer nor during winter. This is what the Torah must be to us – a year-round activity, not reserved only for the synagogue "season." Both in summer and winter, day and night, for old and for young, the study of Torah must be the source and fountain of our life.

As a matter of fact, given the conditions of our society, I dare say that it is more important to emphasize the study of Torah during leisure hours and vacation weeks and months than during our working periods. For it is during these times that we can apply ourselves with greater intensity and concentration, without constant distractions, to what is the truest and noblest purpose of anyone's existence. There was a time when in our synagogues and schools one could see only retired, ancient, superannuated people studying in the old tomes. But for the last fifteen or twenty years the situation has been reversed: Now, all Jewish education seems to be concentrated in the pre-*bar mitzva* years. In other words, the study of Torah was once regarded as exclusively a geriatric activity and now has become a pediatric activity. What it should be is a life-long, mature, constant, and uninterrupted activity of Jewish life – for this indeed is the highest "recreation" – which simply means re-creation, the highest form of creativity known to mankind.

Otherwise we fall to that low level of people who seek means "to kill time" – the most horrendous blasphemy of which any man can be culpable! For to kill time is to spill the blood of existence, to destroy the very soul of a person. All God gives us in this world is time – how dare we speak of killing it? It is only a lightweight upon whom time weighs heavily!

As leisure increases, as many more years free from work are added to the end of a man's life, we must reorient our whole philosophy of education as well. There once was a time when a father's major responsibility and obligation was to train his son in a formal, rewarding occupation. Now, however, we must recognize that the next generation and all those following will have more time to spend in leisure than in work. It therefore becomes a major responsibility for us to spend at least as much energy and effort in training children in the use of their leisure as we do in educating them toward succeeding in their work. "Living" is at least as important as "making a living." And, as we have pointed out, according to the whole Jewish world-view, there basically is no problem. If we will teach our children Torah – and, far more importantly, teach them by personal example that the study of Torah is a life-long activity and not reserved only to the beginning or to the very end of one's career – then we will have succeeded in giving our children the fullest education possible and in discharging our obligations as parents to the fullest satisfaction of our conscience before Almighty God.

The *mishna* in *Berakhot* (4:1) tells us that when Rabbi Neḥunya ben Hakana would leave his study hall, he would offer a brief prayer of thanksgiving. According to the Talmud (*Berakhot* 28b), that prayer read: "I thank you O Lord my God for making my portion amongst those who dwell in the study hall." One of the leading thinkers of the *Musar* movement asked: Since this prayer was recited when Rabbi Neḥunya ben Hakana was leaving the study hall, should he not have thanked God for having thrown his lot amongst those who leave the study hall, rather than amongst those who dwell there? The answer is that this prayer teaches us that even when we leave the study hall, we must still consider ourselves as among those who dwell in the study hall!

So, as so many of us this week make our way to our vacations, to seashore or countryside, to hotel or to cruise or to travel, as we are on the threshold of leaving the study hall of our synagogue for our leisure activity, let us thank and pray to God to help us continue to be among those who dwell in the study hall; that mentally and spiritually we remain in this House of God; that we take with us, wherever we go, its spirit of prayer and consecration, of total loyalty and commitment to the values of God, Torah, and Israel.

The Entebbe Rescue [1]

If we were to search Scripture for an appropriate expression of our relief, joy, and thanksgiving at the heroic and brilliant rescue by Israel of the over one hundred Jewish hostages kept by Arab and German terrorists in the Entebbe Airport in Uganda, one important verse would come to mind: "Now it shall be said concerning Jacob and Israel, what hath God wrought?" (Numbers 23:23).

What indeed hath God wrought! How great and miraculous was the deliverance, how wondrous was the rescue! From the depths of despair, we were brought to the heights of joy and gratitude – but we are mindful of the loss of three lives, and the disappearance of one of the hostages. [2]

Indeed, for the last several days our national mood has been reminiscent of the heady days following the Six-Day War. And yet,

---

1. July 10, 1976.
2. One of the hostages, Dora Bloch, a 74 year-old Jewish woman, had choked on some food while in captivity and had been taken by her captors to a local hospital, where she was during the rescue operation. Idi Amin, the Ugandan dictator, had her killed following the raid.

this very association with the Six-Day War raises problems that were debated then too. Amongst these is, should we really be thanking God for this victory, or congratulating the Israelis who risked so much and achieved so mightily? Should we be reciting this verse, "What hath God wrought?" or the verse immediately following it, "Behold it is a nation which arises as a lioness, and lifts up its head as a lion"? After all, it is these courageous young men who risked their lives – and the prestige of Israel – in a raid concocted so quickly and executed so brilliantly. So, which shall it be: "What hath God wrought," and its religious consequences; or "Behold it is a nation which arises as a lioness," and its political-military ramifications?

This is no idle speculation. Two attitudes strive for supremacy within each of us, and the two attitudes are present in our community as well. One of them, perhaps the minority, is what might be termed quietist. It advocates *bitaḥon*, complete faith in God, to the exclusion of man's strength or power. In fact, it is somewhat contemptuous of man's activities. The other point of view, much more prevalent, is activist. It focuses exclusively on what the teachers of *Musar* called *hishtadlut*, effort or initiative. It disdains appeals to faith, and comes dangerously close to the boastfulness against which Moses warned: "It is my power and the strength of my hand which has made for this success of mine" (Deuteronomy 8:17).

The first attitude is one which responds only with the words "What hath God wrought"; the second knows only the verse, "It is a nation which arises as a lioness."

Secularist man tends to see science and technology and all human achievement as displacing the divine in the world. The secularist mentality is such that it perceives human genius in competition with God's work, and holds that religion is meaningful only when science has no answer and technology no solution – as if faith in God were a function of human ignorance! It sees no reason to exclaim about what God wrought when it knows that achievement is a result of a nation arising like a lioness.

We have here the echoes of the "secular city debate" which was current in theological circles a number of years ago. In a less sophisticated manner, we can always hear such arguments and challenges as,

"Can you still believe in God – or in Torah, or observe the commandments – in a space age?"

Opposed to this is the outlook of religious man who, in his faith, often fails to appreciate the importance of human creativity, of science and technology – even while he makes use of it and enjoys the benefits and advantages that it has brought to civilization. In a way, such an approach is a subtle indication that it accepts the secularist premise that man's achievements are in competition with, and seek to displace those of God's – except that we side with God in this contest and exclaim, "What hath God wrought."

Neither of these, to my mind, is authentically Jewish. I must hasten to add that I deny as well the kind of compromise which attributes success to mankind and failure to God!

There is such a way of thinking which ascribes human vulnerability and natural cataclysms to God and man's triumph to man. In the insurance industry, when we speak of natural disasters or catastrophes, we employ a euphemism, "an act of God!" (Indeed, I heard of an Orthodox Jewish insurance agent who was seeking to sell a policy to an equally pious potential client, and said to him, "Now if there should occur an act of God, God forbid...") Such a mentality recites "What hath God wrought" only at the occasion of bad news. But if there is economic success, or a career triumph, or a military victory, then this mentality is one which then recites, "It is a nation which arises as a lioness," it is a result of my genius, my talent, my competence. But such a division of credit and blame is manifestly unfair.

What should be the authentic Jewish attitude? I believe it is that neither one is adequate! We need both verses – "What hath God wrought," in order to avoid the arrogance that comes from the successful exercise of human power, and "It is a nation which arises as a lioness" to avoid the paralysis of human power that is often the result of spiritual passivity.

There is no fundamental contradiction between the two verses, although we must always live in the tension between them. A truly religious Jew sees God's wisdom in man's wisdom, and God's power in man's power – for God and man, according to Jewish teaching, are partners in Creation, and it is God who delegated to man the role of

His surrogate in the mastery of Creation. If indeed man is "the image of God" (Genesis 1:27), then man's deed must reflect God's personality. In such a case, a manifestation of human wisdom or the benevolent use of human power for creative ends must be seen as a reflection of the character of God. No wonder that the *Halakha* directs us to recite special blessings upon encountering unusually wise or powerful individuals, in which we declare our gratitude to God for sharing His power and wisdom with mere flesh and blood. For us, "It is a nation which arises as a lioness" is a reflection of "What hath God wrought."

If there is no *hishtadlut*, if there are no human initiatives – what the *Zohar* calls "initiative from below" – the world must remain fallow, and the dark forces of nature will reign supreme in the absence of such human creativity. I recall the story of a farmer in Maine who bought an old and dilapidated farm. Slowly, he repaired the sheds, plowed the land, pruned the trees and hedges, fixed up the farmhouse. After he had finished, the local parson came by for a visit and, beholding the scene of this successful renovation, said, "I am glad to see what the Lord has done to this farm." Whereupon the farmer, in typically laconic Yankee fashion, responded, "You should have seen this farm when the Lord had it alone!"

Indeed so. God insists that man become the tool for His creative work. If He has it by Himself, He will refuse to do any more with it.

Similarly, if Israel had not undertaken its brilliant exploit, we would have lost not three or four hostages, but over a hundred, Heaven forbid. Without "It is a nation which arises as a lioness," we would have had no occasion to say "What hath God wrought." Without those Israeli lions, we would not today be thanking God. Perhaps when we are next solicited for the campaign on behalf of Israel, we will not groan and moan and complain, but remember the risks that these young lads of Israel embraced when they undertook this arduous and dangerous maneuver.

And yet – human agency alone cannot be held exclusively responsible for this miracle! I shudder to think what might have been, the untold errors and accidents and slip-ups that might have made a shambles of the entire effort and would not only have resulted in a massacre of the hostages and the would-be rescuers, but in a devastating public reaction to the futile Israeli effort. I can understand the censure of Israel by the French Pilots Association on the basis of a possible failure – though I ordinarily find it difficult to sympathize with anything French these days. Indeed, if not for "What hath God wrought," we would have no occasion for pride which would lead us to exclaim "It is a nation which arises as a lioness." Without God, our lions would be of no avail.

So we offer today our warmest and most deep-felt felicitations to the Israel Defens͏e ͏my, the lions of Israel. Not only Jews, but decent people throughou͏t ͏t͏he ͏world will join us in these congratulations. This is especially true of England, which not too long ago had the uncomfortable experience of having a representative of the Crown humiliated by that psychopath, Idi Amin, when the Ambassador came groveling and bowing and scraping before him.[3] Now, England too can hold up its head higher and exclaim with all the world about Israel, "It is a nation which arises as a lioness."

But no less – and even infinitely more – must we offer our prayer for thanks to Almighty God and exclaim, "What hath God wrought" in so protecting and prospering our Israeli soldiers in this extremely perilous effort.

I cannot help but think, at this occasion, of how God bends man to His purposes, how little we know of what role we play in history. It seems such a short time ago that Israel was banished from UNESCO and the representative of Lebanon came up to the rostrum of the United Nations and arrogantly crowed, "Israel is a country which belongs nowhere!" And now look at what God hath wrought: In the same week that Israel managed this brilliant coup of saving its hostages from Uganda, Lebanon is in the deepest throes of its most agonizing despair, it has effectively ceased to be a nation, it is – and I say this without any special satisfaction – a country which is a non-country, a blot upon the nations of the world. It is itself nowhere. How ironic is the justice that God executes upon the nations of the world. "What hath God wrought!"

The same coordination of an intersection between the divine and the human must always be part of our understanding of the forces

---

3. In 1975, the British Foreign Secretary pleaded with Amin, successfully, to stay the execution of British citizen Denis Hills.

of history, and this understanding must guide us in all our endeavors – not only that of Israel's military and political and economic security, but also in our efforts for Torah whether in Israel, the United States, or the world over.

In offering our congratulations to Israel and our thanks to God Almighty, in expressing both verses in profound appreciation of this historic event in which Israel proved to be so bold, so swift, so quick and so powerful, our lesson is clear: We must learn from this heroic act to inspire ourselves to heroism in pursuit of our spiritual goals as well. And here too we must be bold and swift and quick and powerful. For so we read this afternoon in *Avot* (5:20): "Be bold as the leopard and swift as the eagle and quick as the deer and powerful as the lion. And all this must be done in order to carry out the will of our Father in Heaven."

Pinḥas

Great Ideas are Dangerous[1]

J ewish mysticism teaches a great principle, which it derives from the verse in Ecclesiastes (7:14) that God created the world "one opposite the other." This means, according to the Kabbala, that every manifestation of holiness in the world had an underside of profanity and destructiveness. Hence, when God emanated the ten spheres of holiness there came into being, corresponding to them, the ten spheres of impurity. This underside of evil and impurity that always accompanies the phenomena of sanctity is referred to as the "*sitra aḥra*," "the other side" – a term often applied in Yiddish to the devil or demons.

This is not only a mystical idea, but a universal truth that applies at all times and places.

For instance, love is a great idea, but it can easily be distorted into something powerfully destructive, namely, lust. The same tender and warm feelings of love, when applied to the wrong person, can become illicit and immoral. No wonder that the word *ḥessed* (Leviticus 20:17),

---

1. June 26, 1975.

which is usually used to express the idea of affectionate generosity, is also used by the Torah to describe a particularly ugly form of incest.

Self-confidence is a great attribute. Every parent wants to inculcate this quality in his or her children. Yet by the slightest twist, this great idea reveals its "other side" of impurity, and it becomes arrogance, changing a confident person into an insufferably supercilious one.

Democracy is certainly a great idea, one which has inspired millions. Yet the same idea of power being invested in the people can, if one is not careful, turn into its "other side," and become merely mob-rule. What is a lynch mob, if not democracy distorted?

All of these, and many more, are great ideas which are dangerous. I often use this as a test of an idea. If someone proposes an idea to me, I see if it can become dangerous if it is distorted. If it cannot, then probably the idea is trivial!

Of course, one can simply opt for safety and security by abandoning all great ideas – but that is a living death. Rather, it is incumbent upon us to search out greatness but to beware of going to the extremes, to be always suspicious of taking things to their "logical conclusion," which usually means the "*sitra aḥra*," the "other side."

The same principle applies to the quality of zeal. Without it, commitment has little value and can hardly survive. Judaism cannot do without the passion that goes with zeal. Our *sidra* begins with the personality of Pinḥas, who is the symbol of zeal – *kina* in biblical Hebrew, *kana'ut* in Modern Hebrew. The Children of Israel had sinned with the Midianite women in the cult of the idol Baal Pe'or, and Zimri, one of the princes of the tribe of Simeon, had flaunted his immoral liaison with a Midianite princess before Moses and the Children of Israel. If this had gone unopposed and unpunished, only God knows how dreadful the consequences would have been for Israel then and for all posterity. The priest Pinḥas, in response to the actions of Zimri, took a sword and stabbed the two perpetrators to death. Our *sidra* tells us that because of this act of zeal, Pinḥas was awarded with the High Priesthood as a hereditary gift.

Unquestionably, *kana'ut* is a valuable sentiment. Without this zealousness, without this passion, commitment is at best superficial. Zeal involves self-sacrifice and earnestness.

Such *kana'ut* is not an easy achievement. There may be those who resort to zealousness as a substitute for thinking, but that is not always the case. The zealot is often a lonely man, willing to sacrifice popularity for the sake of his ideals. Consider the difference between the last *sidra* and this one. Read through what the pagan prophet Balaam had to say about our people – a veritable string of adulatory compliments! Every time you feel hesitant and uncertain as a Jew, go back to the prophecies of Balaam and you will emerge much more optimistic and self-confident. And yet, the Rabbis (see, for example, *Avot* 5:19) refer to him as *Bilam harasha*, the evil or wicked Balaam! Contrariwise, Pinḥas, according to many of our commentators, incurred the displeasure and animosity of large numbers of Israelites by his act of zealousness. And he is praised and offered the perpetual High Priesthood in recognition of his act!

Closer to our own time, the founding of the State of Israel in 1948 required a great deal of zealousness. Looking back at that era with the benefit of historical perspective and emotional detachment, many of us who at that time were opposed to the extremist groups now can recognize that the so-called "Stern Gang" and Irgun were indispensable for the success of our venture. And these groups proved far more civilized and moral and humane than the guerrillas of so many other nationalist movements. It is for this reason that we ought to offer our respect and undying gratitude to those two young men who were hanged by the British in 1947 and who this past week were re-interred on Mt. Herzl with honors by all of Israel.

And what is true for the State is true for Judaism. We have survived to this station because of the self-sacrifice of countless zealots, the historical successors of Pinḥas.

That is why I am not overly anxious for our camp, what we call "Modern Orthodoxy," to cut off from the "right wing." The "yeshiva world" and the "hasidic world" are reservoirs of passionate commitment, without which we are wishy-washy, wan, weak, and wavering. Of course I am unhappy with many of their policies. But our very survival may well depend on the degree to which we can become inspired by their zeal and learn to bring passion to our own commitments, no matter how much we may disagree with them on specific issues.

A Commentary for the Ages: Numbers

However, even in the Torah itself we find hints of apprehension that, like all great ideas, *kana'ut* has an "other side," that of destructive fanaticism. The other side of a warm-blood is a hot-headed one. In our *sidra*, Pinḥas is praised and rewarded and yet if we study the verses of today's *sidra* carefully, we can find in them tell-tale signs of reservation and hesitation about zealousness. Our Rabbis (*Yerushalmi Sanhedrin* 9:7) were much more explicit when they said that Pinḥas acted "against the wishes of the Sages."

Thus, one verse (Numbers 25:12) reads, "Therefore say (*emor*), 'Behold I give him [Pinḥas] My covenant of peace.'" However this verse is a bit difficult. Should it not say, "Say unto him" or "Say unto the Children of Israel?" Instead we find the word "*emor*" all by itself. A number of years ago, a student of mine became proficient in Semitic languages and published an article on one verse in the beginning of the Torah, which describes the actions of Cain towards Abel. When we read of the murder by Cain, the Torah says (Genesis 4:8), "And Cain said," but it does not tell us what he said. This student discovered that in cognate languages, the root *amar* frequently means "to puff up" with anger. Thus it means that Cain became angry with Abel and therefore killed him.

I suggest that the same is true for this verse. It means: Therefore, Moses, become angry, show your displeasure, even at the same time that you are rewarding Pinḥas! And give him the covenant of peace, teaching him that zeal must never be sustained, that it is appropriate only for extraordinary moments in history, but that in ordinary life situations there must be only *shalom*, peace. The *brit* (covenant) is meant for the regular ongoing activities of life, and there only peace and not zeal must prevail.

And the next verse reads: "And it shall be for him and his descendants after him for an eternal covenant of the priesthood *taḥat* he was zealous for his God." The word "*taḥat*" is usually translated as, "because he was zealous for his God." I suggest that here the word "*taḥat*" has the meaning of "instead." Thus, Pinḥas, who did something meritorious when he performed his act of zeal, must now learn to adopt a policy of peace and priesthood instead of zeal. Or perhaps "*taḥat*" means, in almost a physical sense, "underneath" – that even when one is zealous,

158

underneath the zeal must always be love and peace. Not vengeance but love, not zeal but peace, are the attributes of hereditary priesthood.

So, in all aspects of contemporary life we must seek out *kana'ut*, but by keeping it confined and restrained and in the context of love and peace, we will avoid the "other side" of fanaticism.

As I have said, I admire the zeal of our right-wing. But *emor* – we must become upset and indignant when it is thoughtless, abusive, uncivilized. At that point, it can well become destructive and self-defeating.

Of course it is not easy to propose clear formulae on how to determine when zeal shades into fanaticism, when passion becomes poisonous.

But if we are conscious of this potential of danger, if we are aware of how destructive great ideas can become, then we will be able to latch on to greatness and avoid the snares and pitfalls of "the other side."

If *emor*, if we are sensitive to the abuses of exalted ideas, then we will attain the *brit shalom*, the blessing and covenant of eternal peace.

Matot-Masei*

* Editor's note: Because of Rabbi Lamm's summer schedule, no sermons were available for *Parashat Matot*. With Rabbi Lamm's approval, we have moved "Knowing the Thoughts of the Almighty" from its original place in *Parashat Balak* to *Parashat Matot*, as the sermon addresses the character of Balaam, whose death is recorded in *Matot*. A few phrases in the original have been modified in order to reflect this change in location.

Knowing the Thoughts of the Almighty [1]

I want to discuss with you this morning a problem which is familiar to all of us, yet, despite its familiarity, is the most sadly neglected. It is a matter which is of central importance in every phase of human life and existence and on every level. And perhaps it would be best for me to state the problem by pointing it out in the context of the villain whose death is recounted in this morning Torah reading (Numbers 31:8), where it is drawn in clear and bold lines.

The character of Balaam is an intensely paradoxical one. He is a person who fluctuates from the heights to the depths, from greatness to pettiness, from genius to perversity. Indeed, Maurice Samuel (in his *Certain People of the Book*) rightly refers to this character as the "The Perverted Genius." That is just what he was – a perverted genius. Our Rabbis (*Sifri* 357:10) indicated the same thing when on the one hand they commented on the verse, "There arose in Israel no one like Moses" (Deuteronomy 34:10), that in Israel there arose no one like Moses, but the nations of the world were given an equivalent to Moses, namely,

---

1. July 7, 1956.

Balaam. And on the other hand, they tell us (*Avoda Zara* 4b) that this man who is comparable to Moses himself was a degraded sexual pervert who regularly committed the most vile form of sodomy with his donkey! Nowhere in the Bible do we find a single personality combining such two extreme opposites within the confines of one: prophet and pervert, genius and degenerate. Here is a man who has intimate contact with the divine, and then sinks to the lowest debasement known to us. He speaks with eloquence unequalled by most of the great prophets of Israel and takes it upon himself, with incredible *chutzpah*, to thwart and frustrate the plans of the Almighty by cursing Israel. A strange and paradoxical person indeed!

Such behavior dos not "just happen." Minor inconsistencies are common to all human beings, but this sharp and jagged contrast is irrational, it is pathological, and must have deeper roots. What, then, are the roots of this eccentric character?

Our Sages pointed to these roots when they expressed great amazement and astonishment about one statement of Balaam's about himself. Recall the famous incident of the talking ass. Here is one of the crucial incidents of the whole Bible, when properly understood (which it generally is not), and one which is highly instructive. Balaam had decided to go and curse Israel, complying with the request of the Moabite king Balak, enemy of our people. Riding on his ass he came between two narrow walls when the animal saw an angel blocking his way. Balaam did not see any angel and struck the poor animal, when the animal turned to him and complained that he did not deserve such treatment – and then Balaam too saw the angel and apologized. There is here a great element of biblical humor, of divine teasing and ridicule of this heathen prophet. An animal can see more than Balaam! And the great Balaam then apologizes to the ass!

And yet soon after that in one of his truly eloquent prophecies, Balaam begins by referring to himself with typical modesty as "*yodei'a da'at Elyon*," "he who knows the thoughts of the Almighty" (Numbers 24:16). Upon which the Rabbis (*Sanhedrin* 105b) declare, in awestruck astonishment at this empty brag, "A man who cannot know the thoughts of a mere animal (*da'at behemto*) can know the thoughts of the Almighty?!" A man who has not the vision of a four-legged beast can boast of divine knowledge? Much more importantly: A man who can so mistreat and so cruelly abuse an innocent ass that the animal turns to him plaintively and says, "Am I not your loyal beast of burden upon whom you have ridden all your life to this day, did I deserve this of you?" (Numbers 22:30) – can a man of such meanness and pettiness and cruelty dare boast of knowing the innermost thoughts of Almighty God?

That is more than a question. It is a devastating condemnation, not only of Balaam but of the type he represents – a type so common, so tragically abundant, that it has colored world history and colors the lives of so many of us. This is the Balaam-type, the kind who "talks with God" as the Yiddish idiom goes, the kind who is *"yodei'a da'at Elyon,"* who professes great faith and great morals and great ethics, who speaks eloquently of his honor and lavishly of his integrity and sincerity, but confines all this to the realm of abstract principles and lets the ethics and morals and faith suffocate in the thin atmosphere of the upper heavens, while in practice he doesn't even know the thoughts of his own animal. He violates the most elementary principles, he practices every conceivable form of treachery and sin. This is the gulf between theory and practice, between talking and doing, the vast abyss which separates professing and performing. This is the root of perverted genius and of the perversion of normal human intelligence and pretense. This is the tragedy of great vision and detestable living, of high principles and low deeds, of prophesying like Moses and practicing the morals of an animal.

If we are ever fooled by eloquent phraseology, it is our own fault. We should have learned from Balaam. It was not long ago that most of us American Jews were carried away like a bunch of hysterical bobbysoxers by the noble eloquence of an American president to whom we all but attributed divinity – only to find that treachery against Jews, his greatest supporters, was not beyond him.[2] We have now experience with the pious protestations of diplomats who talk like monks, whose every political pronouncement is loaded with religious phrases – and yet go ahead to flirt with every petty tyrant in the world, who commit what we might call political sodomy, a la Balaam. Even the most

---

2. This comment is referring to Franklin D. Roosevelt's actions during the Holocaust.

naïve fellow-traveler in our country must by now be sufficiently disgusted with the revelations of the Balaam-like behavior of the despots of Russia – *"yodei'a da'at Elyon,"* and yet "cannot know the thoughts of a mere animal" – people who speak of "democracy" and "freedom" and "people's governments" and can witness without objection so many decades of the world's most brazen one-man tyranny.

That is why we Jews were so careful about too much high talk and too few high deeds. That is why Orthodox Judaism keeps central the *Halakha* – that which has least to do with propounding great doctrines, and most to do with enforcing them in life. How interesting that the one place the *Mishna* does discuss theology (in *Ḥagiga* 2:1), it takes a negative attitude, and says to restrict it. Don't fool yourself by all this sham eloquence of a Balaam, the Rabbis plead. Live the right life, which is far more eloquent in its own way. Jews and Judaism are different from others, a noted Gentile thinker once said. While others have a religion, Jews are religious. We begin not from *"yodei'a da'at Elyon,"* from elaborating lofty ideas, but from *"da'at behemto,"* from instructing in how to live this mundane life, how not to mistreat a mere beast of burden, how to eat meat, how to make a loan, how and what and what not to cook, where to assist another person, how to pray – from a loyal practice of these minutia we then are able to understand the *"da'at Elyon,"* for then we have lived according to the pattern of this same *Elyon.* That is why the individual who speaks a good line of religion but in his business practice follows the competitive code of the jungle and treats a friend with treachery – such a person is not religious in the Jewish sense but in the Balaam sense. He knows all about the thoughts of the Almighty, but cannot divine the simple sentiments of an ass.

It is told of the famous Malbim that he came to a new position in a city not overly known for its learning or piety and was disappointed in the inhabitants' attitudes and behavior. They would promise to do *mitzvot* and they "talked big" but they never followed through. One Shabbat he noticed, before his sermon, that everyone had a habit of kissing the *sefer Torah* with their hands, so in his *derasha* he said, "The trouble with this congregation is that we kiss with our hands and give with our mouths. It would be better if we would kiss with our mouths but give with our hands."

Rabbi Meir, in *Mishna Sanhedrin* 6:5, says that when a righteous person, a *tzadik*, dies the *Shekhina* mourns for him and wails "woe for the head, woe for the arms" – for a true Jewish *tzadik* is one who combines both – an intellectual attitude and a program of action, talking and thinking, doing and living, "*da'at Elyon*" and sympathizing with "*da'at behemto*."

Here is the true Jewish way of living: *rosh* and *zero'a*, head and arm. Separate them, allow a person to feel he has done his duty by just professing ethics and talking religion and believing in morals, and you have made of that person a Balaam, a logical spiritual descendant of this most debased of all false prophets. For that is the essence of false prophecy: prophecy followed by perversion, genius but degenerate, poetry and pettiness.

We who are descended of Moses and not Balaam must live up to the traditions of *nevi'ei ha'emet*, the true prophets. Before pretending to know the thoughts of the Almighty, let us try to commiserate with an animal in pain, with fellow men who seek us out for aid and assistance, with friends whose misery we can lessen and whose joys we can enhance.

The greatest eloquence is in righteous living; the finest poetry is a good deed; the highest philosophy a *mitzva*; and the most precious knowledge of God – the sympathy we extend to all His creatures.

The Disciples of Aaron [1]

The death of Aaron, recorded in this morning's *sidra*, is described in stirring and dramatic detail in the midrash (*Yalkut Shimoni* 787). The people mourned for Aaron even more than they later did for Moses, for Aaron was a man who loved peace and pursued peace. It was an eternal tribute to the first high priest of Israel that Hillel bade us regard ourselves as the disciples of Aaron by emulating his noble qualities – "*oheiv shalom, rodeif shalom, oheiv et habriyot, umekarvan laTorah*" (*Avot* 1:12). These are four in number and deserve to be spelled out clearly for all of us who earnestly desire the ideals that Aaron cherished.

Oheiv shalom: To the person who is ambitious and opportunistic, peace is only a truce, a poor second-best to total victory for his own ruthless pursuits. In order to be a disciple of Aaron, you must not seek peace merely for its utilitarian value, not merely because it is the best arrangement under the conditions that prevail, but because you love peace, because peace is the normal, most desirable state of the world. One of God's names is *Shalom*. *Shalom* is a positive virtue in its own

---

1. RCA Manual, 1960.

right, not merely the absence of strife. Hence, one must not only hate war but love peace. Peace is the kind of harmony that leads to perfection. *Shalom* leads to *shalem*.

Rodeif shalom: To pursue peace means not to be satisfied with finding it, but actively to engage in seeking it out, in creating it where it is lacking. Aaron was a pursuer of peace. The Rabbis (*Avot DeRabbi Natan* 12:4) tell of Aaron going first to one antagonist and then to the other and telling each how the other regrets the state of enmity and wishes that bygones be bygones. As a result of his active efforts, peace would reign.

There is yet another explanation of this felicitous phrase given by a hasidic teacher. Peace, he says, is a virtue only when it unites decent people with each other. But peace amongst people of evil design can only lead to greater harm to the world. Therefore one must "pursue" peace in the sense of chasing it away, when it concerns corrupt and malicious people. If we fail to "pursue" peace in this sense, then the Arab League might prove a more serious threat to Israel, the Chinese and Russians too powerful for the survival of democracy, and the gangsters of the country more influential than the forces of righteousness.

Oheiv et habriyot: The love of fellow man can come from many sources. I may love my fellow human because he is human. In a deeper sense, that means I love another because I love myself; I see myself in him. There is nothing wrong with that kind of humanistic approach. "Love thy neighbor as thyself" (Leviticus 19:18) implies we must first love ourselves. But there is the danger that this kind of love exists only where I feel a kinship of some kind between myself and another person. But where there are pronounced differences in color or belief or background or opinion, this kind of love breaks down. Hence, Hillel tells us, we must be disciples of Aaron who loved "*et habriyot*," "creatures." He loved other people because they were created by God. In loving mankind he loved God, for the love of created and Creator were intimately bound up with each other in his eyes. And when we love a person because that individual is God's creature, then no differences between us can affect that love adversely. Thus, the verse states, "Love thy neighbor as thyself, I am the Lord."

Umekarvan laTorah: The love of fellow creatures may be expressed in many ways. Charity, respect, consideration, economic assistance, appreciation all are signs of such love. But greatest of all is helping your fellow creature find meaning in life, assisting others in appreciating why they are alive and helping them spend their lives in a manner that is worthy and dignified. The highest form of *oheiv et habriyot* is therefore *mekarvan laTorah*. The Netziv used to say that this *mishna* urges us to love not only those who are devout and scholars, *benei Torah*, but also – perhaps especially – those who are distant from Torah. For the *Tanna* pleads with us to love people and bring them close to Torah – which means that they originally were distant from Torah and only through our love were brought close!

By directing our energies towards embodying these noble ideals, we can truly honor the memory of Israel's first high priest, who was mourned by the Children of Israel to an even greater extent than Moses.

About the Author

Rabbi Norman Lamm, former President and Chancellor of Yeshiva University and former Rosh haYeshiva of its affiliated Rabbi Isaac Elchanan Theological Seminary, is one of the most gifted and profound Jewish thinkers today. He was the founding editor of *Tradition*, the journal of Orthodox thought published by the Rabbinical Council of America, and to this convenes the Orthodox Forum, a think tank of rabbis, academicians, and community leaders that meets annually to discuss topics of concern in the Orthodox community. Before assuming the presidency of Yeshiva University, Rabbi Lamm served for many years as Rabbi of The Jewish Center, one of New York City's most prominent and vibrant Orthodox synagogues.

A prolific author in the field of Jewish philosophy and law, a distinguished academician, and a charismatic pulpit rabbi, Rabbi Lamm has made, and continues to make, an extraordinary impact on the Jewish community. With a rare combination of penetrating scholarship and eloquence of expression, he presents a view of contemporary Jewish life that speaks movingly to all.

About the Editor

Stuart W. Halpern serves as an Academic Advisor on the Wilf Campus at Yeshiva University, the Assistant Director of Operations of the Zahava and Moshael Straus Center for Torah and Western Thought at Yeshiva University, and the Assistant Director of Student Programming and Community Outreach of the Bernard Revel Graduate School of Jewish Studies. He received his BA from the University of Pennsylvania, an MA in Psychology in Education from Teachers College at Columbia University, an MA in Bible from Revel, and his doctorate from the Azrieli Graduate School of Jewish Education and Administration. He is the co-editor of the *Mitokh Ha-Ohel* series and serves on the Steering Committee of the Orthodox Forum.

Other works by Norman Lamm:

Rav Kook: Man of Faith and Vision (1965)

A Hedge of Roses: Jewish Insights into Marriage and Married Life (1966)

*The Royal Reach: Discourses on the Jewish Tradition
and the World Today (1970)*

Faith and Doubt: Studies in Traditional Jewish Thought (1971:1986:2006)

*Torah Lishmah: Torah for Torah's Sake in the Works of Rabbi Hayyim
of Volozhin and his Contemporaries (Hebrew 1972, English 1989)*

The Good Society: Jewish Ethics in Action (1974)

*Torah Umadda: The Encounter of Religious Learning and Worldly
Knowledge in the Jewish Tradition (1990:2010)*

*Halakhot Ve'Halikhot (Hebrew): Jewish Law and the Legacy of Judaism:
Essays and Inquiries in Jewish Law (1990)*

The Shema: Spirituality and Law in Judaism (1998)

The Religious Thought of Hasidism: Text and Commentary (1999)

Seventy Faces (two volumes): Articles of Faith (2001)

The Royal Table: A Passover Haggadah (2010)

Festivals of Faith: Reflections on the Jewish Holidays (2011)

The Megillah: Majesty and Mystery (2012)

Derashot LeDorot: A Commentary for the Ages: Genesis (2012)

Derashot LeDorot: A Commentary for the Ages: Exodus (2013)

Derashot LeDorot: A Commentary for the Ages: Leviticus (2013)

*Maggid Books
The best of contemporary Jewish thought from
Koren Publishers Jerusalem Ltd.*

The Complete Guide
Managir

ETSY

SHOP

2025

Step-by-Step Success with Etsy SEO, Marketing, and Social Media Strategies

CARLY JENNINGS-BOWEN

ISBN: 9798346067528

☐

Contents

Introduction

Etsy has become one of the most vibrant and successful platforms for creative entrepreneurs, offering a global marketplace where handmade, vintage, and unique items thrive. Whether you're a seasoned seller looking to expand or a new entrepreneur ready to turn your passion into profit, Etsy offers the perfect opportunity to reach millions of potential buyers. But with evolving tools, policies, and trends, setting up and managing a successful Etsy shop in 2025 requires more than just listing products—success lies in a deep understanding of Etsy SEO, marketing strategies, and customer engagement.

As Etsy continues to grow, so do the opportunities, challenges, and competition. That's where this book comes in. The Complete Guide to Setting Up and Managing an Etsy Shop in 2025 is a practical, step-by-step guide designed to help you navigate every aspect of the platform, from creating your shop and mastering Etsy SEO to leveraging social media platforms like Instagram and TikTok to drive traffic and sales.

In this guide, you'll discover:

How to Set Up Your Etsy Shop: A complete walkthrough for starting your Etsy business, including choosing the right shop name, designing a compelling profile, and developing a product line that attracts buyers.

Mastering Etsy SEO: How Etsy's search algorithm works in 2025, and actionable strategies to improve your product visibility, drive organic traffic, and boost sales.

Marketing Your Etsy Shop: Step-by-step strategies for using Etsy's built-in tools and external platforms like TikTok and Instagram to promote your products and create a loyal customer base.

Optimizing Your Listings: Learn how to craft compelling product descriptions, take high-quality photos, and price your items for maximum profit.

Managing Operations and Scaling: From processing orders and handling shipping to dealing with customer service, this book will help you streamline your operations and scale efficiently.

Etsy's marketplace offers incredible opportunities, but navigating its many tools and features can be overwhelming. Whether you're starting from scratch or looking to grow an existing shop, this book will give you the knowledge and confidence you need to succeed. It's designed to provide practical advice that's up-to-date with Etsy's 2025 policies, ensuring you have everything you need to build a thriving, sustainable business.

By the end of this guide, you'll not only have a fully functioning Etsy shop, but you'll also understand the key strategies to grow your brand, attract the right customers, and manage your business effectively in a fast-changing eCommerce landscape.

Let's get started on building your Etsy success story.

1 Getting Started with Etsy

An Etsy shop requires more than just listing a few products. You need a clear understanding of how the platform works, how to set up your shop for success, and how to stand out in a crowded marketplace. In this chapter, we'll walk you through everything you need to know to get started on Etsy, from creating your seller account and setting up your shop to making your first listings shine.

1. Creating Your Etsy Seller Account

The first step in starting your Etsy business is to create a seller account. If you already have a personal Etsy account, you can easily transition into a seller, but if you're new to the platform, the process is straightforward.

Step-by-Step Guide to Setting Up Your Seller Account:

Sign Up for an Etsy Account: If you don't have an Etsy account yet, visit Etsy's homepage and sign up with your email, Google, or Facebook. You'll need to provide basic details such as your name, email address, and password.

Switch to Seller Mode: Once your account is created, navigate to the "Sell on Etsy" option. Etsy will guide you through the process of setting up a seller account.

Complete Profile Information: Here, you'll fill in the necessary details for your seller account, including country of residence, language, and currency preference. Make sure these reflect your primary customer base, especially if you plan to target international buyers.

Enter Payment and Billing Information: Etsy requires sellers to provide payment details for receiving payouts. You'll need to link a bank account and choose how frequently you want to get paid (e.g., weekly, bi-weekly). Additionally, Etsy will ask for billing information for seller fees, including listing fees and transaction costs.

2. Choosing the Right Shop Name

Your Etsy shop name is one of the most critical aspects of your brand. It's the first impression potential buyers get, so you want it to be memorable, relevant to your products, and SEO-friendly to help you rank higher in search results.

Tips for Choosing a Strong Shop Name:

Keep It Simple and Memorable: Short, catchy names are easier for customers to remember. Avoid overly complex words, unusual spellings, or numbers that could confuse buyers.

Make It Relevant: If possible, incorporate keywords related to your products or niche in the shop name. For example, if you sell eco-friendly jewelry, try to include words like "Eco," "Green," or "Jewels" in your name.

Check for Availability: Etsy doesn't allow duplicate shop names, so before finalizing your name, use Etsy's name availability checker to ensure it's unique. Also, check domain availability if you plan to expand your brand with a standalone website in the future.

Stay Flexible: As your business grows, your product line may expand or shift. Choose a name that isn't too narrow in scope, so you're not limited to one specific product category.

Once you've chosen the perfect name, Etsy will lock it in, and you won't be able to change it later without contacting support—so take your time to get it right.

3. Setting Up Your Shop Profile and Branding

After selecting your shop name, the next step is building your shop's profile and branding. This is where you'll make your shop visually appealing and professional, ensuring you stand out among the competition.

Your Etsy Shop Profile

Shop Title: The shop title is a brief description (140 characters or less) that appears below your shop name on your shop page. This is a great place to include important keywords related to your products. For example, "Handmade Organic Candles | Sustainable & Eco-Friendly."

Shop Banner and Logo: Upload a custom banner and logo that visually represent your brand. A well-designed banner can create a polished, professional look and instantly communicate your shop's style. Etsy provides guidelines on image sizes, so make sure your visuals are high-quality and properly formatted.

About Section: The "About" section is where you tell the story behind your shop. Why did you start your business? What makes your products unique? Buyers on Etsy love personal stories, especially when they can connect with the creator's passion, so use this space to build an emotional connection with potential customers. Include behind-the-scenes photos or videos of your creative process if possible.

4. Crafting Your Shop Policies

Clear, well-defined shop policies help set expectations for your buyers and protect you as a seller. Etsy encourages transparency, and having thorough policies in place will make your shop appear more professional and trustworthy.

Key Policies to Include:

Shipping Policy: Outline your shipping methods, delivery times, and any regions you don't ship to. Be sure to specify whether you offer free shipping or charge a fee. With Etsy's push toward free shipping on orders over a certain amount, you may want to factor that into your pricing strategy.

Return and Exchange Policy: Define your return and exchange policies. Will you accept returns on all products or only under specific conditions (e.g., damaged items)? Who covers the shipping costs for returns?

Payment Policy: Etsy handles most payment processing, but you can clarify which payment methods are accepted and whether you offer any payment plans or custom orders.

FAQs: Include a section for frequently asked questions (FAQs) to address common concerns or inquiries upfront. This could cover topics such as how to care for certain products, sizing information, or whether customizations are available.

5. Creating Your First Product Listings

Now that your shop is set up, it's time to start listing your products. Etsy's product listing process allows you to showcase your items in a way that appeals to customers while optimizing for Etsy's search algorithm.

Step-by-Step Guide to Listing Products:

Product Title: Write a detailed, keyword-rich title for each product. Etsy's search algorithm heavily favors product titles, so include relevant keywords that customers are likely to search for. However, avoid keyword stuffing—make sure the title reads naturally.

Photos and Videos: Etsy allows multiple images and video uploads for each listing, so take full advantage of this feature. Use high-quality, well-lit photos that show your product from different angles. If possible, include lifestyle shots that show your product in use. Etsy now also supports short videos (5–15 seconds) that can help bring your product to life.

Product Description: Your description is where you can dive deeper into your product's details. Be thorough—include the materials used, dimensions, and any special care instructions. This is also a place to tell the story behind the product, appealing to customers on a personal level.

Pricing and Quantity: Set your price based on your cost of materials, labor, Etsy's fees, and desired profit margin. Etsy will show you the total fees associated with each listing, so make sure you're pricing to cover those costs. Also, input the quantity you have available.

Tags and Categories: Etsy allows you to add up to 13 tags per listing. These are essential for Etsy SEO, as they help customers find your product in search results. Use all available tags and include a mix of specific (e.g., "handmade silver earrings") and broad (e.g., "gifts for her") keywords. Choose the appropriate categories and attributes to make your listing easier for shoppers to find.

6. Launching Your Etsy Shop

Once your listings are ready, it's time to officially launch your Etsy shop! Before you go live, double-check your shop's appearance, policies, and listings for completeness and accuracy. Once you're ready:

Hit the "Open Your Shop" button, and your Etsy store will be visible to the public.

Etsy will guide you through a brief onboarding to optimize your first listings, share your shop on social media, and begin marketing efforts.

Congratulations! You've now officially opened your Etsy shop and are ready to start attracting customers.

2 Defining Your Niche and Crafting a Product Line

One of the keys to building a successful Etsy shop is finding the right niche and developing a product line that resonates with your target audience. Etsy is a highly competitive marketplace, and to stand out, it's crucial to offer products that not only align with current trends but also reflect your unique creativity and values. Defining a clear niche helps you position yourself within the market, attract the right customers, and create a cohesive brand.

In this chapter, we'll walk through how to identify your niche, research current market trends, and craft a product line that not only sets you apart but also appeals to Etsy's global audience.

1. Understanding the Importance of Niche Selection

When starting an Etsy shop, you may be tempted to offer a wide variety of products to appeal to as many buyers as possible. However, this broad approach can dilute your brand and make it difficult to attract a loyal customer base. Instead, focusing on a specific niche allows you to develop a reputation as an expert in your area, offering high-quality products that meet the unique needs and desires of a defined group of customers.

Benefits of Defining a Niche:

- **Builds Brand Identity**: A well-defined niche helps establish your brand identity and makes it easier for customers to understand what your shop stands for.

- **Attracts Targeted Customers**: By catering to a specific group, you're more likely to attract customers who are genuinely interested in your products, leading to higher conversion rates and customer loyalty.

- **Reduces Competition**: While Etsy is a large marketplace, narrowing your focus to a niche can help you avoid direct competition with mass-market sellers and bigger brands.

- **Increases Marketing Efficiency**: With a clear niche, your marketing efforts can be more targeted, allowing you to speak directly to the needs and preferences of your ideal customers.

2. Identifying Your Niche

Finding the right niche requires a blend of self-reflection, market research, and understanding of current trends. Your niche should not only reflect your personal interests and creative strengths but also align with market demand.

Self-Assessment: What Are You Passionate About?

Before diving into market research, take time to reflect on your passions, skills, and interests. The most successful Etsy sellers often have a deep connection to their products, and this passion translates into higher-quality items and more authentic branding.

Ask yourself the following questions:

- What products do I enjoy creating the most?

- What skills do I possess that could be translated into sellable products?

- Are there any hobbies or interests I can monetize?

Your niche should stem from your strengths and interests so that you're motivated to continue improving and expanding your product line over time.

Researching Market Trends

Once you have a general idea of what you'd like to create, it's essential to validate your niche by researching market trends. This will help ensure there is demand for your products and that you're not entering an oversaturated market.

How to Research Etsy Trends:

1. **Etsy's Trending Tools**: Etsy itself provides insights into trending items through its "Trending Now" and "Popular Right Now" sections. These tools are a great way to see what's currently in demand across various categories.

2. **Keyword Research**: Use Etsy's search bar to type in potential product ideas and see how many listings appear. If there are too many listings, the niche may be oversaturated. If there are very few, it might indicate low demand. Striking the right balance is key.

3. **Third-Party Tools**: Platforms like Marmalead and eRank are valuable for Etsy-specific keyword and trend research.

These tools allow you to see what products and keywords are trending and provide data on competition and demand.

4. **Google Trends**: Explore broader market trends using Google Trends, which shows how interest in certain topics or products is changing over time. This is helpful for determining whether your niche is growing in popularity or fading.

Analyzing the Competition

Once you've identified a potential niche, examine the competition within that space. Competitor research can provide valuable insights into what works (and what doesn't) and help you identify gaps where your product line can stand out.

Steps for Competitor Analysis:

- **Search for Similar Shops**: Use Etsy's search function to find shops offering similar products. Pay attention to their product listings, customer reviews, and overall branding.

- **Look for Gaps**: What products are your competitors not offering? Is there a variation or customization that's missing in the market? These gaps could present an opportunity for you to offer something unique.

- **Analyze Pricing**: Look at how your competitors are pricing their products. This can give you an idea of what customers are willing to pay and help you position your products competitively.

3. Crafting a Product Line That Stands Out

Once you've defined your niche, the next step is crafting a cohesive product line that reflects your brand's values, style, and uniqueness. Your product line should be both appealing and consistent, making it easy for customers to understand what your shop offers and encouraging them to return for future purchases.

Start Small and Focused

When you first open your Etsy shop, it's a good idea to start with a small, focused product line. This allows you to test the market and gather feedback before expanding. Choose a handful of items that represent the core of your brand and resonate with your target audience.

Example:

If you're starting a shop that sells eco-friendly jewelry, you might begin with a collection of five to ten different styles, focusing on designs that use sustainable materials like recycled metals or ethically sourced gemstones.

Design with Cohesion in Mind

Cohesion across your product line is critical for creating a strong brand identity. Your products should not feel random or disconnected. Instead, aim for consistency in terms of style, color palette, and materials.

Consider the Following for a Cohesive Product Line:

- **Materials**: Use similar materials across your product line to create a unified look and feel. For example, if you sell handmade candles, you might choose to use only organic soy wax and natural essential oils across all your products.

- **Aesthetic**: Keep your design style consistent, whether it's minimalist, boho, rustic, or modern. Customers should be able to identify your products as part of the same brand at a glance.

- **Themes**: Create themed product collections that cater to specific customer needs or occasions (e.g., "Winter Collection" or "Self-Care Essentials").

Offering Customization Options

Customization is a powerful way to stand out on Etsy, as it allows you to cater to individual customer preferences. Whether it's personalized engraving on jewelry, custom colors for home decor items, or made-to-order designs, offering customization can make your products more attractive.

Customization Ideas:

- **Personalized Names or Initials**: Customers love personalized items, from monogrammed tote bags to engraved jewelry. This simple addition can make your products feel more special.

- **Custom Colors or Patterns**: If you create products like art prints or clothing, consider offering custom color choices or fabric patterns to suit individual tastes.

- **Made-to-Order Sizes**: Offer custom sizes for products like furniture or clothing, giving buyers a sense of exclusivity and personalized service.

Developing Variations to Appeal to a Broader Audience

While keeping your product line focused is important, offering variations of your products can help you reach a broader audience without losing the cohesion of your brand. Variations can include different sizes, colors, or materials to suit different customer preferences.

Examples of Product Variations:

- **Jewelry**: Offer the same necklace design in gold, silver, and rose gold.

- **Home Decor**: Provide different sizes of wall art to fit various room types (e.g., small for bedrooms, large for living rooms).

- **Apparel**: Create your signature t-shirt design in multiple color options or fabric types.

4. Testing and Validating Your Products

Before fully committing to a product line, it's important to test and validate your ideas. Testing your products allows you to gather feedback from real customers and make adjustments as needed, ensuring that your final offerings meet market demand.

Ways to Test Your Products:

- **Start with Limited Quantities**: Instead of producing large quantities upfront, start with a limited run of each product. This minimizes risk and allows you to gauge customer interest before scaling up.

- **Gather Feedback from Friends or Family**: Share your products with trusted friends or family members and ask for honest feedback. This can provide valuable insights into potential improvements.

- **Offer Samples or Pre-Orders**: Consider offering a small batch of products as samples or pre-orders to generate interest and test the market. Pre-orders also allow you to gather funding for larger production runs.

Refining Your Product Line Based on Feedback

Once you've launched your initial products, pay close attention to customer feedback and reviews.

Are there recurring complaints about product quality, shipping times, or other aspects of your offerings? Use this information to refine your products, update your listings, and improve the overall customer experience.

5. Pricing Your Products for Profit

Pricing your products is a delicate balance between covering your costs, making a profit, and staying competitive. As a dropshipper or handmade seller, you need to consider both the cost of materials and production time, as well as Etsy fees and shipping expenses.

Factors to Consider When Pricing:

- **Cost of Goods Sold (COGS)**: Add up the total cost of materials, production time, packaging, and shipping. Ensure you're covering these costs before determining your profit margin.

- **Etsy Fees**: Don't forget to account for Etsy's fees, which include listing fees, transaction fees, and payment processing fees.

- **Profit Margin**: Your profit margin should allow for enough revenue to sustain your business and reinvest in growth. While competitive pricing is important, don't undercut yourself by setting prices too low.

- **Competitor Pricing**: Research how similar products are priced on Etsy and other marketplaces. While you don't need to match competitors exactly, this research will give you a benchmark for what customers are willing to pay.

3 Selling Digital Products on Etsy

Etsy is widely known as a marketplace for handmade goods, vintage items, and crafts, but in recent years, selling digital products has emerged as a popular and lucrative niche. Digital products provide a unique opportunity for sellers to create passive income, meaning that after the initial creation, there is little ongoing work involved in fulfilling orders. Digital downloads can be anything from printable artwork and planners to patterns, eBooks, or digital invitations. For entrepreneurs looking for a scalable, low-maintenance way to earn on Etsy, digital products offer endless possibilities.

In this chapter, we'll explore how to sell digital products on Etsy successfully. We'll cover the types of digital products you can sell, how to create them, optimize your listings for SEO, manage customer expectations, and ensure long-term growth in this exciting space.

1. Why Sell Digital Products on Etsy?

Selling digital products comes with several advantages over physical goods:

- **Passive Income**: Once you create a digital product, it can be sold repeatedly without any additional effort on your part. You don't need to worry about inventory, shipping, or production times.

- **Low Overhead Costs**: Selling digital products eliminates the need for physical materials, storage, and shipping costs. You just need the tools to create your digital files, making it a low-cost venture.

- **Scalability**: With digital products, your ability to sell isn't limited by the amount of time you have or the number of products you can produce. You can sell hundreds or thousands of copies with no additional labor.

- **Global Reach**: Digital products are delivered instantly, so they can be sold worldwide without worrying about shipping fees, customs, or long delivery times.

For creatives, designers, and entrepreneurs who want to monetize their skills with minimal ongoing work, digital products are a fantastic way to expand into a scalable business.

2. Types of Digital Products You Can Sell on

Etsy

The range of digital products you can sell on Etsy is broad, allowing you to align your product offerings with your skills and interests. Here are some of the most popular categories of digital products:

a) Printables

Printables are one of the best-selling types of digital products on Etsy. These include items like:

- Planners (daily, weekly, or monthly)
- Calendars
- Wall art or inspirational quotes
- Habit trackers
- Budgeting templates
- Invitations for events (weddings, birthdays, etc.)

Buyers can download these files, print them at home, or send them to a professional printing service.

b) Digital Planners and Stickers

With the rise of tablet devices and apps like GoodNotes or Notability, digital planners and stickers have gained popularity. These are downloadable files that customers can use digitally rather than print out. This includes:

- Digital planners (for organizing schedules, tasks, or projects)

- Digital stickers (for decorating digital notebooks or planners)

- Digital journals and notebooks

c) Patterns and Templates

Etsy is home to a vast community of crafters and makers, so selling digital patterns is a natural fit. Popular products include:

- Sewing patterns

- Knitting or crochet patterns

- DIY project instructions

- Craft templates

These can be downloaded and followed at home, allowing buyers to create their own handmade goods.

d) Educational Resources

Digital educational products like eBooks, workbooks, and printable lesson plans are in high demand. If you have expertise in a specific field, you can monetize that knowledge by creating:

- eBooks on a niche topic

- Printable worksheets for students

- Lesson plans for teachers or homeschooling parents

- Guides and how-to manuals on various subjects

e) Digital Art and Graphics

Graphic designers and artists can sell digital art and design resources, including:

- Printable artwork

- Custom fonts or typography

- SVG (Scalable Vector Graphics) files for Cricut or Silhouette users

- Logos, branding elements, or website templates

These files allow buyers to create their own projects using your artwork.

3. Creating High-Quality Digital Products

Creating a successful digital product requires more than just designing something beautiful—you need to ensure that it meets the needs and expectations of your target audience. Here's how to create digital products that stand out:

a) Understand Your Target Audience

Before you begin designing, research your target audience. What are they looking for? What problems can you solve with your product? Browse popular shops in your niche and read customer reviews to understand what buyers are seeking.

b) Use Professional Design Tools

Investing in good design software is essential for creating high-quality digital products. Tools like **Adobe Illustrator**, **Canva**, or **Procreate** are popular choices for designing printables, patterns, and graphics. Canva, in particular, is user-friendly and offers plenty of templates for beginners.

If you're designing for digital planners or other

tablet-based products, ensure that your files are compatible with the apps and devices your customers are using. GoodNotes, for example, works best with PDF files that can be written on with a stylus.

c) Save Files in the Correct Formats

Ensure your files are saved in the appropriate format for their use. Common file types for digital products include:

- **PDFs**: Ideal for printables, eBooks, and templates.

- **JPEG/PNG**: Used for digital artwork, printables, or web graphics.

- **SVG**: Required for cutting machine files used in Cricut and Silhouette projects.

- **ZIP**: If your product contains multiple files, consider bundling them into a ZIP file to make it easier for customers to download everything at once.

4. Listing and Optimizing Your Digital Products on Etsy

To succeed in selling digital products on Etsy, you need to create compelling listings optimized for

Etsy's search algorithm. Here's how:

a) Writing SEO-Friendly Titles and Descriptions

SEO (Search Engine Optimization) is key to making sure your digital products are discoverable. Use keyword research tools like **EverBee** or **Marmalead** to find relevant, high-traffic keywords related to your product. Include these keywords in your product title, description, and tags.

For example, if you're selling printable wall art, your title could be something like: *"Printable Wall Art, Modern Minimalist Art, Instant Download, Boho Print, Digital Art for Home Decor, 8x10"*

In your description, clearly explain what the product is, what the customer will receive, how they can use it, and how to download it.

b) Product Images

Even though digital products aren't physical items, product images are still crucial. Buyers need to see what they are purchasing. Create mockups or lifestyle images to show your printables or digital artwork in real-world settings. Tools like Canva can help you create beautiful mockups with ease.

c) Provide Clear Instructions

Since customers may not be familiar with how to use digital files, especially if they need to print them, include clear instructions in the description or a downloadable guide. Explain how to download the files, print them, or use them in apps like GoodNotes or Procreate.

5. Managing Customer Expectations and Support

When selling digital products, managing customer expectations is key to avoiding misunderstandings and negative reviews.

a) Clear Download Instructions

Provide detailed instructions for how customers can download their files after purchase. Etsy automatically sends an email to the buyer with a link to download the files, but you can also include additional instructions in the listing description or the thank-you message.

b) Digital Product Policies

Since digital products are often non-refundable due to their nature, clearly state your refund policy upfront. Let customers know that once the file is downloaded, the sale is final. However, if they experience any technical difficulties, offer to assist them.

c) Handling Customer Inquiries

Be prepared to answer questions about file types, compatibility, and printing. Offering great customer service, even for digital products, can lead to positive reviews and repeat business.

6. Promoting Your Digital Products

Just like physical products, digital products need marketing to succeed. Here's how to promote them effectively:

a) Pinterest Marketing

Pinterest is an ideal platform for promoting digital products like printables, planners, and digital art. Create eye-catching pins that link directly to your Etsy listings. Since Pinterest functions as a visual search engine, it can drive a lot of traffic to your shop.

b) Instagram and TikTok

Use Instagram and TikTok to showcase how your digital products can be used. Share behind-the-scenes content of you creating the designs, or show tutorials on how to use the products (e.g., how to use digital planners in GoodNotes). These platforms are great for engaging with your audience and building brand awareness.

c) Collaborate with Influencers

Partner with influencers who align with your brand and target market. You could offer free digital products in exchange for a review or feature on their social media channels, helping you reach a wider audience.

7. Legal Considerations for Selling Digital Products

Digital products come with their own set of legal considerations. It's important to understand copyright laws and licensing agreements to avoid legal issues down the road.

a) Copyright Protection

When you create original digital products, they are automatically protected by copyright law. However, it's a good idea to include a disclaimer in your product descriptions stating that the files are for personal use only and cannot be resold or redistributed.

b) Licensing and Usage

If you're using third-party elements, such as fonts, stock photos, or design elements, make sure you have the proper commercial licenses. Many design resources available online require a commercial license for selling products made with them.

c) Trademark Considerations

Avoid using trademarked names or phrases (like brand names or popular slogans) in your digital products unless you have explicit permission. Violating trademark laws can lead to legal action or the removal of your listings.

4 Creating Your Etsy Shop and Listing Products

Once you've defined your niche and crafted a cohesive product line, it's time to bring your Etsy shop to life. This stage is crucial because your shop's layout, presentation, and product listings will determine whether visitors stay, browse, and ultimately make a purchase. A well-optimized shop with thoughtfully designed product listings can significantly increase your chances of success on Etsy.

In this chapter, we'll walk you through the process of creating your Etsy shop, from setting up its appearance and branding to listing your first products in a way that attracts buyers and optimizes visibility in Etsy's search engine.

1. Setting Up Your Etsy Shop

Setting up your Etsy shop is more than just filling in information—it's about creating a visually appealing and user-friendly experience that conveys your brand identity and gives customers confidence to buy. Every detail, from your shop banner to the policies you establish, contributes to how potential customers perceive your shop.

Creating a Memorable Shop Appearance

When a potential buyer visits your shop, the first thing they see is your shop's layout, banner, and branding. It's important to create a professional yet inviting environment that draws people in.

Key Elements of Your Etsy Shop's Appearance:

- **Shop Banner**: Your banner is the large image at the top of your shop page, and it's one of the first things customers see. Use a high-quality banner image that reflects your brand. This could be a collage of your products, a lifestyle shot showing your items in use, or a simple, well-designed graphic with your shop name.

- **Shop Logo**: Your logo should represent your brand's identity. Even if your shop name is your personal name, having a logo helps make your shop appear more professional. Etsy recommends uploading a 500 x 500 pixel image for your shop icon.

- **Shop Title**: The shop title appears directly under your shop name and serves as a brief description of your business. Etsy allows up to 140 characters, so use this space to describe what your shop offers while incorporating relevant keywords to help improve your search ranking. For example: "Handcrafted Jewelry | Eco-Friendly | Personalized Gifts."

- **Shop Announcement**: The shop announcement section is a short message displayed at the top of your shop. Use it to communicate important updates, such as promotions, shipping delays, or new products. Keep it concise but informative.

Shop Sections for Better Navigation

Etsy allows you to create different sections within your shop to organize your products. This feature not only makes it easier for customers to navigate but also improves your shop's SEO by adding another layer of keyword optimization.

Creating Shop Sections:

- **Organize by Product Type**: If you sell different types of products (e.g., earrings, necklaces, rings), create separate sections for each category.

- **Organize by Theme**: Alternatively, you can organize by themes or collections, such as "Holiday Gifts," "Best Sellers," or "Eco-Friendly Products."

Each section can include up to 20 characters in its title, so choose names that are both descriptive and search-friendly.

2. Writing a Compelling "About" Section

The "About" section of your Etsy shop is a chance to tell your story and connect with potential buyers. This section isn't just a formality—it's a powerful tool for building trust with your audience and differentiating your brand.

What to Include in Your "About" Section:

- **Your Story**: Share the story behind your shop. Why did you start your business? What inspires your products? Customers love knowing the passion and creativity that goes into handmade and unique items. A personal touch helps build a connection.

- **Your Creative Process**: Describe how your products are made. Do you use eco-friendly materials? Are your items crafted by hand or sourced from vintage collections? Giving insights into your process adds authenticity and value.

- **Behind-the-Scenes Photos or Videos**: Etsy allows you to upload images or videos in your "About" section. Show your workspace, materials, or you creating the products to build transparency and engagement.

- **Your Mission or Values**: Highlight any ethical or environmental practices that set your brand apart. Etsy shoppers often value sustainability and ethical sourcing, so if these align with your brand, make sure to showcase them.

3. Establishing Shop Policies

Clear and transparent shop policies are critical for building trust with customers. They set expectations and provide clarity about shipping, returns, and other important details. Well-defined policies can also help protect you from disputes or misunderstandings.

Key Policies to Include:

- **Shipping Policies**: Be upfront about shipping methods, estimated delivery times, and any restrictions (e.g., international shipping). If you offer free shipping, mention it here and highlight whether you use tracking. It's also a good idea to include information on how you handle lost or delayed shipments.

- **Returns and Exchanges**: Clearly outline your return and exchange policies. Will you accept returns? Who covers return shipping costs? Be transparent about any exceptions or conditions, such as only accepting returns on certain types of products.

- **Payment Methods**: Etsy handles most payment processing, but it's helpful to let customers know what payment methods are available, such as credit cards, PayPal, and Etsy Gift Cards.

By establishing clear policies, you not only protect yourself from potential disputes but also create an environment where customers feel confident purchasing from your shop.

4. Crafting Your Product Listings

Your product listings are the core of your Etsy shop. A great listing has several key components: a compelling title, high-quality images, a detailed description, and proper tags and attributes. Together, these elements help you sell your product and optimize its visibility in Etsy's search results.

Optimizing Your Product Titles

Your product title is one of the most critical factors for Etsy SEO. It's essential to strike a balance between writing a title that's keyword-rich but also reads naturally for customers.

Tips for Writing Effective Product Titles:

- **Use Keywords Strategically**: Place the most important keywords at the beginning of your title. This could include the product type, material, or style. For example, if you're selling a handmade leather journal, a strong title might be: "Handmade Leather Journal – Personalized Notebook with Rustic Cover."

- **Be Descriptive, Not Overstuffed**: While keywords are important, avoid keyword stuffing. Keep your titles clear, concise, and easy to read. Instead of cramming in as many words as possible, focus on the primary features and selling points of your product.

High-Quality Product Images and Videos

Product images are one of the most important factors that influence whether a buyer will make a purchase. Etsy allows multiple photos and videos for each listing, giving you the opportunity to showcase your product from different angles and in various settings.

Best Practices for Product Photos:

- **Use Natural Light**: Natural light often provides the best results for product photography, giving your images a clean, true-to-life look. Avoid harsh lighting that can distort colors or create unappealing shadows.

- **Show Multiple Angles**: Include several images showing different angles, close-ups, and details of your product. If relevant, show your product in use to help customers visualize how it fits into their lives.

- **Maintain Consistency**: Use a consistent background and style across all your product photos to create a cohesive and professional appearance for your shop.

Product Videos:

- Etsy allows you to add short videos (5–15 seconds) to your product listings. Use videos to show your product in motion or provide a 360-degree view. Videos are a powerful way to engage customers and can increase your chances of making a sale.

Writing Detailed Product Descriptions

Your product description is your opportunity to provide in-depth information about your item. Be detailed, but also make sure the description is easy to read and organized.

Elements of a Great Product Description:

- **Describe the Key Features**: Include details such as materials, dimensions, weight, colors, and variations. If your product is customizable, mention the customization options available.

- **Highlight Benefits**: Don't just list features—explain how your product benefits the customer. Why should they choose your item over similar ones? For example, if your product is made from eco-friendly materials, explain how it contributes to sustainable living.

- **Use Bullet Points for Clarity**: Break down important details with bullet points to make the description easy to scan. Buyers often skim product descriptions, so make the key points stand out.

Using Tags, Categories, and Attributes for SEO

Tags, categories, and attributes play a vital role in Etsy SEO, helping your listings appear in relevant search results. Properly optimizing these fields ensures your products get the visibility they deserve.

How to Use Tags Effectively:

- **Include Relevant Keywords**: Etsy allows up to 13 tags per listing, so use all of them to include keywords that describe your product. Use a mix of broad terms (e.g., "handmade jewelry") and specific terms (e.g., "rose gold earrings").

- **Think Like a Buyer**: Consider the phrases a buyer would use when searching for your product. Use both singular and plural versions of keywords where appropriate.

Choosing Categories and Attributes:

- **Select the Right Category**: Choosing the right category helps Etsy organize your listings and show them to the right audience. Be specific when selecting categories.

- **Attributes**: Etsy provides additional attributes such as color, size, and material. Using these attributes helps Etsy match your products with buyers searching for those specific features.

5. Pricing Your Products

Pricing your products can be tricky, especially in a competitive marketplace like Etsy. You need to balance covering your costs, turning a profit, and offering a competitive price that attracts buyers.

Factors to Consider When Pricing:

- **Cost of Materials**: Calculate the cost of all materials involved in making your product, including packaging and shipping supplies.

- **Time and Labor**: Don't forget to factor in the time it takes to create, package, and ship each item. Your labor should be included in the price to ensure you're compensated for your work.

- **Etsy Fees**: Etsy charges listing fees, transaction fees, and payment processing fees, all of which impact your bottom line. Make sure to price your items to account for these costs.

- **Competitive Pricing**: Research similar items on Etsy to gauge how much other sellers are charging. While you don't have to undercut your competition, it's essential to ensure your prices are within a reasonable range for your market.

5 Crafting Your Shop Policies

One of the most important aspects of running a successful Etsy shop is establishing clear, well-defined shop policies. Having transparent policies helps build trust with your customers, ensures that expectations are set upfront, and reduces the risk of misunderstandings or disputes down the road. Etsy buyers tend to value transparency, and knowing exactly what to expect regarding shipping, returns, payments, and exchanges is crucial for providing a positive shopping experience.

In this chapter, we'll walk you through the process of crafting your Etsy shop policies, explaining why each section is vital and offering practical guidance on how to structure them effectively. From shipping to returns, your policies not only protect you as a seller but also help you foster trust and credibility with your customers.

1. Why Clear Shop Policies Matter

Clear shop policies are essential because they serve as a contract between you and your customers. Well-written policies clarify how your business operates and what buyers can expect after they place an order. Additionally, these policies are your first line of defense if any issues arise, such as disputes over shipping, refunds, or product quality.

Benefits of Having Well-Defined Policies:

- **Builds Trust**: Customers are more likely to shop from stores with clear, transparent policies. Knowing the shop's guidelines creates confidence in the purchase.

- **Reduces Misunderstandings**: If customers know your policies upfront, they'll be less likely to raise complaints or disputes about issues like shipping times or returns.

- **Helps with Conflict Resolution**: Should a conflict arise, having a documented policy in place gives you a fair way to handle the situation, ensuring both you and the buyer are on the same page.

- **Improves Customer Experience**: Transparent communication leads to fewer surprises and a smoother buying experience, which can lead to repeat purchases and positive reviews.

2. Essential Shop Policies to Include

When crafting your shop policies, there are a few essential sections that every Etsy shop should include. These cover the key areas of shipping, payments, returns, exchanges, and more. Each policy needs to be clear, concise, and easy to understand. Let's break down each section and explore how to create policies that work for both you and your customers.

a) Shipping Policy

Shipping is often the first area where buyers have questions. They want to know how long it will take for their order to arrive, what shipping methods you use, and whether international shipping is available. Your shipping policy should address all these aspects.

What to Include in Your Shipping Policy:

- **Processing Time**: Clearly state how long it takes to process an order before it's shipped. This is different from shipping time, as processing involves the time needed to prepare and package the product. Example: "Orders are processed within 3-5 business days."

- **Estimated Delivery Time**: Outline the expected delivery times for domestic and international orders. Keep in mind that shipping times may vary depending on the location of the buyer and the shipping method chosen. You may also want to provide a general range, such as "5-7 business days for domestic orders" and "10-21 business days for international orders."

- **Shipping Carriers and Methods**: Specify which shipping carriers you use (e.g., USPS, FedEx, DHL) and whether you offer standard, expedited, or tracked shipping options.

- **International Shipping**: If you ship internationally, be sure to mention any specific countries or regions you do not ship to, as well as the possibility of customs fees or import taxes, which are typically the responsibility of the buyer.

- **Shipping Costs**: Explain whether you charge a flat rate for shipping, use variable rates based on location, or offer free shipping. If you provide free shipping, indicate the conditions under which it applies (e.g., "Free shipping on orders over $50").

Example of a Shipping Policy:

All orders are processed within 3-5 business days. We offer free standard shipping on all domestic orders over $50. For international orders, shipping times vary between 10-21 business days, depending on the destination. Buyers are responsible for any customs fees or import taxes. All orders will be shipped via USPS or DHL, and tracking information will be provided once the order has shipped.

b) Return and Exchange Policy

Returns and exchanges are a crucial part of eCommerce, especially when selling products like clothing, jewelry, or home decor. A return policy sets expectations for customers in the event they are unsatisfied with their purchase or need to exchange an item. It's important to be clear and consistent with your terms to avoid misunderstandings.

What to Include in Your Return and Exchange Policy:

- **Eligibility for Returns**: Specify which products are eligible for returns and which are not. For example, many sellers do not accept returns on custom or personalized items, digital downloads, or sale items.

- **Time Frame for Returns**: State how long customers have to request a return after receiving their order. Common time frames are 14, 30, or 60 days. Example: "Returns must be requested within 14 days of delivery."

- **Condition of Returned Items**: Be specific about the condition items must be in to qualify for a return. Example: "Items must be returned in their original condition and packaging."

- **Who Pays for Return Shipping**: Clarify whether the buyer or the seller is responsible for return shipping costs. In many cases, buyers cover return shipping unless the item arrived damaged or was incorrect.

- **Process for Exchanges**: If you offer exchanges, explain how customers can request one, whether they need to send back the original item first, and how long the exchange process takes.

Example of a Return and Exchange Policy:

We accept returns on non-custom items within 14 days of delivery. Items must be returned in their original, unused condition. Buyers are responsible for return shipping costs. Unfortunately, we do not accept returns on personalized or digital items. If you would like to request an exchange, please contact us within 14 days, and we will guide you through the process.

c) Payment Policy

Etsy handles payment processing through Etsy Payments, making it easy for sellers to accept a variety of payment methods. However, it's still important to outline your payment policy, especially if you offer any custom payment arrangements or accept payments outside of Etsy's usual methods.

What to Include in Your Payment Policy:

- **Accepted Payment Methods**: List the types of payment you accept (e.g., credit cards, PayPal, Etsy gift cards). Since Etsy Payments handles the majority of transactions, most payment methods will be automatically supported, but it's helpful to clarify for your buyers.

- **Deposits or Payment Plans**: If you sell high-priced or custom items, you might offer deposits or payment plans. Outline the terms for these payment arrangements, including any conditions for cancellations or refunds of deposits.

- **Taxes and Fees**: Indicate whether your prices include applicable taxes, or if taxes will be calculated at checkout. Mention any specific regional taxes or import duties that may apply to international buyers.

Example of a Payment Policy:

We accept all major credit cards, PayPal, and Etsy gift cards through Etsy Payments. Please note that buyers are responsible for any customs duties or taxes for international orders. If you're interested in a payment plan for custom orders, please contact us to discuss terms.

d) Custom Order Policy

If your shop offers custom or made-to-order items, a custom order policy is essential. Custom orders often involve unique requirements, longer processing times, and different return policies compared to regular items. Be clear about how you handle these types of orders.

What to Include in Your Custom Order Policy:

- **Processing Times for Custom Orders**: Let customers know how long it will take to complete a custom order from the time the order is placed. Example: "Custom orders are made to order and typically take 2-3 weeks to complete."

- **Customization Options**: Specify what customization options are available, such as personalized text, color choices, or material options. Make it clear whether any limits or restrictions apply.

- **Approval Process**: Explain how customers can submit customization details and whether you'll provide a proof or design approval before creating the product.

- **Return and Refund Policy for Custom Orders**: Most sellers do not accept returns on custom items, but if you do, clarify the conditions. If custom items cannot be returned, make sure this is stated clearly to avoid confusion.

Example of a Custom Order Policy:

Custom orders typically take 2-3 weeks to complete, depending on the complexity of the request. We offer a range of customization options, including personalized engraving and color choices. Once we receive your order, we will send you a proof for approval. Please note that custom items are non-refundable unless they arrive damaged or defective.

3. FAQs (Frequently Asked Questions)

Including an FAQ section in your shop policies helps answer common questions and reduces the number of customer inquiries you receive. FAQs can cover anything from product care instructions to shipping times or customization options.

Example FAQs:

- *Q: How long will it take for my order to arrive?*
  - *A: Our processing time is 3-5 business days, and delivery typically takes 5-7 business days for domestic orders. International orders may take*

up to 21 business days.

- *Q: Can I request a custom order?*

  - *A: Yes! We offer customization on select items. Please see our Custom Order Policy for details.*

- *Q: Do you ship internationally?*

  - *A: Yes, we ship worldwide. Please be aware that international shipping times may vary, and buyers are responsible for any customs fees.*

4. Keeping Your Policies Updated

As your Etsy shop evolves, you may need to update your policies to reflect changes in your offerings, shipping carriers, or other aspects of your business. Etsy makes it easy to update your policies at any time, but be sure to notify your customers of significant changes, especially if they impact existing orders.

Tips for Updating Policies:

- **Notify Customers**: If you make major updates to your policies (e.g., changes to return policies or shipping times), consider posting an announcement in your shop or sending a message to affected customers.

- **Regular Reviews**: Periodically review your shop policies to ensure they align with your current business practices and industry standards.

6 Maximizing Sales with Etsy Ads

Etsy Ads are a powerful tool for increasing the visibility of your products and driving more traffic to your shop. While Etsy's organic traffic and SEO optimization can get your products in front of buyers, Etsy Ads give you an additional boost by placing your listings prominently in search results, category pages, and other high-visibility spots across the platform.

Running Etsy Ads requires a balance between strategy and budget management. When done correctly, ads can significantly increase your sales and help you grow your business, but to see the best results, it's crucial to understand how and when to use them effectively. This chapter will guide you through how Etsy Ads work, how to set up and manage successful ad campaigns, and how to make data-driven decisions that maximize your return on investment (ROI).

We'll also address a common question for new sellers: *Should you start running Etsy Ads before or after turning a profit?* Let's dive into how Etsy Ads can elevate your shop and when to begin using them.

1. How Etsy Ads Work

Etsy Ads are a pay-per-click (PPC) advertising system, meaning you only pay when someone clicks on your ad. Your product ads appear in key locations on Etsy, such as search results, related listings, and category pages. Etsy uses your daily budget to automatically promote your products, and the cost of a click can vary depending on competition for specific keywords.

Key Features of Etsy Ads:

- **Pay-per-click (PPC)**: You're charged only when someone clicks on your ad, not when the ad is displayed.

- **Automatic Placement**: Etsy automatically decides where your ads are displayed based on buyer behavior, keyword relevancy, and competition.

- **Budget Control**: You set a daily budget, and Etsy optimizes your ad placement accordingly, ensuring you don't exceed your spending limit.

- **Keyword Optimization**: Etsy uses the keywords in your listings to determine when and where to show your ads, making SEO optimization crucial even for paid ads.

Ads work best when they're part of a larger strategy that includes SEO optimization, strong product photography, and a compelling product description. You can't rely solely on ads to drive sales—your products need to be attractive and well-presented to convert clicks into purchases.

2. When Should You Start Running Etsy Ads?

One of the most frequently asked questions among new sellers is whether they should start running Etsy Ads immediately or wait until they've turned a profit. While there's no one-size-fits-all answer, there are several factors to consider when deciding the best time to invest in Etsy Ads.

Running Etsy Ads Before Turning a Profit:

Starting Etsy Ads before turning a profit can be beneficial if:

- **You Need to Increase Visibility**: If you're a new shop without much organic traffic, ads can help you get your listings in front of potential buyers more quickly. Etsy Ads can act as a fast-track to visibility, especially if your products are in a competitive niche where it's hard to gain traction with SEO alone.

- **You Want to Test Product Demand**: Running ads early can help you test the demand for your products. If your ads are generating clicks but not converting into sales, it may indicate that you need to adjust your product descriptions, pricing, or photos.

- **You're Building Brand Awareness**: Ads can help new shops build awareness and trust. Even if buyers don't purchase right away, repeated exposure to your products can lead to future sales. It's common for buyers to browse multiple times before making a decision, so getting your shop in front of them early can be advantageous.

Caution: If you run Etsy Ads before turning a profit, it's essential to have a clear budget and monitor your ad performance closely. You don't want to overspend before fully understanding your shop's profitability. Ads can boost visibility, but they won't guarantee sales, so make sure you can afford the investment without hurting your business's finances.

Running Etsy Ads After Turning a Profit:

Waiting to run Etsy Ads until after you've turned a profit can be a more cautious, data-driven approach. By focusing on organic traffic first and proving that your shop can generate sales without ads, you reduce the risk of spending money on advertising without knowing if your products will convert.

Starting ads after you've turned a profit makes sense if:

- **You Want to Maximize Your ROI**: Once your shop is profitable, you can use Etsy Ads to amplify what's already working. Running ads on listings that already perform well can lead to even greater sales, giving you a clearer idea of the return on your advertising investment.

- **You Have a Better Understanding of Your Shop's Data**: By waiting until you've made sales, you'll have more data on which products sell best, what price points work, and what your customers are looking for. This allows you to create more targeted ad campaigns and spend your budget on the most promising products.

- **You Want to Scale Confidently**: If you've already turned a profit, running ads becomes part of your scaling strategy. Ads can help you reach a wider audience, but now you're doing it from a position of strength, knowing that your products and pricing are already proven.

Caution: If you wait too long to start Etsy Ads, you may miss out on early growth opportunities. The key is to balance your organic growth with paid ads to maximize your shop's potential.

Final Recommendation:

You can run Etsy Ads both before and after turning a profit, but it's crucial to understand your goals. If you're running ads before turning a profit, focus on visibility and testing your market, but keep a close eye on your budget. If you wait until you've turned a profit, you're in a better position to use ads strategically for scaling. In either case, start small, monitor your results, and adjust your ad strategy as you learn more about what works for your shop.

3. Setting Up Your First Etsy Ads Campaign

Setting up an Etsy Ads campaign is straightforward, but the key to success is choosing the right budget, selecting the products you want to promote, and monitoring performance. Let's walk through the process of creating your first campaign.

Step-by-Step Guide to Setting Up Etsy Ads:

1. **Navigate to Etsy Ads**: In your Etsy shop dashboard, click on "Marketing" and then select "Etsy Ads." Here, you'll be able to set

up your campaign and manage existing ones.

2. **Set a Daily Budget**: Etsy allows you to set a daily budget for your ads. Start with a small amount—around $1 to $5 per day—to test your ads before scaling up. Etsy will automatically distribute your budget across your selected listings to maximize visibility.

3. **Choose Which Listings to Promote**: Etsy gives you the option to promote all your listings or select specific ones. It's often best to start by promoting a few of your best-selling or most popular listings. This gives you a better chance of generating sales from ads.

4. **Use Automatic Bidding**: Etsy Ads operate on a bidding system where you compete with other sellers for ad space. Etsy automatically manages bids based on your daily budget to ensure you get the best placement for your ads. For most sellers, automatic bidding is effective and simplifies the process.

5. **Launch Your Ads**: Once you've selected your budget and listings, you're ready to launch your ads. Etsy will display your promoted listings to relevant shoppers

based on their search queries, interests, and buying behavior.

4. Analyzing and Optimizing Your Etsy Ads

Launching your ads is just the first step. To get the most out of your ad campaigns, you'll need to regularly analyze their performance and make adjustments as necessary. Etsy provides a detailed dashboard where you can track key metrics like clicks, impressions, conversion rates, and ad spend.

Key Metrics to Monitor:

- **Impressions**: This shows how many times your ad was displayed to potential buyers. High impressions mean your ads are getting seen, but low clicks could indicate that your product titles or images need improvement.

- **Clicks**: The number of times shoppers clicked on your ad. A healthy click-through rate (CTR) shows that your ad is attracting attention. If your CTR is low, you may need to improve your product photos, titles, or pricing.

- **Sales from Ads**: This metric tracks how many sales were made directly from clicks on your ads. This is the most important metric for determining the success of your campaign.

- **Cost-per-Click (CPC)**: The amount you're paying for each click. The lower your CPC, the more cost-effective your ad campaign is.

- **Return on Investment (ROI)**: To calculate your ROI, divide the revenue generated from ads by the amount spent on those ads. A positive ROI means your ads are generating more sales than they cost.

5. Best Practices for Etsy Ads Success

To maximize the success of your Etsy Ads, it's important to follow a few best practices:

Start Small and Scale

Begin with a modest daily budget and a few key products. Monitor your results for at least a week or two before increasing your budget or adding more listings. This allows you to test the waters without overspending.

Promote High-Converting Listings

Focus on promoting products that are already performing well organically. These listings are more likely to convert from ad traffic, maximizing your ROI. Avoid spending money on products with low conversion rates until you've optimized them.

Use Strong Photos and Titles

Since Etsy Ads rely heavily on your existing product titles, photos, and descriptions, make sure they are optimized for both SEO and conversions. Your ads need to stand out in search results, so invest time in improving your listing presentation.

Optimize Based on Data

Regularly review your ad performance metrics and make adjustments. If certain listings aren't performing well, remove them from your ad campaign and focus on the ones with higher conversions. Adjust your daily budget based on what's working.

Seasonal Campaigns

Take advantage of holidays and peak shopping periods (like Black Friday or Christmas) by increasing your ad budget during these times. More shoppers are browsing Etsy during peak seasons, giving you a better chance to capitalize on increased traffic.

7 Marketing Your Etsy Shop Beyond Etsy

While Etsy provides a fantastic platform for reaching millions of potential customers, relying solely on Etsy's marketplace traffic may limit the growth of your shop. To build a sustainable and thriving Etsy business, it's essential to take charge of your marketing efforts and drive traffic from outside the platform. Diversifying your marketing strategy allows you to reach new audiences, establish a broader brand presence, and foster a loyal customer base beyond the Etsy ecosystem.

In this chapter, we'll explore how to effectively market your Etsy shop on external platforms, including social media, email marketing, and partnerships. By expanding your marketing efforts beyond Etsy, you can increase visibility, boost sales, and create a community of dedicated customers.

1. Why Marketing Beyond Etsy Matters

Etsy is a competitive marketplace, and while it offers valuable tools like Etsy Ads and SEO optimization, depending solely on its internal traffic can limit your shop's potential. External marketing allows you to:

- **Expand Your Reach**: Reach new audiences who may not actively search on Etsy but would be interested in your products.

- **Build Brand Loyalty**: By marketing through your own channels (such as social media or email), you can create stronger connections with your customers, build a recognizable brand, and increase the likelihood of repeat sales.

- **Diversify Your Traffic Sources**: Relying only on one platform leaves your business vulnerable to algorithm changes or shifts in marketplace dynamics. By bringing in traffic from multiple channels, you ensure a more stable and consistent flow of customers.

Now, let's explore some of the most effective ways to market your Etsy shop outside of Etsy itself.

2. Using Social Media to Drive Traffic

Social media platforms are one of the most powerful tools available for Etsy sellers to market their products. By building a presence on platforms like Instagram, TikTok, and Pinterest, you can connect with potential buyers, showcase your products, and build a community around your brand. Each platform offers unique opportunities to engage with your target audience and direct traffic back to your Etsy shop.

a) Instagram: Visual Storytelling and Shopping Integration

Instagram is a visual-first platform, making it perfect for promoting handmade, vintage, and artistic products. With Instagram's built-in shopping features, you can now create a seamless path for customers to discover your products and make purchases.

How to Market Your Etsy Shop on Instagram:

- **Set Up an Instagram Shop**: Connect your Etsy shop to Instagram by setting up an Instagram Shop. This allows you to tag products in posts and stories, making it easy for followers to browse and purchase directly from your Instagram profile.

- **Post Consistently**: Consistency is key to building an engaged audience. Post high-quality photos and videos of your products, behind-the-scenes content, and customer testimonials. Use Instagram's "Stories" and "Reels" features to increase engagement and showcase your products in action.

- **Leverage Hashtags**: Use relevant hashtags to make your posts discoverable to new audiences. Mix broad hashtags (#handmade, #vintage, #etsyshop) with more niche-specific tags (#bohojewelry, #sustainablefashion) to target your ideal customers.

- **Engage with Your Audience**: Respond to comments, answer direct messages, and engage with your followers. Building relationships on Instagram can help create a loyal customer base that regularly returns to your shop.

b) TikTok: Short-Form Video Marketing for Etsy Sellers

TikTok has become one of the most popular social media platforms for short-form video content, and it presents a unique opportunity for Etsy sellers to reach a massive, engaged audience. TikTok users love discovering new products through creative, entertaining videos, making it an ideal platform for showcasing your products in action.

How to Market Your Etsy Shop on TikTok:

- **Create Engaging Videos**: TikTok's algorithm prioritizes engaging content, so focus on creating videos that are fun, creative, and visually appealing. Show off how your products are made, feature customer unboxings, or demonstrate how your products can be used in everyday life.

- **Jump on Trends**: TikTok is driven by trends. Stay up-to-date with viral challenges, popular music, and trending hashtags, and find ways to incorporate them into your content. Using trending sounds and participating in challenges can increase the visibility of your videos.

- **Leverage TikTok Ads**: TikTok Ads allow you to target specific audiences based on their interests, behaviors, and demographics. Running targeted ads on TikTok can help increase your visibility and drive traffic to your Etsy shop.

- **Collaborate with Influencers**: Influencers on TikTok can help amplify your brand's reach. Partner with micro-influencers who align with your niche to create sponsored content that showcases your products.

c) Pinterest: A Visual Search Engine for Etsy Sellers

Pinterest acts more like a visual search engine than a traditional social media platform. Users on Pinterest are often looking for inspiration and ideas, making it an excellent platform for showcasing your products in a visually appealing way and driving traffic to your Etsy shop.

How to Market Your Etsy Shop on Pinterest:

- **Create "Buyable" Pins**: Pinterest now offers "Buyable Pins," which allow users to purchase products directly from Pinterest. Ensure your product images are linked to your Etsy listings, so interested buyers can easily shop.

- **Pin Consistently**: Like Instagram, Pinterest rewards consistent activity. Regularly pin images of your products, blog content (if applicable), and related lifestyle images to increase your visibility on the platform.

- **Optimize Pins with Keywords**: Pinterest uses keywords to organize content, so optimize your pin descriptions with relevant keywords. Think about what your target audience might search for and use those terms in your pin titles and descriptions.

- **Create Product Boards**: Organize your products into themed boards (e.g., "Gifts for Her," "Eco-Friendly Home Decor") to make it easy for users to discover and save your products.

3. Building an Email Marketing List

Email marketing remains one of the most powerful ways to communicate directly with your customers and drive repeat purchases. Unlike social media, where content can be missed or ignored, emails land directly in your customers' inboxes, giving you a direct line of communication.

Why Email Marketing is Important for Etsy Sellers:

- **Builds Customer Loyalty**: Email allows you to build ongoing relationships with your customers, keeping them informed about new products, sales, and promotions.

- **Drives Repeat Purchases**: With email campaigns, you can encourage past customers to return to your Etsy shop with exclusive offers or product updates.

- **Increases Control Over Your Marketing**: Email marketing gives you control over how and when you communicate with your audience, unlike social media algorithms which can limit your reach.

Steps to Build and Grow an Email List:

1. **Collect Emails from Buyers**: Etsy automatically collects customer emails for order confirmation and updates, but you can encourage customers to sign up for

your newsletter or promotional emails with incentives like exclusive discounts or early access to new products.

2. **Create a Lead Magnet**: A lead magnet is an incentive offered to potential customers in exchange for their email address. It could be a special discount, free shipping, or a downloadable guide related to your product niche (e.g., "How to Style Your New Earrings").

3. **Send Regular Updates**: Send emails consistently, whether it's monthly updates, seasonal promotions, or holiday discounts. Make sure your emails provide value by offering useful content, exclusive offers, or personalized product recommendations.

4. **Use Email Marketing Tools**: Tools like Mailchimp, Klaviyo, and ConvertKit allow you to create professional email campaigns, segment your audience based on their shopping behavior, and track the performance of your emails.

4. Partnering with Influencers and Collaborators

Collaborating with influencers or other small businesses can help expand your reach and introduce your Etsy shop to new audiences. By working with influencers, you can leverage their existing following and tap into communities of potential buyers who trust their recommendations.

How to Partner with Influencers:

- **Find Influencers in Your Niche**: Look for influencers who align with your brand's values and products. Micro-influencers (those with smaller, but highly engaged audiences) can be especially effective for Etsy sellers.

- **Offer Free Products for Reviews**: Many influencers are willing to showcase products in exchange for free samples. Choose influencers who have a loyal following and are known for authentic reviews to ensure your products are being showcased genuinely.

- **Collaborate on Giveaways**: Partner with influencers for product giveaways. This not only boosts your visibility but also encourages user engagement and can help grow your social media following.

5. Leveraging Etsy's Integration with External Platforms

Etsy has been expanding its integration capabilities, allowing sellers to connect their shops with external platforms and tools more easily. This enables you to automate parts of your marketing, simplify the customer shopping experience, and increase your visibility outside of Etsy.

How Etsy Integrates with External Platforms:

- **Social Media Integrations**: Etsy allows sellers to link their shops directly to Instagram and Pinterest, making it easier for followers to browse and shop your products without leaving the social media platforms. Set up your Instagram Shopping or Pinterest Buyable Pins to streamline the shopping experience.

- **Marketing Tools**: Etsy integrates with marketing tools like Mailchimp for email marketing and Google Analytics to track website traffic and user behavior. Use these tools to gather insights into your audience and refine your marketing strategies.

- **Shipping Tools**: Etsy integrates with third-party shipping platforms like ShipStation and Pirate Ship, making it easier to manage orders and shipping logistics, especially if you're promoting products on multiple platforms.

6. Paid Advertising Beyond Etsy Ads

While Etsy Ads are an effective way to promote your products within the Etsy platform, paid advertising outside Etsy can drive traffic from other sources and expand your audience even further. Platforms like Facebook, Instagram, and Google Ads offer advanced targeting options that allow you to reach specific audiences based on their interests, behaviors, and demographics.

How to Use External Paid Advertising:

- **Facebook and Instagram Ads**: Facebook Ads Manager allows you to create highly targeted campaigns based on user data. You can promote your Etsy listings to users who have shown interest in similar products or behaviors. Retargeting ads can also be used to reach people who visited your Etsy shop but didn't make a purchase.

- **Google Shopping Ads**: Google Shopping Ads display your products when users search for related items on Google. Listing your products on Google Shopping can significantly increase your visibility to buyers who are actively searching for items like yours.

- **Budgeting for External Ads**: Start small with a modest daily budget and track your ad performance to see which platforms and ad types work best for your Etsy shop. Use data from your campaigns to adjust your strategy over time.

8 Managing Orders and Shipping

Efficient order management and reliable shipping are crucial to running a successful Etsy shop. Your ability to process orders promptly and ensure items reach customers in good condition can make or break your shop's reputation. Buyers expect transparency, clear communication, and timely delivery, and meeting (or exceeding) these expectations helps build trust and encourages repeat purchases.

In this chapter, we'll walk you through the best practices for managing orders, handling shipping logistics, and dealing with potential issues like delays or lost packages. Additionally, we'll cover how to streamline your workflow by utilizing Etsy's latest order management tools and integrating with third-party shipping platforms to ensure smooth, efficient operations.

1. Managing Your Etsy Orders

Once a customer places an order, the clock starts ticking. Etsy tracks order status, and buyers expect regular updates as their purchase moves from "Processing" to "Shipped." Managing your orders efficiently means staying on top of the entire process from when the order is received to when the item is delivered to the buyer's door.

Order Management Tools on Etsy

Etsy offers several built-in tools that help you manage your orders with ease. Let's explore how to use them to streamline your process and reduce the risk of missed or delayed orders.

a) Etsy's Order Dashboard

The Etsy Order Dashboard gives you a comprehensive view of all your active orders. You can see the order details, including the buyer's information, product purchased, and any customization requests, all in one place.

Key Features of the Order Dashboard:

- **Order Status Tracking**: View orders that are "New," "In Progress," and "Completed" to keep track of where each order is in the process.

- **Order Filters**: Use filters to sort orders by status, shipping destination, or processing date. This is particularly helpful if you have a large volume of orders.

- **Messaging Customers**: Directly message customers from the dashboard to clarify order details, update them on processing times, or respond to questions.

b) Bulk Order Processing

If you're handling a high volume of orders, Etsy offers a bulk processing feature that allows you to mark multiple orders as "shipped" or "complete" at once. This saves time and helps you keep track of progress during busy periods.

c) Custom Order Requests

For sellers offering custom or personalized products, managing custom orders requires extra attention. Etsy's Custom Order Request feature lets buyers provide customization details directly through the platform, making it easier to track and manage personalized requests.

Best Practices for Managing Custom Orders:

- **Communicate Clearly**: Confirm all customization details with the buyer before starting the order to avoid any misunderstandings.

- **Set Realistic Expectations**: Provide clear processing times for custom orders, and let buyers know if it will take longer than standard items.

2. Processing and Packaging Orders

Efficient order processing and professional packaging go a long way in creating a positive experience for your customers. Once an order is placed, your goal is to package it securely and get it shipped out as quickly as possible.

Order Processing Best Practices

- **Prioritize Processing Times**: Make sure to follow the processing times listed in your shop. If you consistently ship orders faster than expected, you'll earn positive reviews and build customer loyalty. For made-to-order or custom products, set a realistic timeline and update buyers on progress.

- **Double-Check Order Details**: Before shipping an order, verify that all items match what the buyer purchased. For custom orders, ensure that any personalization is accurate.

Professional Packaging

Your product's packaging is often the first physical interaction a buyer has with your shop, so making it look professional and secure is important. Well-designed packaging not only protects your items during shipping but also reflects your brand's quality and care.

Packaging Tips:

- **Use Proper Shipping Materials**: Ensure that fragile items are packaged with enough padding (such as bubble wrap, packing peanuts, or foam). For less fragile items, consider eco-friendly packaging materials like recyclable paper or cardboard.

- **Brand Your Packaging**: Consider including a branded touch in your packaging, such as custom stickers, thank-you notes, or branded tissue paper. This small effort enhances the unboxing experience and leaves a lasting impression on the customer.

- **Include a Personal Touch**: A handwritten thank-you note or a small freebie can go a long way in delighting your customers and encouraging them to leave a positive review or make a repeat purchase.

3. Shipping Your Orders

Shipping is a critical component of your Etsy business, and selecting the right shipping options and carriers can make a big difference in customer satisfaction. Etsy provides several tools and integrations to help streamline the shipping process and make it as cost-effective as possible.

a) Choosing the Right Shipping Options

Depending on your product type, size, and destination, shipping can vary significantly. Offering multiple shipping options allows customers to choose between standard, expedited, and sometimes even same-day shipping, depending on their needs.

Shipping Options to Consider:

- **Standard Shipping**: This is the most commonly used option and typically the least expensive. Ensure your customers know the estimated delivery times upfront.

- **Expedited Shipping**: Some customers may be willing to pay more for faster delivery. Offering priority or express shipping options can meet this demand, especially during holidays or special events.

- **International Shipping**: If you offer international shipping, make sure your listings are clear about delivery times and potential customs duties or fees. Use services that offer international tracking for better customer confidence.

b) Etsy Shipping Labels

Etsy provides a shipping label service that integrates with major carriers like USPS, FedEx, and DHL, allowing you to print shipping labels directly from your Etsy dashboard. Using Etsy's shipping labels offers several benefits:

- **Discounted Rates**: Etsy partners with carriers to offer discounted shipping rates to sellers, helping you save on shipping costs.

- **Automatic Tracking**: When you use Etsy's shipping labels, the tracking information is automatically uploaded to the buyer's order, keeping them informed about the status of their shipment.

- **Streamlined Process**: Printing labels from Etsy saves time by eliminating the need to manually enter shipping details on carrier websites. Everything is handled within Etsy's system.

How to Use Etsy Shipping Labels:

1. From your Order Dashboard, click on "Print Shipping Label" for the order you're processing.

2. Choose the correct package size and weight, and select your preferred shipping method.

3. Review the shipping cost, then print the label directly from Etsy.

After printing the label, all that's left is to package your order, attach the label, and drop it off at the nearest carrier location.

4. Using Third-Party Shipping Tools

While Etsy's shipping labels work well for many sellers, third-party shipping platforms can offer additional features, such as more advanced tracking, bulk shipping options, and even better discounts for certain carriers. Integrating these platforms with your Etsy shop can streamline your shipping operations even further.

Popular Third-Party Shipping Tools:

- **ShipStation**: ShipStation integrates with Etsy to provide multi-carrier shipping options, advanced tracking, and inventory management. You can sync orders from Etsy, print labels in bulk, and manage shipments across multiple sales channels.

- **Pirate Ship**: Known for offering excellent discounts on USPS shipping rates, Pirate Ship integrates with Etsy and allows you to batch print labels, track shipments, and calculate shipping rates in advance.

- **Shippo**: Shippo provides a wide range of carrier options, discounted rates, and tools for printing labels, tracking orders, and managing returns. Like ShipStation, Shippo works across multiple sales platforms, making it ideal if you're selling on other sites in addition to Etsy.

5. Handling Shipping Issues

Occasionally, things may go wrong during the shipping process—packages can get delayed, lost, or damaged in transit. While these issues are often out of your control, how you handle them can significantly impact customer satisfaction.

Dealing with Delayed or Lost Packages

- **Be Proactive with Communication**: If a buyer's order is delayed, reach out to them before they contact you. Let them know the status of their order and provide tracking details if possible. Buyers appreciate being kept in the loop.

- **Work with Your Carrier**: If a package is lost or significantly delayed, you can file a claim with your shipping carrier. Most major carriers offer insurance or reimbursement for lost packages, especially if you used tracking.

- **Offer a Solution**: If an item is lost and cannot be replaced, offer the buyer a refund or the option to select another product. This shows goodwill and helps maintain customer trust, even if the issue was caused by the shipping carrier.

Handling Damaged Items

If a product arrives damaged, it's important to resolve the issue quickly and professionally. Here's what to do:

- **Request Photos**: Ask the buyer to send photos of the damaged item and packaging. This helps you understand what went wrong and provides evidence if you need to file an insurance claim with the carrier.

- **Offer a Replacement or Refund**: Offer to send a replacement product (if available) or provide a full refund. The quicker you address the issue, the more likely you are to retain the customer's trust.

- **Improve Packaging**: If damaged items become a recurring problem, consider improving your packaging materials. Ensure fragile items are well-protected with extra padding or double-walled boxes.

6. Providing Excellent Post-Purchase Support

Once an order is shipped, your interaction with the customer shouldn't end. Offering great post-purchase support helps build customer loyalty and encourages repeat purchases.

Follow-Up Messages

After an order has been delivered, send a follow-up message thanking the customer for their purchase and encouraging them to reach out if they have any issues. Etsy allows you to automate these messages, making it easy to stay in touch without extra effort.

Encouraging Reviews

Positive reviews are essential for building trust on Etsy. After a successful delivery, gently remind customers to leave a review. You can include a thank-you note in the package or follow up via Etsy's messaging system to ask for feedback.

Handling Returns and Exchanges

Even with clear policies, returns and exchanges are bound to happen. Handle these requests promptly and professionally, ensuring the process is as smooth as possible for the customer. Quick and fair handling of returns increases the likelihood of retaining a customer.

9 Building Customer Loyalty

True long-term success depends on building and maintaining customer loyalty. A loyal customer base not only brings in consistent revenue but also becomes your brand's greatest advocate, spreading the word about your shop and helping you grow organically. Repeat customers are more likely to leave positive reviews, make larger purchases, and recommend your products to others, making customer loyalty one of the most valuable assets you can cultivate for your Etsy shop.

In this chapter, we'll explore strategies for building strong relationships with your customers, offering excellent post-purchase experiences, and creating incentives to keep buyers coming back. By focusing on loyalty, you'll ensure sustainable growth for your Etsy business.

1. Why Customer Loyalty Matters

Loyal customers are the foundation of a thriving business. While marketing and advertising efforts bring in new buyers, it's often more cost-effective to retain existing ones. Moreover, repeat customers tend to spend more per transaction and have a higher lifetime value than first-time buyers.

Key Benefits of Building Customer Loyalty:

- **Increased Repeat Purchases**: Loyal customers return to your shop time and again, providing you with consistent revenue.

- **Positive Word-of-Mouth**: Satisfied customers are more likely to recommend your products to friends, family, and social media followers.

- **Higher Average Order Value (AOV)**: Studies show that repeat customers often spend more per order compared to new customers.

- **Better Reviews**: Happy, loyal customers are more likely to leave glowing reviews, which can drive more sales and improve your shop's reputation.

Let's explore some practical strategies for fostering customer loyalty in your Etsy shop.

2. Providing Exceptional Customer Service

One of the most effective ways to build customer loyalty is by providing exceptional customer service. Shoppers are more likely to return if they feel valued and receive prompt, helpful responses to their inquiries.

Key Elements of Great Customer Service:

- **Quick Response Time**: Respond to customer inquiries and messages as quickly as possible, ideally within 24 hours. Etsy provides message notifications, making it easy to stay on top of customer communication. A quick, friendly response goes a long way in creating a positive impression.

- **Personalization**: When possible, personalize your interactions with customers. Address them by name, reference previous orders, and provide tailored recommendations. Personal touches show that you care about each customer individually.

- **Resolve Issues with Grace**: Mistakes happen. Whether it's a delayed shipment or an incorrect item, how you handle the situation can make or break the relationship. Always offer solutions—such as refunds, replacements, or store credit—

quickly and professionally. A smooth resolution turns a potential negative experience into a positive one.

Going the Extra Mile:

- **Follow-Up After Purchase**: After a customer receives their order, send a follow-up message thanking them for their purchase. Ask if they're happy with the product and if there's anything else you can assist them with. This simple gesture shows that you value their satisfaction.

- **Offer Solutions Before Problems Arise**: For example, if you foresee a shipping delay, notify the customer in advance and offer a discount for the inconvenience. Proactive communication can turn potential frustration into appreciation.

3. Creating a Memorable Unboxing Experience

The unboxing experience is your opportunity to make a lasting impression on customers. A well-packaged, thoughtfully presented product can turn a one-time buyer into a loyal customer.

Elements of a Great Unboxing Experience:

- **High-Quality Packaging**: Invest in packaging materials that not only protect your products but also enhance the buyer's experience. Use branded boxes, tissue paper, and thank-you cards to create a cohesive, professional presentation.

- **Include a Personal Touch**: Handwritten thank-you notes, personalized messages, or small extras (like a free sample or sticker) can leave a lasting impression. It shows that you value your customers beyond the transaction.

- **Encourage Social Sharing**: Include a small card encouraging customers to share their unboxing experience on social media and tag your shop. Many buyers enjoy showcasing their purchases, and this can help you reach new audiences organically.

4. Implementing a Customer Loyalty Program

A customer loyalty program rewards repeat customers and incentivizes them to keep coming back. Etsy doesn't have a built-in loyalty program feature, but you can create one manually by offering discounts, rewards, or exclusive perks to returning customers.

How to Build a Simple Loyalty Program:

- **Offer Discounts for Repeat Purchases**: Provide returning customers with a discount code for their next purchase. For example, offer 10% off their next order after completing their first purchase.

- **Create a Points System**: Consider implementing a points-based system where customers earn points for each purchase. After accumulating a certain number of points, they can redeem them for discounts or free products. Keep it simple so that customers understand how the program works.

- **Reward Referrals**: Encourage customers to refer your shop to friends by offering both the referrer and the new customer a discount on their next purchase. Word-of-mouth referrals are one of the most effective ways to grow your customer base.

- **Exclusive Offers for Loyal Customers**: Send special promotions, early access to new products, or invitations to sales events to your most loyal customers. This makes them feel valued and keeps them engaged with your brand.

Tracking Loyalty Program Participation:

- Keep track of loyal customers manually or through a simple spreadsheet. Make notes on when customers qualify for discounts or exclusive offers based on their purchase history.

- Alternatively, email marketing tools like Mailchimp or Klaviyo can help you track customer behavior and automate loyalty emails.

5. Personalized Email Marketing

Email marketing is one of the most effective tools for nurturing customer relationships. With personalized emails, you can keep customers engaged, informed about new products, and incentivized to return to your shop.

Building Your Email List:

- **Collect Emails at Checkout**: Etsy collects buyer email addresses during the checkout process, which you can use (with permission) for future marketing.

- **Offer an Incentive**: Encourage customers

to sign up for your email list by offering a small discount or exclusive access to promotions.

Creating Engaging Email Campaigns:

- **Send Regular Updates**: Keep your customers informed about new product releases, seasonal promotions, or limited-time offers. Sending emails regularly keeps your brand top of mind.

- **Personalize Your Messages**: Use your customers' names in email subject lines or the email body to make your communications feel more personal. You can also segment your email list based on customer behavior to send targeted messages, such as recommending products based on previous purchases.

- **Offer Exclusive Discounts**: Reward your email subscribers with exclusive discounts or special offers that are only available to them. This creates a sense of exclusivity and encourages customers to remain engaged.

6. Encouraging Customer Reviews

Positive reviews on Etsy help build your shop's reputation and influence potential buyers. Happy customers are more likely to leave positive feedback, and the more reviews you have, the more trust you build with new buyers.

How to Encourage Reviews:

- **Ask for Feedback**: After an order has been delivered, send a polite message thanking the customer and asking them to leave a review if they're happy with their purchase. Make it easy by including a direct link to the review page.

- **Offer an Incentive**: While Etsy prohibits offering discounts or rewards in exchange for reviews, you can follow up with a thank-you coupon after a review is left as a gesture of appreciation.

- **Respond to Reviews**: Take the time to thank customers for their positive reviews. If a customer leaves a negative review, respond professionally and offer to resolve the issue. Customers appreciate seeing that you care about their experience, even if things didn't go perfectly.

7. Engaging with Customers on Social Media

Building customer loyalty also extends to how you interact with your audience on social media. Engaging with your customers on platforms like Instagram, TikTok, or Facebook creates a community around your brand, fostering loyalty and encouraging repeat purchases.

Tips for Social Media Engagement:

- **Respond to Comments and Messages**: Make an effort to respond to comments, questions, and direct messages promptly. Engaging with your followers builds a sense of connection and shows that you value their support.

- **Share User-Generated Content**: Encourage your customers to post photos of your products in use and tag your shop. Sharing these posts on your social media accounts not only provides social proof but also makes customers feel valued.

- **Host Giveaways and Contests**: Engage your followers by hosting occasional giveaways or contests. Ask customers to share their favorite products or tag friends for a chance to win a prize. These events build excitement and encourage participation.

- **Provide Exclusive Updates**: Use your social media platforms to give loyal followers a sneak peek at new products, special offers, or upcoming events. This keeps your audience engaged and feeling "in the know."

8. Handling Negative Feedback Positively

No matter how well you run your Etsy shop, negative feedback is inevitable. How you handle it can have a significant impact on customer loyalty. Responding professionally to complaints or negative reviews can turn a dissatisfied customer into a loyal one.

Steps to Handle Negative Feedback:

- **Acknowledge the Problem**: Respond to the customer promptly, acknowledging their concerns and apologizing for any inconvenience.

- **Offer a Solution**: Whether it's a refund, replacement, or another solution, ensure the customer knows you're willing to make things right. Taking responsibility and providing a resolution can turn a negative experience into a positive one.

- **Follow Up**: After resolving the issue, follow up with the customer to ensure they're satisfied with the outcome. This extra step shows you care about their experience and value their business.

10 Scaling Your Etsy Shop

Efficient order management and reliable shipping are crucial to running a successful Etsy shop. Your ability to process orders promptly and ensure items reach customers in good condition can make or break your shop's reputation. Buyers expect transparency, clear communication, and timely delivery, and meeting (or exceeding) these expectations helps build trust and encourages repeat purchases.

In this chapter, we'll walk you through the best practices for managing orders, handling shipping logistics, and dealing with potential issues like delays or lost packages. Additionally, we'll cover how to streamline your workflow by utilizing Etsy's latest order management tools and integrating with third-party shipping platforms to ensure smooth, efficient operations.

1. Managing Your Etsy Orders

Once a customer places an order, the clock starts ticking. Etsy tracks order status, and buyers expect regular updates as their purchase moves from "Processing" to "Shipped." Managing your orders efficiently means staying on top of the entire process from when the order is received to when the item is delivered to the buyer's door.

Order Management Tools on Etsy

Etsy offers several built-in tools that help you manage your orders with ease. Let's explore how to use them to streamline your process and reduce the risk of missed or delayed orders.

a) Etsy's Order Dashboard

The Etsy Order Dashboard gives you a comprehensive view of all your active orders. You can see the order details, including the buyer's information, product purchased, and any customization requests, all in one place.

Key Features of the Order Dashboard:

- **Order Status Tracking**: View orders that are "New," "In Progress," and "Completed" to keep track of where each order is in the process.

- **Order Filters**: Use filters to sort orders by status, shipping destination, or processing date. This is particularly helpful if you have a large volume of orders.

- **Messaging Customers**: Directly message

customers from the dashboard to clarify order details, update them on processing times, or respond to questions.

b) Bulk Order Processing

If you're handling a high volume of orders, Etsy offers a bulk processing feature that allows you to mark multiple orders as "shipped" or "complete" at once. This saves time and helps you keep track of progress during busy periods.

c) Custom Order Requests

For sellers offering custom or personalized products, managing custom orders requires extra attention. Etsy's Custom Order Request feature lets buyers provide customization details directly through the platform, making it easier to track and manage personalized requests.

Best Practices for Managing Custom Orders:

- **Communicate Clearly**: Confirm all customization details with the buyer before starting the order to avoid any misunderstandings.

- **Set Realistic Expectations**: Provide clear processing times for custom orders, and let buyers know if it will take longer than standard items.

2. Processing and Packaging Orders

Efficient order processing and professional packaging go a long way in creating a positive experience for your customers. Once an order is placed, your goal is to package it securely and get it shipped out as quickly as possible.

Order Processing Best Practices

- **Prioritize Processing Times**: Make sure to follow the processing times listed in your shop. If you consistently ship orders faster than expected, you'll earn positive reviews and build customer loyalty. For made-to-order or custom products, set a realistic timeline and update buyers on progress.

- **Double-Check Order Details**: Before shipping an order, verify that all items match what the buyer purchased. For custom orders, ensure that any personalization is accurate.

Professional Packaging

Your product's packaging is often the first physical

interaction a buyer has with your shop, so making it look professional and secure is important. Well-designed packaging not only protects your items during shipping but also reflects your brand's quality and care.

Packaging Tips:

- **Use Proper Shipping Materials**: Ensure that fragile items are packaged with enough padding (such as bubble wrap, packing peanuts, or foam). For less fragile items, consider eco-friendly packaging materials like recyclable paper or cardboard.

- **Brand Your Packaging**: Consider including a branded touch in your packaging, such as custom stickers, thank-you notes, or branded tissue paper. This small effort enhances the unboxing experience and leaves a lasting impression on the customer.

- **Include a Personal Touch**: A handwritten thank-you note or a small freebie can go a long way in delighting your customers and encouraging them to leave a positive review or make a repeat purchase.

3. Shipping Your Orders

Shipping is a critical component of your Etsy business, and selecting the right shipping options and carriers can make a big difference in customer satisfaction. Etsy provides several tools and integrations to help streamline the shipping process and make it as cost-effective as possible.

a) Choosing the Right Shipping Options

Depending on your product type, size, and destination, shipping can vary significantly. Offering multiple shipping options allows customers to choose between standard, expedited, and sometimes even same-day shipping, depending on their needs.

Shipping Options to Consider:

- **Standard Shipping**: This is the most commonly used option and typically the least expensive. Ensure your customers know the estimated delivery times upfront.

- **Expedited Shipping**: Some customers may be willing to pay more for faster delivery. Offering priority or express shipping options can meet this demand, especially during holidays or special events.

- **International Shipping**: If you offer

international shipping, make sure your listings are clear about delivery times and potential customs duties or fees. Use services that offer international tracking for better customer confidence.

b) Etsy Shipping Labels

Etsy provides a shipping label service that integrates with major carriers like USPS, FedEx, and DHL, allowing you to print shipping labels directly from your Etsy dashboard. Using Etsy's shipping labels offers several benefits:

- **Discounted Rates**: Etsy partners with carriers to offer discounted shipping rates to sellers, helping you save on shipping costs.

- **Automatic Tracking**: When you use Etsy's shipping labels, the tracking information is automatically uploaded to the buyer's order, keeping them informed about the status of their shipment.

- **Streamlined Process**: Printing labels from Etsy saves time by eliminating the need to manually enter shipping details on carrier websites. Everything is handled within Etsy's system.

How to Use Etsy Shipping Labels:

1. From your Order Dashboard, click on "Print Shipping Label" for the order you're processing.

2. Choose the correct package size and weight, and select your preferred shipping method.

3. Review the shipping cost, then print the label directly from Etsy.

After printing the label, all that's left is to package your order, attach the label, and drop it off at the nearest carrier location.

4. Using Third-Party Shipping Tools

While Etsy's shipping labels work well for many sellers, third-party shipping platforms can offer additional features, such as more advanced tracking, bulk shipping options, and even better discounts for certain carriers. Integrating these platforms with your Etsy shop can streamline your shipping operations even further.

Popular Third-Party Shipping Tools:

- **ShipStation**: ShipStation integrates with Etsy to provide multi-carrier shipping options, advanced tracking, and inventory management. You can sync orders from Etsy, print labels in bulk, and manage shipments across multiple sales channels.

- **Pirate Ship**: Known for offering excellent discounts on USPS shipping rates, Pirate Ship integrates with Etsy and allows you to batch print labels, track shipments, and calculate shipping rates in advance.

- **Shippo**: Shippo provides a wide range of carrier options, discounted rates, and tools for printing labels, tracking orders, and managing returns. Like ShipStation, Shippo works across multiple sales platforms, making it ideal if you're selling on other sites in addition to Etsy.

---

5. Handling Shipping Issues

Occasionally, things may go wrong during the shipping process—packages can get delayed, lost, or damaged in transit. While these issues are often out of your control, how you handle them can significantly impact customer satisfaction.

Dealing with Delayed or Lost Packages

- **Be Proactive with Communication**: If a buyer's order is delayed, reach out to them before they contact you. Let them know the status of their order and provide tracking details if possible. Buyers appreciate being kept in the loop.

- **Work with Your Carrier**: If a package is lost or significantly delayed, you can file a claim with your shipping carrier. Most major carriers offer insurance or reimbursement for lost packages, especially if you used tracking.

- **Offer a Solution**: If an item is lost and cannot be replaced, offer the buyer a refund or the option to select another product. This shows goodwill and helps maintain customer trust, even if the issue was caused by the shipping carrier.

Handling Damaged Items

If a product arrives damaged, it's important to resolve the issue quickly and professionally. Here's what to do:

- **Request Photos**: Ask the buyer to send photos of the damaged item and packaging. This helps you understand what went wrong and provides evidence if you need to file an insurance claim with the carrier.

- **Offer a Replacement or Refund**: Offer to send a replacement product (if available) or provide a full refund. The quicker you address the issue, the more likely you are to retain the customer's trust.

- **Improve Packaging**: If damaged items become a recurring problem, consider improving your packaging materials. Ensure fragile items are well-protected with extra padding or double-walled boxes.

6. Providing Excellent Post-Purchase Support

Once an order is shipped, your interaction with the customer shouldn't end. Offering great post-purchase support helps build customer loyalty and encourages repeat purchases.

Follow-Up Messages

After an order has been delivered, send a follow-up message thanking the customer for their purchase and encouraging them to reach out if they have any issues. Etsy allows you to automate these messages, making it easy to stay in touch without extra effort.

Encouraging Reviews

Positive reviews are essential for building trust on Etsy. After a successful delivery, gently remind customers to leave a review. You can include a thank-you note in the package or follow up via Etsy's messaging system to ask for feedback.

Handling Returns and Exchanges

Even with clear policies, returns and exchanges are bound to happen. Handle these requests promptly and professionally, ensuring the process is as smooth as possible for the customer. Quick and fair handling of returns increases the likelihood of retaining a customer.

, spreading the word about your shop and helping you grow organically. Repeat customers are more likely to leave positive reviews, make larger purchases, and recommend your products to others, making customer loyalty one of the most valuable assets you can cultivate for your Etsy shop.

In this chapter, we'll explore strategies for building strong relationships with your customers, offering excellent post-purchase experiences, and creating incentives to keep buyers coming back. By focusing on loyalty, you'll ensure sustainable growth for your Etsy business.

---

1. Why Customer Loyalty Matters

Loyal customers are the foundation of a thriving business. While marketing and advertising efforts bring in new buyers, it's often more cost-effective to retain existing ones. Moreover, repeat customers tend to spend more per transaction and have a higher lifetime value than first-time buyers.

Key Benefits of Building Customer Loyalty:

- **Increased Repeat Purchases**: Loyal customers return to your shop time and again, providing you with consistent revenue.

- **Positive Word-of-Mouth**: Satisfied customers are more likely to recommend your products to friends, family, and social media followers.

- **Higher Average Order Value (AOV)**: Studies show that repeat customers often spend more per order compared to new customers.

- **Better Reviews**: Happy, loyal customers are more likely to leave glowing reviews, which can drive more sales and improve your shop's reputation.

Let's explore some practical strategies for fostering customer loyalty in your Etsy shop.

---

2. Providing Exceptional Customer Service

One of the most effective ways to build customer loyalty is by providing exceptional customer service. Shoppers are more likely to return if they feel valued and receive prompt, helpful responses to their inquiries.

Key Elements of Great Customer Service:

- **Quick Response Time**: Respond to customer inquiries and messages as quickly as possible, ideally within 24 hours. Etsy provides message notifications, making it easy to stay on top of customer communication. A quick, friendly response goes a long way in creating a positive impression.

- **Personalization**: When possible, personalize your interactions with customers. Address them by name, reference previous orders, and provide tailored recommendations. Personal touches show that you care about each customer individually.

- **Resolve Issues with Grace**: Mistakes happen. Whether it's a delayed shipment or an incorrect item, how you handle the situation can make or break the relationship. Always offer solutions—such as refunds, replacements, or store credit— quickly and professionally. A smooth resolution turns a potential negative experience into a positive one.

Going the Extra Mile:

- **Follow-Up After Purchase**: After a customer receives their order, send a follow-up message thanking them for their purchase. Ask if they're happy with the product and if there's anything else you can assist them with. This simple gesture shows that you value their satisfaction.

- **Offer Solutions Before Problems Arise**: For example, if you foresee a shipping delay, notify the customer in advance and offer a discount for the inconvenience. Proactive communication can turn potential frustration into appreciation.

3. Creating a Memorable Unboxing Experience

The unboxing experience is your opportunity to make a lasting impression on customers. A well-packaged, thoughtfully presented product can turn a one-time buyer into a loyal customer.

Elements of a Great Unboxing Experience:

- **High-Quality Packaging**: Invest in packaging materials that not only protect your products but also enhance the buyer's experience. Use branded boxes, tissue paper, and thank-you cards to create a cohesive, professional presentation.

- **Include a Personal Touch**: Handwritten thank-you notes, personalized messages, or small extras (like a free sample or sticker) can leave a lasting impression. It shows that you value your customers beyond the transaction.

- **Encourage Social Sharing**: Include a small card encouraging customers to share their unboxing experience on social media and tag your shop. Many buyers enjoy showcasing their purchases, and this can help you reach new audiences organically.

---

4. Implementing a Customer Loyalty Program

A customer loyalty program rewards repeat customers and incentivizes them to keep coming back. Etsy doesn't have a built-in loyalty program feature, but you can create one manually by offering discounts, rewards, or exclusive perks to returning customers.

How to Build a Simple Loyalty Program:

- **Offer Discounts for Repeat Purchases**: Provide returning customers with a discount code for their next purchase. For example, offer 10% off their next order after completing their first purchase.

- **Create a Points System**: Consider implementing a points-based system where customers earn points for each purchase. After accumulating a certain number of points, they can redeem them for discounts or free products. Keep it simple so that customers understand how the program works.

- **Reward Referrals**: Encourage customers to refer your shop to friends by offering both the referrer and the new customer a discount on their next purchase. Word-of-mouth referrals are one of the most effective ways to grow your customer base.

- **Exclusive Offers for Loyal Customers**: Send special promotions, early access to new products, or invitations to sales events to your most loyal customers. This makes them feel valued and keeps them engaged with your brand.

Tracking Loyalty Program Participation:

- Keep track of loyal customers manually or through a simple spreadsheet. Make notes on when customers qualify for discounts or exclusive offers based on their purchase history.

- Alternatively, email marketing tools like Mailchimp or Klaviyo can help you track customer behavior and automate loyalty emails.

---

5. Personalized Email Marketing

Email marketing is one of the most effective tools for nurturing customer relationships. With personalized emails, you can keep customers engaged, informed about new products, and incentivized to return to your shop.

Building Your Email List:

- **Collect Emails at Checkout**: Etsy collects buyer email addresses during the checkout process, which you can use (with permission) for future marketing.

- **Offer an Incentive**: Encourage customers to sign up for your email list by offering a small discount or exclusive access to promotions.

Creating Engaging Email Campaigns:

- **Send Regular Updates**: Keep your customers informed about new product releases, seasonal promotions, or limited-time offers. Sending emails regularly keeps your brand top of mind.

- **Personalize Your Messages**: Use your customers' names in email subject lines or the email body to make your communications feel more personal. You can also segment your email list based on customer behavior to send targeted messages, such as recommending products based on previous purchases.

- **Offer Exclusive Discounts**: Reward your email subscribers with exclusive discounts or special offers that are only available to them. This creates a sense of exclusivity and encourages customers to remain engaged.

6. Encouraging Customer Reviews

Positive reviews on Etsy help build your shop's reputation and influence potential buyers. Happy customers are more likely to leave positive feedback, and the more reviews you have, the more trust you build with new buyers.

How to Encourage Reviews:

- **Ask for Feedback**: After an order has been delivered, send a polite message thanking the customer and asking them to leave a review if they're happy with their purchase. Make it easy by including a direct link to the review page.

- **Offer an Incentive**: While Etsy prohibits offering discounts or rewards in exchange for reviews, you can follow up with a thank-you coupon after a review is left as a gesture of appreciation.

- **Respond to Reviews**: Take the time to thank customers for their positive reviews. If a customer leaves a negative review, respond professionally and offer to resolve the issue. Customers appreciate seeing that you care about their experience, even if things didn't go perfectly.

7. Engaging with Customers on Social Media

Building customer loyalty also extends to how you interact with your audience on social media. Engaging with your customers on platforms like Instagram, TikTok, or Facebook creates a community around your brand, fostering loyalty and encouraging repeat purchases.

Tips for Social Media Engagement:

- **Respond to Comments and Messages**: Make an effort to respond to comments, questions, and direct messages promptly. Engaging with your followers builds a sense of connection and shows that you value their support.

- **Share User-Generated Content**: Encourage your customers to post photos of your products in use and tag your shop. Sharing these posts on your social media accounts not only provides social proof but also makes customers feel valued.

- **Host Giveaways and Contests**: Engage your followers by hosting occasional giveaways or contests. Ask customers to share their favorite products or tag friends for a chance to win a prize. These events build excitement and encourage participation.

- **Provide Exclusive Updates**: Use your social media platforms to give loyal followers a sneak peek at new products, special offers, or upcoming events. This keeps your audience engaged and feeling "in the know."

---

8. Handling Negative Feedback Positively

No matter how well you run your Etsy shop, negative feedback is inevitable. How you handle it can have a significant impact on customer loyalty. Responding professionally to complaints or negative reviews can turn a dissatisfied customer into a loyal one.

Steps to Handle Negative Feedback:

- **Acknowledge the Problem**: Respond to the customer promptly, acknowledging their concerns and apologizing for any inconvenience.

- **Offer a Solution**: Whether it's a refund, replacement, or another solution, ensure the customer knows you're willing to make things right. Taking responsibility and providing a resolution can turn a negative experience into a positive one.

- **Follow Up**: After resolving the issue, follow up with the customer to ensure they're satisfied with the outcome. This extra step shows you care about their experience and value their business.

Conclusion

Building customer loyalty is essential for the long-term success of your Etsy shop. By providing exceptional customer service, creating memorable unboxing experiences, and offering personalized communication, you can foster strong relationships that lead to repeat business and positive word-of-mouth.

In the next chapter, we'll focus on scaling your Etsy shop and automating certain aspects of your business to handle increased demand without sacrificing quality. Let's continue building on the foundation of trust and loyalty you've established with your customers!

4o

You said:

write Chapter 9: Crafting Successful Etsy Ad Campaigns

ChatGPT said:

ChatGPT

Chapter 9: Crafting Successful Etsy Ad Campaigns

Advertising is a powerful tool for driving more traffic and sales to your Etsy shop, but it requires a strategic approach to make the most of your investment. Etsy Ads allow you to promote your products directly to shoppers within the platform, making your listings more visible in search results, categories, and other key placements across the site. A well-crafted ad campaign can significantly boost your shop's visibility, attract more customers, and increase your revenue.

However, running a successful Etsy ad campaign

is not just about spending money; it's about understanding your target audience, choosing the right products to promote, setting a realistic budget, and continuously analyzing your campaign's performance to optimize for success.

In this chapter, we'll guide you through the process of creating effective Etsy ad campaigns, including how to select the best products to advertise, how to set and manage your ad budget, and how to monitor and optimize your ads for maximum return on investment (ROI).

---

1. Understanding How Etsy Ads Work

Before diving into the specifics of setting up and managing Etsy Ads, it's essential to understand how Etsy's advertising system works. Etsy Ads use a pay-per-click (PPC) model, meaning you only pay when someone clicks on your promoted listing. Etsy automatically decides where to place your ads, whether in search results, related listings, or other high-traffic areas.

Key Features of Etsy Ads:

- **Pay-per-click (PPC)**: You are only charged when someone clicks on your ad, not when it's displayed. This makes it a cost-effective way to drive targeted traffic to your shop.

- **Automatic Placement**: Etsy's algorithm places your ads in the best possible locations based on user behavior, search queries, and relevancy. The more optimized your listings are (titles, descriptions, photos), the better your ads will perform.

- **Daily Budget Control**: You set a daily budget for your ads, which Etsy will use to maximize exposure. Once your daily budget is reached, Etsy will stop showing your ads for the day.

- **Automatic Bidding**: Etsy manages the bidding process for you, determining how much to bid on each click to ensure optimal placement for your ads based on your budget.

Etsy Ads are a great tool for increasing product visibility, but to make the most of them, you need a clear strategy.

---

2. Choosing the Right Products to Advertise

Not every product in your shop is an ideal candidate for advertising. Promoting the right listings can maximize your returns, while promoting low-conversion products can waste your ad budget. The key is to select products that have the potential to convert into sales.

How to Choose Products to Advertise:

- **Best Sellers**: Focus on promoting products that already sell well organically. These items have proven appeal, and advertising them will likely increase their visibility and sales even further.

- **Seasonal Products**: If you sell products that are tied to specific seasons, holidays, or events (such as Christmas decorations or Valentine's Day gifts), advertising them during peak periods can help you capitalize on seasonal demand.

- **High-Profit Margins**: Choose products with healthy profit margins. Since Etsy Ads are a paid investment, you want to ensure that the profit from each sale is worth the cost of the ad. Low-margin products might not provide enough return to justify the ad spend.

- **New Products**: If you've recently launched a new product line and want to drive initial traffic to it, consider running ads to generate awareness and sales. However, monitor performance closely to ensure the ads are delivering a return.

Products to Avoid Advertising:

- **Low-Performing Products**: If a product hasn't been selling well organically, it may not perform well in ads either. Before advertising, make sure the product listing is optimized and there is demonstrated demand for the item.

- **Low-Price Products**: Products with low prices may not generate enough profit to offset the cost of advertising. Be cautious about promoting inexpensive items unless you're bundling them with higher-priced goods.

---

3. Setting a Realistic Budget for Etsy Ads

When running Etsy Ads, it's essential to set a daily budget that aligns with your business goals and financial capacity. Etsy allows you to control how much you spend each day on ads, which gives you flexibility, especially if you're just starting with paid advertising.

How to Set Your Daily Budget:

- **Start Small and Scale**: If you're new to Etsy Ads, start with a modest daily budget—around $1 to $5 per day. This allows you to test how your ads perform without committing too much upfront. As you begin to see results and learn which products convert best, you can gradually increase your budget.

- **Align Your Budget with Your Profit Margins**: Your ad spend should reflect your profit margins. If you're promoting products with high-profit margins, you can afford to spend more on advertising. However, if your margins are tight, be conservative with your budget.

- **Monitor and Adjust**: One of the advantages of Etsy Ads is that you can adjust your daily budget at any time. If you notice that your ads are performing well and driving sales, you can increase your budget to capitalize on the momentum. Conversely, if the ads aren't delivering results, you can lower or pause your budget to avoid overspending.

Calculating Return on Investment (ROI) for Etsy Ads:

- **Track Sales from Ads**: Etsy provides data on how much revenue your ads generate, making it easy to calculate your ROI. Divide the total revenue generated from ads by your ad spend to determine if the campaign is profitable.

- **Monitor Clicks and Conversions**: It's important to track how many clicks your ads receive and how many of those clicks convert into sales. A high click-through rate (CTR) with a low conversion rate may indicate that your product listing needs improvement.

---

4. Creating and Managing Your Etsy Ad Campaign

Once you've selected the products to promote and set your budget, it's time to create and manage your ad campaign. Etsy Ads are easy to set up, but it's crucial to regularly monitor performance and make adjustments to ensure you're maximizing your results.

Step-by-Step Guide to Setting Up an Etsy Ad Campaign:

1. **Access Etsy Ads**: From your shop dashboard, navigate to the "Marketing" tab and select "Etsy Ads." This will take you to the ad campaign setup page.

2. **Set Your Daily Budget**: Enter the amount you're willing to spend per day. Remember, Etsy will not exceed this budget, and you can adjust it at any time.

3. **Choose Which Listings to Promote**: You can choose to promote all your listings or select specific products. It's usually best to start by promoting a few high-converting products rather than your entire inventory.

4. **Launch Your Ads**: Once your budget and listings are selected, you can launch your campaign. Etsy will automatically place your ads in relevant search results and other placements across the platform.

5. Monitoring and Optimizing Your Ads

The key to a successful Etsy ad campaign is continuous optimization. By analyzing performance data and making adjustments, you can improve your ads over time and ensure they're driving profitable results.

Metrics to Monitor:

- **Impressions**: This is the number of times your ad is shown to potential buyers. A high number of impressions indicates that your ad is being seen, but if it's not converting into clicks, you may need to adjust your listing or keywords.

- **Click-Through Rate (CTR)**: The CTR measures how many people clicked on your ad compared to how many saw it. A low CTR may indicate that your listing title, photo, or description isn't compelling enough to attract clicks.

- **Cost-per-Click (CPC)**: This is the amount you're paying for each click on your ad. A high CPC can eat into your profits, so monitor this metric and try to keep it as low as possible without sacrificing visibility.

- **Sales from Ads**: The ultimate measure of success is how many sales your ads generate. Track which listings are driving the most sales and focus your budget on those high-performing products.

Tips for Optimizing Etsy Ads:

- **Refine Your Listings**: If your ads are getting clicks but not converting into sales, review the product listings. Ensure that your product descriptions are clear, your photos are high-quality, and your pricing is competitive.

- **Test Different Products**: Don't be afraid to experiment with different products. If certain listings aren't performing well, try promoting new products or different combinations of items to see what resonates with your audience.

- **Adjust Your Budget Based on Performance**: If you're seeing strong results from your ads, consider increasing your daily budget to capitalize on the success. Conversely, if an ad isn't performing well, reduce your spend or pause the campaign to avoid wasting money.

- **Monitor Seasonality**: Adjust your ad strategy based on seasonal demand. For example, during holiday seasons, you may want to increase your budget to capture more sales, while in slower periods, you can scale back your ad spend.

---

6. Understanding the Impact of Etsy's Algorithm on Ads

Etsy's search algorithm plays a crucial role in how your ads are displayed. The algorithm considers various factors, including the relevance of your keywords, the quality of your listings, and the overall performance of your shop. Therefore, optimizing your shop and listings for SEO not only improves your organic traffic but also enhances the effectiveness of your paid ads.

SEO Tips to Boost Your Etsy Ad Campaigns:

- **Optimize Titles and Tags**: Ensure that the product titles and tags for your advertised listings include relevant keywords that shoppers are likely to search for. Etsy uses these keywords to determine when and where to show your ads.

- **Use High-Quality Photos**: Visuals play a significant role in driving clicks. Make sure your product images are well-lit, high-resolution, and showcase your items from multiple angles.

- **Keep Your Listings Active**: Etsy favors active shops that regularly add new products and update listings. Keep your shop fresh and engaging by updating listings, adding new items, and responding to customer inquiries.

- **Earn Positive Reviews**: A strong track record of positive reviews boosts your shop's credibility and increases your chances of getting more visibility in both organic and paid placements.

7. Maximizing Returns During Key Sales Periods

Advertising during peak shopping seasons, such as holidays, special events, or major sales periods, can drive significant sales growth. Etsy shoppers are particularly active during key times like Christmas, Valentine's Day, and Mother's Day, making these ideal opportunities to increase your ad budget and maximize returns.

Tips for Running Ads During Sales Periods:

- **Increase Your Budget for High-Demand Products**: If you have products that are popular during certain holidays or seasons, increase your daily budget to boost their visibility during these times.

- **Promote Discounts or Special Offers**: If you're running a sale or offering a discount, highlight these promotions in your ad campaign. Shoppers are more likely to click on listings that advertise limited-time deals.

- **Prepare Your Shop in Advance**: Ensure your shop is fully optimized and stocked before key sales periods. Update your listings, review your shipping policies, and make sure you're ready to handle increased traffic and orders.

11   Navigating   Etsy's   Latest Updates and Changes

Etsy is a dynamic platform, continually evolving to improve both the seller and buyer experience. As the marketplace grows and trends shift, Etsy regularly introduces updates to its policies, features, and tools. These changes can affect everything from fees and shipping policies to how products are promoted and discovered. Staying informed about these updates is essential for ensuring that your shop stays competitive and compliant with Etsy's rules.

In this chapter, we'll guide you through some of the most recent and significant updates on Etsy and explain how to adapt your shop accordingly. From new tools that streamline operations to policy changes that impact fees and shipping, understanding Etsy's latest developments will help you make informed decisions and take advantage of new opportunities.

1. Understanding Etsy's Platform Updates

Etsy periodically introduces new features, policies, and platform improvements designed to enhance the experience for both sellers and buyers. These updates are driven by changes in the eCommerce landscape, customer feedback, and Etsy's desire to stay competitive with other platforms.

Why It's Important to Stay Updated:

- **Compliance**: Etsy occasionally updates its seller policies, and failing to comply with these changes could result in warnings, penalties, or even suspension of your shop.

- **Opportunities**: New features and tools can provide opportunities to improve your shop's performance, streamline operations, or reach more customers. Being among the first to adopt new tools can give you a competitive edge.

- **Cost Management**: Etsy may adjust its fee structure or shipping requirements. Understanding these changes helps you plan for any potential impact on your pricing or profit margins.

Let's explore some of the key areas where Etsy has recently introduced updates and how to navigate these changes.

2. Fee Structure Changes

One of the most important aspects of running an Etsy shop is understanding the platform's fee structure. Etsy generates revenue through a combination of listing fees, transaction fees, and payment processing fees. Occasionally, Etsy adjusts these fees to reflect changes in the marketplace or to support new seller tools.

Recent Changes to Etsy's Fee Structure:

- **Transaction Fees**: Etsy charges a transaction fee on each sale you make, which is a percentage of the total sale price (including shipping). If Etsy has recently increased this fee, you may need to adjust your product pricing to maintain profitability.

- **Offsite Ads Fees**: Etsy's Offsite Ads program, which promotes your products on external platforms like Google and Facebook, also carries a fee. This fee is charged when a sale results from a customer clicking on an offsite ad. The fee can vary depending on your shop's revenue and whether you're opted into the program. It's important to monitor the impact of Offsite Ads on your margins and adjust your participation if necessary.

- **Payment Processing Fees**: When customers use Etsy Payments, a processing fee is applied to each transaction. Etsy Payments supports a variety of payment methods, and staying informed about processing fees allows you to understand the full cost of each sale.

How to Adapt to Fee Changes:

- **Adjust Your Pricing**: If fees have increased, consider adjusting your product pricing to cover the additional costs. Be mindful of your target market, and avoid pricing yourself out of competitiveness while still protecting your profit margins.

- **Promote Higher-Margin Products**: Focus on promoting products with higher profit margins, as these will be less affected by fee increases and ensure that your ads and marketing efforts yield positive returns.

3. Etsy's Shipping Updates

Shipping is a critical aspect of running an Etsy shop, and Etsy frequently updates its shipping policies and tools to enhance the customer experience. Sellers need to stay updated on these changes to ensure they are offering the most competitive and customer-friendly shipping options.

Key Shipping Updates on Etsy:

- **Free Shipping Incentives**: Etsy has continued to emphasize free shipping as a way to boost sales. Sellers are encouraged to offer free shipping on orders over a certain amount, as this can improve your shop's visibility in search results and increase customer conversion rates. If you opt into Etsy's free shipping program, your listings are prioritized in the marketplace.

- **Shipping Labels and Integration**: Etsy offers discounted shipping labels for sellers who ship domestically and internationally. Recent updates have made it easier to integrate Etsy's shipping labels with third-party carriers, providing more options for tracking, handling, and managing orders.

- **International Shipping Requirements**: Etsy has improved its international shipping tools, helping sellers manage customs forms and taxes more easily. If you ship internationally, it's important to stay on top of these updates to ensure your packages meet legal requirements and avoid shipping delays.

How to Adapt to Shipping Changes:

- **Offer Free Shipping**: If free shipping is feasible for your business, consider implementing it on orders over a set threshold. This can make your listings more attractive to buyers and help increase your overall sales volume.

- **Use Etsy's Shipping Labels**: Take advantage of Etsy's discounted shipping rates and integrated shipping label tools to streamline the shipping process. This can save you time and money, particularly for high-volume orders.

- **Monitor International Orders**: If you sell internationally, familiarize yourself with the latest customs requirements and fees. Use Etsy's international shipping tools to make sure your customers have a smooth and transparent buying experience.

4. SEO and Search Algorithm Updates

Etsy's search algorithm, which determines how products are ranked in search results, is constantly being updated to improve relevance and user experience. Recent changes in Etsy's SEO (Search Engine Optimization) practices can have a significant impact on how your listings perform in search results.

Recent SEO Updates on Etsy:

- **Improved Relevancy**: Etsy's algorithm continues to prioritize relevancy when displaying search results. This means that your product listings must closely match what buyers are searching for in terms of keywords, tags, and product descriptions. The more relevant your listings are to a search query, the more likely they are to appear higher in search results.

- **Listing Quality Score**: Etsy uses a Listing Quality Score to determine the placement of your products in search results. This score takes into account factors like conversion rate, customer reviews, and whether your listings are updated regularly. High-quality listings with positive reviews and frequent sales are more likely to be shown to potential buyers.

- **Mobile Optimization**: With more buyers shopping on mobile devices, Etsy has been optimizing its search and display features for mobile users. Sellers should ensure their product images and descriptions are mobile-friendly and easy to read on smaller screens.

How to Adapt to SEO and Search Algorithm Changes:

- **Use Relevant Keywords**: Regularly update your product titles, descriptions, and tags to include keywords that reflect what buyers are searching for. Use Etsy's search bar to see what phrases are trending and incorporate them naturally into your listings.

- **Monitor Listing Performance**: Keep an eye on which of your listings perform well and which may need improvement. Update low-performing listings with better photos, descriptions, and keywords to improve their ranking.

- **Encourage Reviews**: Positive customer reviews play a significant role in boosting your Listing Quality Score. Encourage satisfied customers to leave reviews, and be proactive in addressing any negative feedback.

5. Etsy's Expanded Marketing and Promotional Tools

Etsy has introduced several new marketing tools and features that allow sellers to better promote their shops and reach a larger audience. These tools range from in-platform advertising options to integrations with social media and email marketing platforms.

Recent Marketing Tool Updates:

- **Etsy Ads Enhancements**: Etsy has improved its ad platform, making it easier for sellers to set up campaigns, monitor performance, and adjust budgets. With Etsy Ads, you can promote specific listings across the platform, helping your products appear higher in search results, category pages, and related listings.

- **Social Media Integration**: Etsy has enhanced its integration with social media platforms like Instagram and Pinterest. These integrations make it easier for sellers to promote their products on external platforms, driving traffic back to their Etsy shops.

- **Discounts and Sales**: Etsy has streamlined the process of running sales and offering discounts. You can now schedule sales in advance, target specific products or categories, and use promotional tools to highlight your offers across the platform.

How to Leverage Etsy's Marketing Tools:

- **Run Strategic Ad Campaigns**: Use Etsy Ads to promote your best-selling or high-conversion listings. Monitor your ad campaigns closely and adjust your daily budget based on performance. Focus on advertising products with high profit margins to maximize your return on investment.

- **Promote on Social Media**: Take advantage of Etsy's social media integrations to create seamless shopping experiences on platforms like Instagram and Pinterest. By showcasing your products on these visual platforms, you can drive more traffic to your Etsy shop and increase sales.

- **Schedule Sales and Discounts**: Use Etsy's sale scheduling tool to plan promotions around key shopping periods, such as holidays or seasonal events. Offering limited-time discounts can create urgency and encourage buyers to make a purchase.

6. Policy Updates and Compliance Requirements

Etsy regularly updates its seller policies and guidelines to ensure compliance with legal requirements and maintain a safe marketplace for buyers and sellers. It's important to stay informed about these policy changes to avoid potential violations.

Key Policy Updates:

- **Prohibited Items**: Etsy has expanded its list of prohibited items to ensure that products sold on the platform comply with legal and ethical standards. This includes restrictions on counterfeit items, illegal goods, and certain health-related products. Make sure you review Etsy's latest policies to ensure your listings are compliant.

- **Intellectual Property**: Etsy takes intellectual property (IP) rights seriously, and recent updates have made it easier for copyright holders to report infringements. If you create custom or personalized products, be mindful of any trademarks, logos, or copyrighted designs you may be using.

- **Tax and Regulatory Changes**: Etsy may update its tax collection policies in response to local or international regulations. This includes the collection of sales tax in certain regions or compliance with new eCommerce tax laws. Stay informed about Etsy's tax policies to ensure you're handling sales tax correctly.

How to Stay Compliant with Etsy's Policies:

- **Regularly Review Etsy's Policies**: Make it a habit to check Etsy's policies page for any updates or changes that might affect your shop. This ensures that you're aware of new regulations and requirements.

- **Handle Intellectual Property Responsibly**: If you create custom or personalized items, be cautious about using copyrighted materials. If you're unsure whether something is protected by IP laws, consult with an attorney or refer to Etsy's resources on IP compliance.

- **Stay on Top of Tax Requirements**: Depending on your location and the regions you ship to, Etsy may collect and remit sales tax on your behalf. Make sure you understand Etsy's tax policies and how they apply to your business.

7. Taking Advantage of Etsy's New Tools and Features

Etsy continuously rolls out new tools and features to help sellers grow their businesses. By staying informed and embracing these innovations, you can improve your shop's performance and streamline your operations.

Recent Tool Updates:

- **Advanced Analytics**: Etsy has enhanced its seller dashboard with more detailed analytics. This allows you to track your shop's performance, monitor visitor behavior, and analyze sales trends more effectively. Use this data to make informed decisions about pricing, marketing, and inventory management.

- **Shop Customization Tools**: Etsy has introduced new customization options for shop layouts, allowing you to personalize your shop's appearance and create a more branded experience for customers. This includes the ability to create custom shop banners, logos, and featured product sections.

- **Improved Shipping Tools**: Etsy's integration with third-party shipping providers has been expanded, making it easier to manage shipping, print labels, and track packages. This is particularly useful for sellers who handle a high volume of orders or ship internationally.

How to Use Etsy's Latest Tools:

- **Leverage Analytics for Growth**: Dive into Etsy's advanced analytics to identify trends in your shop's performance. Use this data to optimize your product listings, adjust your pricing strategy, and focus on high-conversion products.

- **Customize Your Shop's Appearance**: Take advantage of Etsy's customization tools to create a professional, branded shop that reflects your unique style. A well-designed shop layout can improve customer experience and increase conversion rates.

- **Streamline Your Shipping Process**: Use Etsy's improved shipping tools to simplify your order fulfillment process. Integrate with third-party carriers to get better shipping rates and reduce the time spent managing logistics.

12 Tools and Resources for Your Etsy Business

Running a successful Etsy shop involves much more than just creating beautiful products. To streamline your operations, optimize your listings, and grow your business, it's crucial to leverage the right tools and resources. These tools can help you manage everything from product research and SEO optimization to order fulfillment and customer communication.

In this chapter, we'll cover some of the most effective tools and resources available to Etsy sellers, with a particular focus on helping you save time, make data-driven decisions, and scale your business. Whether you're looking to streamline your workflow, improve your Etsy SEO, or gain insights into trending products, the right tools can make a significant impact on your shop's success.

1. EverBee: Product Research and Etsy SEO Tool

EverBee is a powerful tool designed specifically for Etsy sellers to help with product research, keyword analysis, and Etsy SEO. One of the biggest challenges for Etsy sellers is identifying products with strong demand and low competition. EverBee simplifies this process by providing data-driven insights into what's trending, which products are performing well, and which keywords you should target to improve your shop's visibility.

Key Features of EverBee:

- **Product Analytics**: EverBee allows you to analyze top-performing products within your niche. You can see estimated monthly sales, revenue, and listing details of successful products, helping you identify trends and opportunities.

- **Keyword Research**: Understanding which keywords customers are using to find products similar to yours is critical for Etsy SEO. EverBee helps you find high-volume, low-competition keywords to optimize your listings and increase your shop's visibility.

- **Revenue Estimation**: EverBee provides revenue estimates for individual products, giving you insight into what's selling well and at what price points. This helps you determine whether it's worth adding similar products to your own shop.

- **Niche Research**: The tool is especially

helpful for identifying profitable niches that you may not have considered. By analyzing trends and sales data, you can spot new opportunities for expanding your product line.

How to Use EverBee to Grow Your Etsy Shop:

- **Optimize Your Listings**: Use the keyword research feature to identify relevant, high-performing keywords for your product titles, tags, and descriptions. This improves your chances of ranking higher in Etsy search results.

- **Discover Trending Products**: Analyze top sellers in your category to spot trends early. You can either create similar products or introduce complementary items that align with current demand.

- **Plan New Product Launches**: Use the revenue estimation tool to evaluate the potential profitability of new products before launching them. This helps you make informed decisions about where to invest your time and resources.

By incorporating EverBee into your research process, you can make data-driven decisions that increase your shop's visibility and sales.

2. Marmalead: Etsy SEO and Keyword Optimization

Marmalead is another essential tool for Etsy sellers looking to improve their search rankings. Etsy's search engine relies heavily on keywords to determine which listings appear in search results, and Marmalead helps you identify the best keywords to use in your titles, tags, and descriptions.

Key Features of Marmalead:

- **Keyword Search Volume**: Marmalead provides data on the search volume of specific keywords, helping you choose the ones most likely to drive traffic to your listings.

- **Keyword Competition**: It's not just about using popular keywords—it's about finding the right balance between search volume and competition. Marmalead helps you identify keywords with high search volume and low competition.

- **Real-Time SEO Grading**: Marmalead grades your listings based on how well-optimized they are for Etsy search. This grading system shows you where you can improve, such as adding more relevant keywords or adjusting your product descriptions.

- **Trend Data**: Marmalead provides insights into seasonal trends, showing when certain keywords are likely to perform better throughout the year. This is especially useful for holiday or event-based products.

How to Use Marmalead for Etsy Success:

- **Optimize Existing Listings**: Run your existing listings through Marmalead's SEO grading tool to identify areas for improvement. Update titles, descriptions, and tags with high-performing keywords to increase your visibility in search results.

- **Discover New Keywords**: Use the keyword research tool to find long-tail keywords that your competitors may be overlooking. These keywords often have lower competition but still attract relevant buyers.

- **Prepare for Seasonal Trends**: Plan your product launches and promotions around seasonal trends by analyzing when certain keywords start to spike in popularity. This helps you stay ahead of the competition during peak shopping periods.

Marmalead is a great tool for sellers who want to take their Etsy SEO to the next level and ensure their listings are fully optimized for maximum visibility.

3. eRank: Comprehensive Etsy Analytics and SEO Tool

eRank is a powerful all-in-one tool that offers a wide range of features for Etsy sellers, including keyword research, competitor analysis, and detailed shop analytics. Whether you're looking to optimize your SEO, track your shop's performance, or analyze your competitors, eRank provides valuable insights that can help you make informed decisions.

Key Features of eRank:

- **Keyword Tool**: Similar to Marmalead and EverBee, eRank's keyword tool helps you find the best keywords to use in your product listings by providing data on search volume, competition, and seasonal trends.

- **Competitor Tracking**: eRank allows you to track your competitors by monitoring their listings, sales, and performance. This helps you understand what's working for other sellers in your niche and adjust your strategy accordingly.

- **Listing Audit**: eRank's listing audit feature reviews your product listings and identifies areas for improvement, such as missing keywords, poor-quality images, or incomplete descriptions.

- **Shop Performance Metrics**: eRank provides detailed reports on your shop's performance, including traffic, sales, conversion rates, and customer behavior. These insights help you identify what's working and where you can improve.

How to Use eRank to Improve Your Etsy Shop:

- **Spy on Competitors**: Use the competitor tracking feature to monitor top-performing shops in your niche. By understanding their strategies, you can adapt your own listings, keywords, and marketing tactics to stay competitive.

- **Audit Your Listings**: Run a listing audit to

see how well-optimized your products are for Etsy search. Make the recommended changes to improve your SEO, increase traffic, and ultimately boost sales.

- **Track Your Progress**: Regularly check eRank's performance metrics to monitor your shop's growth. Use this data to refine your marketing strategies, adjust your product offerings, and identify potential areas for expansion.

eRank is an invaluable tool for Etsy sellers who want to optimize their shop's performance and stay ahead of the competition through data-driven insights.

4. Canva: Design and Branding Tool

Canva is a user-friendly design tool that allows you to create professional-looking graphics for your Etsy shop. Whether you need to design product images, social media posts, or custom branding materials, Canva provides the templates and tools to help you stand out visually.

Key Features of Canva:

- **Templates for Everything**: Canva offers thousands of customizable templates for product listings, social media posts, email banners, and more. This makes it easy to create cohesive, visually appealing content for your shop.

- **Brand Kit**: With Canva's brand kit feature, you can store your brand's colors, fonts, and logos in one place. This ensures consistency across all of your shop's visuals, from your Etsy banner to your Instagram posts.

- **Customizable Graphics**: Canva's drag-and-drop interface allows you to create custom graphics for your Etsy shop with ease. You can add text, overlays, icons, and other design elements to make your listings and marketing materials look professional.

- **Product Photography Enhancements**: Canva allows you to edit and enhance product photos by adding text overlays, background removal, and filters. This is especially useful if you want to create custom product images for your shop's promotions or social media.

How to Use Canva for Your Etsy Shop:

- **Design Custom Etsy Banners**: Create a professional and cohesive shop banner using Canva's templates. This is an easy way to make your Etsy shop look polished and visually appealing to potential customers.

- **Create Social Media Content**: Use Canva to design eye-catching social media posts for platforms like Instagram, TikTok, and Pinterest. Well-designed graphics will help you promote your products and build brand awareness.

- **Enhance Product Images**: Use Canva's editing tools to enhance your product photos, add promotional text, or create visually appealing product collages. High-quality images increase your chances of making sales.

Canva is an essential tool for Etsy sellers who want to create stunning visuals without the need for advanced design skills or expensive software.

5. QuickBooks: Accounting and Financial Management

QuickBooks is a popular accounting tool that helps Etsy sellers manage their finances, track expenses, and stay on top of taxes. Running a small business requires keeping accurate financial records, and QuickBooks makes it easier to manage your Etsy shop's financials.

Key Features of QuickBooks:

- **Income and Expense Tracking**: QuickBooks automatically tracks your income from Etsy sales and allows you to categorize expenses related to your shop, such as shipping costs, materials, and marketing.

- **Sales Tax Management**: QuickBooks can help you calculate and file sales taxes, making it easier to stay compliant with tax regulations in different states or countries.

- **Profit and Loss Reporting**: Generate profit and loss reports to get a clear picture of your shop's financial health. This helps you understand where your revenue is coming from and where you might need to cut costs.

- **Invoicing and Payments**: If you work with custom orders or wholesale clients, QuickBooks allows you to send professional invoices and receive payments directly through the platform.

How to Use QuickBooks for Your Etsy Shop:

- **Track Your Expenses**: Automatically categorize your business expenses in QuickBooks, making it easier to monitor your spending and budget for future investments in your shop.

- **Stay on Top of Taxes**: Use QuickBooks to track and file your sales taxes, ensuring you stay compliant with state and local tax regulations.

- **Monitor Your Profitability**: Regularly check your profit and loss statements to see how well your shop is performing financially. This helps you make informed decisions about pricing, product expansion, and marketing strategies.

QuickBooks is an essential tool for Etsy sellers who want to keep their financial records organized, stay compliant with tax regulations, and better understand their shop's profitability.

6. The Brand Creators YouTube Channel: Educational Resources for Etsy Sellers

The Brand Creators YouTube Channel is an invaluable resource for Etsy sellers looking to learn the ins and outs of building a successful eCommerce business. Hosted by experienced entrepreneurs, the channel offers practical tips and strategies for growing your Etsy shop, optimizing your listings, and marketing your products effectively.

What You'll Learn from the Brand Creators YouTube Channel:

- **Etsy SEO Best Practices**: The channel covers in-depth strategies for improving your shop's SEO, helping you rank higher in Etsy search results and attract more traffic to your listings.

- **Product Research**: Learn how to find trending products, analyze competitors, and choose products with high demand and low competition. The channel also dives into how to validate product ideas before launching them in your shop.

- **Marketing Strategies**: The Brand Creators channel offers practical advice on promoting your Etsy shop on social media, using email marketing, and running effective Etsy ad campaigns. These strategies help you build a loyal customer base and drive consistent sales.

- **Scaling Your Etsy Business**: As your shop grows, the channel provides insights into automating processes, outsourcing tasks, and managing increased demand to scale your business without burning out.

Why You Should Watch the Brand Creators Channel:

- **Actionable Advice**: The channel focuses on providing actionable steps that Etsy sellers can implement immediately, whether you're just starting out or looking to grow your existing shop.

- **Expert Guidance**: The hosts of Brand Creators have years of experience in the eCommerce space, and they regularly share insights from their own journeys, helping you avoid common pitfalls and accelerate your growth.

- **Regular Updates**: Stay informed about the latest trends, tools, and Etsy updates by following the channel. Regular content ensures you're always equipped with the most current knowledge for growing your Etsy shop.

Incorporating the insights from the Brand Creators YouTube channel into your Etsy business strategy can help you optimize your listings, improve your marketing, and scale your shop for long-term success.

13 Frequently Asked Questions (FAQ)

Running an Etsy shop can be both exciting and challenging, and sellers often encounter similar questions as they navigate the platform. This chapter is designed to answer some of the most frequently asked questions that arise when managing an Etsy business, from understanding Etsy's fees to boosting your shop's SEO and handling returns. Whether you're just starting or looking to fine-tune your operations, this FAQ section will provide quick and concise answers to help you along the way.

1. How do Etsy fees work?

Etsy fees are an important aspect of running your shop, and understanding them ensures you price your products correctly to maintain profitability.

- **Listing Fee**: Etsy charges a $0.20 USD fee for each listing, which is active for four months or until the item sells.

- **Transaction Fee**: Etsy takes a 6.5% commission on the total order amount, including the price of the product and shipping costs.

- **Payment Processing Fee**: Etsy charges a payment processing fee based on your location. For example, in the U.S., this fee is typically 3% + $0.25 per transaction.

- **Offsite Ads Fee**: If a customer clicks on an Offsite Ad and makes a purchase, Etsy charges an additional fee between 12-15%, depending on your annual shop revenue.

These fees can add up, so make sure to incorporate them into your pricing strategy to ensure you maintain a healthy profit margin.

2. What can I do if my product isn't showing up in Etsy search results?

If your product isn't appearing in search results, several factors could be influencing its visibility:

- **SEO Optimization**: Ensure your listing titles, tags, and descriptions are optimized with relevant keywords. Use tools like EverBee, Marmalead, or eRank to research high-traffic keywords.

- **Relevance**: Make sure your product details (title, description, tags) accurately match what shoppers are searching for.

- **Listing Quality**: Etsy prioritizes listings that convert well and have high engagement, so improve your photos, descriptions, and price points to increase your conversion rate.

- **Listing Activity**: Fresh listings are often given more exposure, so regularly update or renew your listings to maintain visibility.

Keep testing and updating your listings until they gain traction in Etsy's search algorithm.

3. How can I boost my Etsy shop's SEO?

Improving your Etsy shop's SEO is key to appearing higher in search results. Here are a few strategies:

- **Use Relevant Keywords**: Research and use keywords that shoppers are likely to search for. Include these keywords in your titles, tags, and descriptions.

- **Optimize Your Product Titles**: Make sure your titles are descriptive, keyword-rich, and easy to read. Place the most important keywords at the beginning of your title.

- **High-Quality Photos**: Etsy ranks listings that get clicks and conversions higher. Eye-catching, professional photos can lead to more clicks and purchases.

- **Customer Reviews**: Encourage positive reviews. Listings with high ratings and reviews are more likely to rank higher.

- **Renew Listings Regularly**: Frequently updated and newly listed products often get a temporary boost in search results.

These strategies, combined with consistent SEO optimization, can help increase your shop's visibility over time.

4. What's the best way to handle customer returns and complaints?

Handling returns and complaints professionally is important for maintaining a good reputation:

- **Clear Policies**: Clearly state your return and refund policies in your shop so customers know what to expect.

- **Communicate Promptly**: If a customer has an issue, respond quickly. Acknowledge their concern and work toward a solution, whether it's a refund, replacement, or other resolution.

- **Stay Polite and Professional**: Even if the complaint feels unreasonable, remaining calm and courteous can help de-escalate the situation and prevent negative reviews.

- **Offer Solutions**: Always provide a fair solution to the customer. Offering a replacement or partial refund can often satisfy the buyer and avoid damaging your shop's reputation.

Handling complaints with care can turn a potential negative experience into a positive one.

5. How do I optimize my shop for international shipping?

International shipping can expand your customer base, but it requires careful planning:

- **Research Shipping Costs**: Use Etsy's shipping calculator or third-party tools like Pirate Ship to estimate international shipping costs. Be transparent with customers about these costs in your listings.

- **Customs and Duties**: Let international customers know they may be responsible for customs fees or import duties. Be clear about this in your shop policies to avoid surprises.

- **Shipping Times**: Provide accurate delivery time estimates for international orders, as they often take longer than domestic shipments.

- **Package Carefully**: Ensure your packaging protects your products during long-distance shipping. Use proper padding and durable materials.

By setting clear expectations, you can successfully manage international orders while avoiding customer dissatisfaction.

6. When should I start using Etsy Ads?

You can start running Etsy Ads at any point, but here are some key considerations:

- **Before You Turn a Profit**: Running ads before turning a profit can help increase visibility and test market demand. However, keep a close eye on your budget and ensure you're not overspending on ads that aren't delivering results.

- **After You Turn a Profit**: Waiting until after you've turned a profit allows you to reinvest earnings into advertising. At this stage, you'll have more data on what products perform best, and you can focus your ad budget on listings that are likely to convert.

Whether you start ads early or after you've seen organic sales, make sure you're tracking performance and adjusting your strategy accordingly.

7. What's the difference between Etsy Ads and Offsite Ads?

Etsy offers two types of ads, each with distinct purposes:

- **Etsy Ads**: These are internal ads that promote your listings within Etsy's marketplace. You pay on a cost-per-click (CPC) basis, meaning you're charged only when someone clicks on your ad.

- **Offsite Ads**: These ads promote your products on external platforms like Google, Facebook, and Instagram. You don't pay for clicks—only when a sale is made as a direct result of someone clicking through from an Offsite Ad. The fee for Offsite Ads is between 12-15%, depending on your shop's revenue.

Both types of ads can help increase visibility, but make sure to analyze which option fits best for your shop's growth goals and budget.

8. How can I protect my designs and products from being copied?

While Etsy does take steps to enforce intellectual property (IP) rights, it's important to take proactive measures to protect your designs:

- **Register Your Designs**: If applicable, consider registering your designs or trademarks with the relevant IP authorities in your country.

- **Watermark Photos**: Use watermarks on your product images to discourage others from copying them directly.

- **Report Infringements**: If you find that your designs are being copied, use Etsy's "Report a Violation" process to notify Etsy about the infringement.

- **Consult an IP Attorney**: If you're unsure whether your work is at risk of infringement, it may be helpful to consult with an IP attorney to understand your rights and the steps you can take to protect them.

Taking these steps can help safeguard your original designs and keep your shop's brand unique.

9. Can I use copyrighted or trademarked materials in my Etsy products?

Using copyrighted or trademarked materials without permission is against Etsy's policies and could lead to penalties or account suspension. To avoid violating intellectual property laws:

- **Obtain Permission**: If you want to use trademarked logos or copyrighted designs, get explicit permission from the rights holder.

- **Create Original Designs**: Avoid using any materials, characters, or logos that you don't own the rights to. Focus on creating unique products that reflect your original ideas.

- **Check for Trademarked Phrases**: Even

common phrases may be trademarked, so always double-check whether you need permission to use certain words or images in your designs.

Failing to follow these guidelines could result in Etsy removing your listings or even suspending your account, so it's crucial to ensure your products comply with IP laws.

10. How do I handle slow sales periods on Etsy?

Every business experiences fluctuations, and slow sales periods are normal. Here are some tips for boosting sales during slow times:

- **Run a Sale or Offer Discounts**: Sales and special offers can create urgency and encourage buyers to purchase during quieter periods.

- **Optimize Listings**: Use slow periods to improve your SEO, update product photos, and refresh descriptions. This can help your shop perform better in search results over time.

- **Promote on Social Media**: Engage with your audience on platforms like Instagram,

Pinterest, and TikTok. Posting regularly and running promotions on social media can help drive traffic to your Etsy shop.

- **Add New Products**: Expanding your product line or adding seasonal items can attract new customers and keep existing ones interested.

Staying proactive during slow periods ensures that your shop remains top-of-mind for potential buyers, even when sales aren't as frequent.

14 Conclusion: Your Roadmap to Etsy Success

As you embark on or continue your journey as an Etsy seller, you now have the tools, strategies, and insights to build a thriving business on one of the world's most popular eCommerce platforms. The Etsy marketplace is a dynamic environment that rewards creativity, persistence, and strategic thinking. Whether you're just starting or looking to scale, understanding the nuances of Etsy's ecosystem will help you stand out, attract loyal customers, and achieve sustainable growth.

Let's recap the essential steps outlined in this guide that will lead you to Etsy success.

1. Defining Your Niche and Crafting a Product Line

One of the most critical steps in building a successful Etsy shop is defining a clear niche and offering a cohesive product line. Finding your niche ensures you attract the right customers and stand out in a crowded marketplace. Crafting a high-quality product line, built on uniqueness and demand, gives you the foundation for long-term success. The key is balancing passion with market trends, understanding your audience, and creating products that meet their needs.

2. Optimizing Your Etsy Shop for Visibility

SEO (Search Engine Optimization) is essential for increasing your visibility on Etsy. By optimizing your product titles, descriptions, and tags with relevant, high-volume keywords, you improve your chances of ranking higher in search results. Using tools like **EverBee**, **Marmalead**, and **eRank**, you can conduct data-driven research to find the most effective keywords and trends, ensuring your products are seen by the right audience.

In addition, presenting your shop with professional branding—including an engaging shop banner, logo, and cohesive product photography—helps build trust and encourages buyers to explore your listings.

3. Marketing Beyond Etsy

To drive consistent traffic to your Etsy shop, you need to go beyond relying solely on Etsy's internal search. Social media platforms like Instagram, TikTok, and Pinterest are invaluable tools for promoting your products, engaging with potential customers, and building a loyal community. In addition to social media, email marketing and influencer collaborations can help grow your brand and encourage repeat purchases.

Leveraging tools like **Canva** for stunning visual content and engaging storytelling through social media is a great way to build brand loyalty. Always remember that visibility is just as important as creating great products.

4. Managing Operations Efficiently

Effective order management and professional shipping practices ensure a smooth customer experience, which is key to maintaining high ratings and positive reviews. By utilizing Etsy's built-in order management tools and integrating with third-party shipping services, you can streamline your fulfillment process, saving time and ensuring your products reach customers quickly and safely.

Having well-defined shop policies for shipping, returns, and custom orders helps set clear expectations for buyers, minimizing misunderstandings and complaints. Great customer service, including prompt communication and timely problem resolution, will turn one-time buyers into loyal customers.

5. Running Successful Etsy Ads

Etsy Ads provide an opportunity to boost your visibility and sales, but they need to be used strategically. By focusing your ad spend on high-converting, best-selling products, you can maximize the return on your investment. Regularly monitoring your ad campaigns and adjusting your budget based on performance data ensures that your ads remain effective and aligned with your overall business goals.

6. Adapting to Etsy's Latest Updates

Etsy is an ever-evolving platform, and staying updated with its latest changes is essential for continued success. Whether it's adjustments to fees, new features like improved shipping tools, or SEO algorithm updates, being proactive about changes will keep your shop competitive and compliant with Etsy's guidelines.

Regularly review Etsy's announcements and use tools like **QuickBooks** to track your finances and adjust to any changes in Etsy's fee structure or tax regulations.

7. Scaling and Growing Your Business

As your Etsy shop gains momentum, the next step is scaling your business. This involves expanding your product line, increasing marketing efforts, and automating processes to handle a growing customer base. Outsourcing tasks, such as hiring virtual assistants or partnering with production services, allows you to focus on product development and business strategy. Additionally, introducing new sales channels, such as a standalone website, can diversify your revenue streams and reduce dependency on a single platform.

Building a sustainable business requires continuous learning, refinement of your processes, and adaptation to industry trends. Staying engaged with your customers, improving your offerings, and testing new marketing strategies will keep your shop thriving.

Your Path to Success

Achieving success on Etsy is a journey that requires dedication, creativity, and strategy. By following the steps outlined in this guide, you have all the knowledge and tools necessary to take your shop to the next level. From defining your niche and optimizing your listings to mastering Etsy Ads and marketing your brand across social media, each action you take will bring you closer to your goals.

Your Etsy shop has the potential to not only bring in sales but to become a thriving, sustainable business that reflects your passion and creativity. Continue to innovate, stay up-to-date with the latest tools and trends, and engage with your customers to build a brand that stands the test of time.

Final Thoughts

The landscape of eCommerce and online retail is constantly evolving, but Etsy remains a powerful platform for creative entrepreneurs to showcase their products and connect with a global audience. Your journey to Etsy success will be shaped by your ability to adapt, learn, and grow along the way.

As you move forward, keep in mind that success doesn't happen overnight. It's built step by step, through consistent effort, smart decision-making, and a commitment to your brand's values. Whether you're looking to turn a side hobby into a full-time business or simply expand your reach as a creative entrepreneur, the roadmap is in your hands.

Printed in Dunstable, United Kingdom

63694521R00111